The Talmud

The Talmud

WHAT IT IS AND WHAT IT SAYS

JACOB NEUSNER

ROWMAN & LITTLEFIELD PUBLISHERS, INC.
Lanham • Boulder • New York • Toronto • Oxford

ROWMAN & LITTLEFIELD PUBLISHERS, INC.

Published in the United States of America
by Rowman & Littlefield Publishers, Inc.
A wholly owned subsidary of The Rowman & Littlefield Publishing Group, Inc.
4501 Forbes Boulevard, Suite 200, Lanham, Maryland 20706
www.rowmanlittlefield.com

PO Box 317
Oxford
OX2 9RU, UK

British Library Cataloguing in Publication Information Available

Library of Congress Cataloging-in-Publication Data

Neusner, Jacob, 1932–
 The Talmud : what it is and what it says / Jacob Neusner.
  p. cm.
 Includes bibliographical references and index.
 ISBN-13: 978-0-7425-4670-7 (cloth)
 ISBN-10: 0-7425-4670-5 (cloth)
 ISBN-13: 978-0-7425-4671-4 (pbk.)
 ISBN-10: 0-7425-4671-3 (pbk.)
 1. Talmud—Introductions. I. Title.
 BM503.5.N4945 2006
 296.1'2061—dc22   2006005565

Printed in the United States of America

♾™The paper used in this publication meets the minimum requirements of American
National Standard for Information Sciences—Permanence of Paper for Printed Library
Materials, ANSI/NISO Z39.48-1992.

CONTENTS

PREFACE vii

CHAPTER 1. HISTORY: THE WORLD IN WHICH THE TALMUD CAME INTO BEING 1

CHAPTER 2. WHAT IS THE MISHNAH? 19

CHAPTER 3. WHAT IS THE GEMARA? 45

CHAPTER 4. THE TWO TALMUDS 71

CHAPTER 5. HOW IS THE TALMUD PART OF THE TORAH? 99

CHAPTER 6. HOW IS THE SAGE PART OF THE TORAH? 119

CHAPTER 7. HOW DOES THE TALMUD PRESENT GOD? 133

GLOSSARY 155

SOURCES OF RABBINIC TEXTS 157

INDEX 159

Preface

Imagine the questions that will demand answers when colonists from earth move to the moon. With all the problems of technology solved, the work of rebuilding civilization will get under way. In the beginning society and culture will have to be invented from scratch. The pioneers will ask questions thought settled on earth, questions of law, politics, and the social order. They will need a cookbook of culture, composed of recipes for sustaining civilization.

For the ever-renewing communities of Judaism the Talmud has been and is that transcendent, enduring cookbook of culture. It contains the record for Israelites wherever they are located of what is to be done, how it is to be done, and why to do it. It transmits the givens of Judaic civilization, gifts out of time, the heritage of the ages for the generations to come.

The Talmud is relevant to contemporary Judaism for two reasons. First, it is the authoritative source for law and theology of Judaism. It is relevant wherever and whenever Judaism is practiced. But, second, there is a more particular reason for its relevance—that is because it was produced in response to a situation comparable to that of Jews in the world today. It is the outcome of a generation that has confronted calamity.

A catastrophe akin to the loss of European Jewry in 1933–1945 precipitated the processes of cultural reconstruction that culminated in the recording of the Talmud. It was the destruction of the Temple and metropolitan center of Jerusalem in 70 CE, which made necessary a new beginning. The Jews after 70 had to reinvent themselves from a political entity to a community of like-minded individuals. Defeated by Rome after a bloody rebellion, they faced the loss of the millennial center of pilgrimage and divine service and the end of their political autonomy. And making the crisis acute, not merely chronic, this was the second time around, for in 586 BCE they had confronted a comparable crisis. At that time they had found in the Torah of Moses that guide they required for the restoration and renewal of their civilization. Now what was to be done? The Talmud answered that question and has continued to serve as the Jews' cookbook of culture from the first centuries of the Common Era to the present day.

For the Jews through their long history have pioneered time and again, beginning afresh first here and then there. The Talmud has been and is now important because for two thousand years it has recorded and transmitted the eternal truths and the laws everywhere deemed authoritative. This it did with sufficient concreteness to define norms, and sufficient abstractness to accommodate unprecedented circumstances. And the Talmud continues today to define all Orthodox Judaisms, to form a reference point for Conservative, Reconstructionist, and Reform Judaisms, and to serve as a rich resource for those that today would build a Jewish secular culture as well. As they made the passage from one country to another, putting down roots in the Middle East and North Africa, Spain and Portugal, Morocco and Algeria, Britain and France and Central Europe, the Balkans and the Eastern European territories of Rumania, Lithuania, Poland, and Ukraine, eastward on the Silk Road to China and southeastward to India and westward to the United States and Canada and Latin America, the Jews adapted the Talmud's eternal verities to local circumstances. Wherever they settled, whatever languages they spoke, they created a community that replicated a single set of values in common, a uniform culture. One law, one theology defined the indicative traits of communities of Judaism wherever they were located and whenever, from late antiquity to modern times, they flourished. A single book explains how this came about.

What was held in common vastly exceeded local variation, and the Torah— initially the Five Books of Moses, Genesis, Exodus, Leviticus, Numbers, and Deuteronomy—as interpreted by the Talmud was and is the reason. "The Torah" refers to the Hebrew Scriptures of ancient Israel (aka "the Old Testament"). Its laws, theology, and narrative are reframed by "the Talmud," meaning the Talmud of Babylonia (the Bavli). A continuous corpus of commentaries and law codes based on that Talmud defined the pattern that would be reproduced wherever Jews formed communities of Judaism. Another Talmud, the Talmud of the Land of Israel (the Yerushalmi or Jerusalem Talmud) appeared as well. In this book we meet both Talmuds, but mainly the Talmud of Babylonia, and define what it is and what it says.

What makes the Talmud engaging is its mode of re-presenting the Torah: through sustained analysis and argument. Specifically, doing more than systematizing the law, the Talmud encourages analysis. Its unfolding dialogue and contention invite successive generations to join in the inquiry into system and order. The Talmud shows how to apply reason and to practice logic. Through a constant flood of questions and answers, disputes and debates, the Talmud invites us to participate in its arguments and to make its issues our own. In presenting the Torah the Talmud preserves diverse opinion and encourages argument and analysis in an open-ended conversation. Here we listen for echoes of that conversation, aspiring to join in.

This primer of seven chapters accomplishes three things, answering fundamental questions of history (where and when?), literature (what is this writing?), and religion (what is in this writing and why does it matter?).

First, in chapter 1, I introduce the document in its historical setting. The Talmud derived from Jewish administrations in the Roman Empire, in the Land of Israel, and in Iran, in Babylonia, reflecting the judgment of the judges and administrators who ran the small claims courts that the respective empires left in local hands. We should not suppose that in the period in which the Talmud was taking shape the Rabbis defined the conduct and culture of the Jews of Babylonia or the Land of Israel. Every page of the Talmud records tension between the Rabbinic sages and the ordinary folk whose affairs they administered. It was only much after 600 CE that that Judaism set the norms of communal law and theology. In the Talmud, therefore, we possess the Rabbinic sages' program for the definition of Israel, meaning the community of Judaism that traced its origins back to the Israel of the Land of Israel recorded in Scripture, or the Torah, instruction, of God to Moses at Sinai and later prophetic revelation.

Second comes the Talmud as a piece of writing. In chapters 2 through 4, I answer the question, what is the Talmud? The Talmud is in two parts, and it exists in two versions. The Talmud is made up of the Mishnah, a law code, and the Gemara, an Aramaic word meaning "learning," a commentary to that code. And it is in a version produced in the Land of Israel circa 400 CE and another written in Babylonia circa 600 CE. Chapter 2 identifies the Mishnah that serves both Talmuds, and chapter 3 spells out the principal trait of the Gemara, its analytical argument. Chapter 4 describes the two Talmuds and explains why the second of the two took priority.

Third come the religious perspectives of the Talmud, in the form of three basic questions, concerning the standing, within the Torah of Moses, of the Talmud and the Rabbinic sage, and the justice of God as revealed by the legal system of Judaism.

In chapters 5 through 7, I answer the question, what is in the Talmud? First, in chapter 5, I show how the Talmud relates to the Torah, how the Talmud is part of the Torah. Second, in chapter 6, I ask how the Rabbinic sage is part of the Torah. Finally, how does the Talmud justify God's disposition of Israel, the holy people: the question of the destruction of the Temple in 70—what are we to do now?—answered through the laws of the Mishnah and the analysis of the Gemara. In chapter 7, I show how God is represented in the coherent statement of the Mishnah and the Gemara—all-powerful, just, and merciful—and how the Talmud proves that proposition from the Torah.

I cite in English translation that is close to the Hebrew and Aramaic of the original very ample abstracts of the Talmud so that readers have a direct encounter with the ancient writing in its own manner of expression. These abstracts are meant to illustrate the general traits that any passage of the Talmud exhibits. In this way readers are prepared for further encounters with this classic writing.

I benefited from the comments of anonymous readers of the original manuscript and especially from the guidance of my editor, Brian Romer, at Rowman & Littlefield.

Jacob Neusner

1

History: The World in Which the Talmud Came Into Being

Who Speaks through the Talmud?

The Rabbi—a holy man sanctified by his knowledge of the Torah that God gave to Moses at Sinai—speaks through the Talmud. He is not a prophet, not a priest, and not a king, but he is defined as a unique authority by his capacity to interpret and apply the Torah. That capacity comes about because the Rabbinic sage has mastered the oral traditions handed on from master to disciple from Sinai to the present hour. The Talmud records those traditions.

The particular religious system, the Judaism that the Talmud sets forth, is called Rabbinic Judaism—for the title *Rabbi*, meaning "my lord," of its authorities— or Talmudic Judaism—for the name of the principal document of that Judaism. It is referred to as formative Judaism, because the particular Judaic system of the Rabbis took shape in the first six centuries of the Common Era, generally called "late antiquity." In the setting of theology of Judaism it is called, especially, *normative* Judaism, the Judaism that sets the norms of right and wrong, that is, for the status as authoritative that in medieval and modern times was attained by the Talmud and those that were and today are its masters.

But most accurately it is called the Judaism of the dual Torah, referring to the narrative critical to Rabbinic Judaism. The story tells that at Sinai God revealed to Moses Torah or instruction in two media. One medium is the written Torah preserved in the Five Books of Moses, and the other is the oral Torah, a memorized tradition handed on in a chain of tradition. Each name for this Judaism serves in its context—historical, theological, literary, and religious—but "the Judaism of the dual Torah" comes closest to what is absolutely unique to the Talmud in the context of Judaism, that is, the doctrine of an oral tradition possessed and handed on by the Rabbinic sages. They qualified for authority through learning in the Torah and in the oral traditions that give the Torah shape and proportion and structure. But that formal matter does not tell us what the Rabbi actually did or why his principal legacy, the Talmud, proved definitive.

Perspective through comparison with other types of Israelite leaders helps place the Talmud in Israelite context. With roots deep in Scripture's Wisdom tradition represented by Proverbs, Job, and Ecclesiastes (Hebrew title: Qoheleth) going back to an age well before the first century of the Common Era, the Rabbi represents a new kind of authority in the community of Judaism. Scripture put forth authorities who were prophets, like Moses, or priests in charge of service to God, like Aaron, or kings, like David and Solomon. But the Rabbi was not a prophet, not a priest, not a king. A prophet spoke in God's name the actual words dictated by God and exercised authority deriving from direct encounter with God. He prophesied concerning practical matters but exercised little or no political authority based on coercion and force. Representing God's stake in holy Israel, the priest qualified by genealogy in the priestly line begun by Aaron administered the divine service in the Temple of Jerusalem. There daily offerings propitiated God and atoned for the sin of all Israel, viewed as a corporate, moral entity. A king managed public policy and exercised secular rule. He had an army and spoke for the ethnic community, Israel as a licit, recognized political entity within the Roman Empire. That arrangement prevailed until the end of the secular monarchy after King Herod (who died in 4 BCE). Later on, as we shall see, secular authority with imperial recognition was exercised by the patriarch—in Hebrew, *nasi,* the ruler of the Jewish ethnic group in the Land of Israel.

How does the Rabbi relate to the patriarch, the political head of the Jewish community? It is an ambiguous relationship, involving two kinds of power, military and intellectual. A story recorded in the Talmud of the Land of Israel portrays the Rabbi's relationship with the patriarch. The Rabbi was the master of the Torah, and the patriarch held office only with Roman imperial support, including Gothic troops to enforce his will. We can readily understand how armed force trumped intellectual and moral authority. But what we see is that the patriarch paid attention to the teachings of the Torah set forth by the sage.

Here is how matters are portrayed, emphasizing the unique qualification of the Rabbi in Torah learning:

YERUSHALMI HORAYOT 3:1 I:1

R. SIMEON B. LAQISH SAID, "A RULER WHO SINNED—THEY ADMINISTER LASHES TO HIM BY THE DECISION OF A COURT OF THREE JUDGES."

What is the law as to restoring him to office?

Said R. Haggai, "By Moses! If we put him back into office, he will kill us!"

If the ruler sins, he is flogged. If he is restored to office, he is going to take vengeance upon those that flogged him. The patriarch of the day, Judah the Patriarch, who is the Roman-recognized head of the Jewish ethnic group in the Land of Israel (aka Palestine), the sponsor of the Mishnah, the authoritative code of the law of Judaism, took offense. Here is what happened.

R. Judah the Patriarch heard this ruling [of Simeon b. Laqish's] and was outraged. He sent a troop of Goths to arrest R. Simeon b. Laqish. [R. Simeon b. Laqish] fled to the Tower, and some say, it was to Kefar Hittayya.

The next day R. Yohanan went up to the meeting house, and R. Judah the Patriarch went up to the meeting house. He said to him, "Why does my master not state a teaching of Torah?"

[Yohanan] began to clap with one hand [only].

[Judah the Patriarch] said to him, "Now do people clap with only one hand?"

He said to him, "No, nor is Ben Laqish here [and just as one cannot clap with one hand only, so I cannot teach Torah if my colleague, Simeon b. Laqish, is absent]."

[Judah] said to him, "Then where is he hidden?"

He said to him, "In the Tower."

He said to him, "You and I shall go out to greet him."

R. Yohanan sent word to R. Simeon b. Laqish, "Get a teaching of Torah ready, because the patriarch is coming over to see you."

The patriarch and the sage agreed to greet the hidden authority and to make peace. This is what happened when they met. Simeon b. Laqish greeted Judah the Patriarch in a conciliatory teaching, praising him by comparing him to God redeemed Israel from Egypt.

[Simeon b. Laqish] came forth to receive them and said, "The example that you [Judah] set is to be compared to the paradigm of your Creator. For when the All-Merciful came forth to redeem Israel from Egypt, he did not send a messenger or an angel, but the Holy One, blessed be he, himself came forth, as it is said, 'For I will pass through the land of Egypt that night' (Ex. 12:12)—and not only so, but he and his entire retinue.

"[What other people on earth is like thy people Israel, whom God went to redeem to be his people' (2 Sam. 7:23).] 'Whom God went' [sing.] is not written here, but 'Whom God went' [plural—meaning, he and all his retinue]."

Judah was conciliated and brought up the sore subject that had originally outraged him.

[Judah the Patriarch] said to him, "Now why in the world did you see fit to teach this particular statement [that a ruler who sinned is subject to lashes]?"

He said to him, "Now did you really think that because I was afraid of you, I would hold back the teaching of the All-Merciful? [And lo, citing 1 Sam. 2:23F.,] R. Samuel b. R. Isaac said, '[Why do you do such things? For I hear of your evil dealings from all the people.] No, my sons, it is no good report that I hear the people of the Lord spreading abroad. [If a man sins against a man, God will mediate for him; but if a man sins against the Lord, who can intercede for him? But they would not listen to the voice of their father, for it was the will of the Lord to slay them' (1 Sam. 2:23–25).] [When] the people of the Lord spread about [an evil report about a man], they remove him [even though he is the patriarch]."

The importance of the story is to underscore the unique qualification of the Rabbi, source of knowledge of the law, superior to all other authorities in Jewry. The Rabbi matched none of the other types of leader—prophet, priest, king—but encompassed traits of all of them. He enjoyed a special relationship with God, like the prophet. His Torah study was equivalent to Temple offerings after the Temple was destroyed. The sage administered the affairs of Jewry as part of the government of the Jewish patriarchs of the Land of Israel and Babylonia. For the Rabbinic sages the media for direct communication with Heaven did not include prophecy.

That point is made in so many words on the Babylonian Talmud's commentary at Mishnah tractate Sotah 9:12A. The Mishnah's rule states, "When the former prophets died out, the Urim and Tummim were cancelled." In that context, the Talmud cites a teaching that alleges that with the end of the latter prophets, Haggai, Zechariah, and Malachi, the direct inspiration of God for the prophets came to an end in Israel. What that means is that there were no further holy writings, beyond those of the Hebrew Scriptural canon (as then understood), in which it would be alleged, "God spoke to me, saying . . . " The system could find ample space for teachings of the Torah not in writing, that is, documents alleged to originate in the oral tradition that formed part of the revelation of Sinai—but no more written ones.

The Rabbi held that prophecy ceased in its earlier form, known to us from Scripture, and communication with God became the domain of the Rabbinic sages through their teaching of the Torah. We see in the following passage the way in which the Rabbinic sages pursue an issue through contentious argument, raising objections and answering them. Here the issue is the relationship of the sages to the gift of prophecy.

Bavli Baba Batra 1:6 II.4/12A–B

Said R. Abdimi of Haifa, "From the day on which the house of the sanctuary was destroyed, prophecy was taken away from prophets and given over to sages."

So are sages not also prophets?

This is the sense of the statement: Even though it was taken from the prophets, it was not taken from sages.

Said Amemar, "And a sage is superior to a prophet: 'And a prophet has a heart of wisdom' (Ps. 90:12). Who is compared to whom? Lo, the lesser is compared to the greater."

Said Abbayye, "You may know that [sages retain the power of prophecy,] for if an eminent authority makes a statement, it may then be stated in the name of some other eminent authority [who can have gotten it only by prophecy]."

Said Raba, "So what's the problem? Maybe both were born under the same star."

Rather, said Raba, "You may know that that is so, for an eminent authority may say something, and then the same thing may be reported [12B] in the name of R. Aqiba bar Joseph."

Said R. Ashi, "So what's the problem? Maybe as to this particular matter both were born under the same star."

Rather, said R. Ashi, "You may know that it is the case, because an eminent authority may say something, and then the same thing may be reported as a law revealed by God to Moses at Mount Sinai."

But perhaps the sage just makes a good guess [literally: is no better than a blind man groping about to a window]?

But doesn't the sage give a reason for what he says [so it cannot be merely a good guess]!

Moses is the best example of a prophet. But in the Talmud and its companion writings he is treated as the original Rabbi and is called, in Talmudic

Judaism, "Moshe Rabbenu," "Our lord, Moses," "our Rabbi Moses." His prophetic standing and gifts were not emphasized, rather his role as master of the Torah.

Bavli Erubin 5:1 I.43/54B

Our Rabbis have taught on Tannaite authority [that is, as a tradition deriving from the masters who set forth the Mishnah, sages who flourished in the first two centuries of the Common Era]:

What is the order of Mishnah teaching? Moses learned it from the mouth of the All-Powerful. Aaron came in, and Moses repeated his chapter to him and Aaron went forth and sat at the left hand of Moses. His sons came in and Moses repeated their chapter to them, and his sons went forth. Eleazar sat at the right of Moses, and Itamar at the left of Aaron.

Then the elders entered, and Moses repeated for them their Mishnah chapter. The elders went out. Then the whole people came in, and Moses repeated for them their Mishnah chapter. So it came about that Aaron repeated the lesson four times, his sons three times, the elders two times, and all the people once.

Then Moses went out, and Aaron repeated his chapter for them. Aaron went out. His sons repeated their chapter. His sons went out. The elders repeated their chapter. So it turned out that everybody repeated the same chapter four times.

The traditions of the Rabbis thus are represented as originating at Sinai, and their procedures of memorizing the traditions go back to the original revelation of the Torah. So Moses is represented as God's disciple, the essential Rabbi, and Aaron as Moses' disciple, and onward through time. Moses also exercised political leadership as ruler of Israel in the wilderness. He supervised the service of God in the holy offerings made by his brother, Aaron the priest. He was sage, king, and prophet. So the Rabbis claimed for themselves to carry forward the multifaceted model of Moshe Rabbenu.

But it was in their own way and in their own context. What did that mean in concrete terms? The Talmud provides a narrative of what the Rabbi actually did in the setting of the Jewish community of Talmudic times in Babylonia. Here the Rabbi emerges as civil administrator in a broad moral context. His study of the Torah was deemed the counterpart of sacrifices offered by the priesthood. He governed the community of Israel in the Land of Israel and in Babylonia as a bureaucrat and clerk. So he combined traits of prior Israelite authorities.

Here we see him in action and identify what set him apart from all of them and made him unique in Israelite context:

Bavli Taanit 20B–21A [V.3]

Said Raba to Rafram bar Pappa, "Would the master report to us some of those lovely things that R. Huna used to do?"

He said to him, "Of his childhood I remember nothing. As to his old age, I recall that every stormy day they would drive him about in a golden carriage and he would make the rounds of the entire town and would have destroyed every shaky wall. If it was possible for the owner, the owner would build it, and if it was not possible, he would build it out of his own resources. On every Friday he would send a messenger to the market, and all vegetables that the market gardeners had left over he would buy and throw into the river."

Oughtn't he to have given the vegetables to the poor?

[It was done] lest they rely on him and not come to buy any for themselves.

And why not throw them to the animals?

He took the view: food fit for human consumption is not to be thrown to animals.

Then he oughtn't to buy it at all?

It would mislead the gardeners in the future [who would then bring an inadequate supply of vegetables to market].

When he came across a healing remedy, he would fill a jug of water with it and hang it above his doorstep and announced, "Who wants, let him come and take."

And there are those who say, a medicine for Sibetha [a disease that affects those that fail to wash hands before eating], he had learned and he would leave a jugful of water and proclaim, "Whoever needs it let him come [and wash his hands] to save his life from danger."

When he would wrap bread for a sandwich for a meal, he would open the door to his house and proclaim, "Whoever is in need, let him come and eat."

Said Raba, "All of these things I can carry out, except for this last, which I cannot carry out [21a] because there are so many impoverished people in Mehoza."

The Rabbi administered the community of the town like a mayor or city manager. He took responsibility for public health and safety, making sure that shaky walls did not fall down and bury people in the streets. He might use his own funds for that purpose. He saw to the maintenance of stable prices in the market place. This he did by assuring the market gardeners of a market for their produce. So they would bring their produce to market on a regular basis. He would provide medicines for healing. He secured food for the starving. The Rabbi thus took on himself responsibility for the welfare, material and moral, of the Jewish community. But these tasks were not particular to the Rabbi.

Prophet, priest, and king—all models are necessary, but none is sufficient to define the Rabbi. What made the Rabbi unique is conveyed by the story before us, the implicit exercise of criticism and rational explanation. What he did required and received reasoned analysis, so that we are left with a model and an example of intelligent conduct. Alone among Jewish authorities of various types, the Rabbi brought to the administration of the community traditions of learning that were the result of much rational reflection upon the public interest. Here in our initial encounter with the Talmud in its own words we see its paramount trait: questions and answers, reasoned dialogue. This is where the Talmud enters in. Its manifest inclusion of disputes and debates, challenges and responses, is unique in the writings of Judaism from Scripture to the Talmud. There is no counterpart effort to record a reasoned dialogue of disagreement and confrontation in Scripture, nor in any writing of any community of Judaism down to the Talmud, not, for example, in the Dead Sea Scrolls. But from the Talmud forward, rational contention in a reasoned manner proved commonplace.

What is particular to the Rabbi is the record of implicit criticism that accompanies the stories of the holy man: Why didn't he do this, why didn't he do that? And sound reason underscores his action. He had his reasons and acted on his principles. We therefore have more than the record of what he did, which in context makes sense but out of the concrete context hardly pertains. What are people to do who live in a different world from one circumscribed by market gardeners and shaky walls? The answer lies in the Talmud's anonymous analysis of his actions, which shades over into an account of intelligent criticism of public policy in abstraction. That brings us to the Talmud and to the age in which it emerged.

As I said, it was an age in which, in the international multicultural empires of Rome and Iran, ethnic-religious communities such as the Jews administered their own affairs. The setting of the Talmud in the two ordinarily tolerant empires, Rome and Iran, afforded the opportunity to produce a document of intracommunal contention over law and theology defining an ethnic-religious community such as the one that called itself "Israel."

The Age and Location that Produced the Talmud

Religious freedom and cultural toleration, characteristics of the Greco-Roman pagan world, left their enduring imprint on the West. Out of late antiquity, the first six centuries of the Common Era (CE = AD), Western civilization received its heritage of enduring works of law and philosophy, religion and theology: Roman law, the Bible (Old Testament and New Testament) of Christianity, and the Torah (written and oral) of Judaism. Not only so, but also at the very end, in the early seventh century CE, Islam embodied in the Quran arose to compete with Christianity throughout the Mediterranean world. The story of the West can be told in terms of that competition. That is the context, the axial age, in which we encounter the Talmud, which records the oral part of the Torah. But among the enduring classics of Roman law and Christian theology, and Judaic law and theology, only the Talmud joined in a single coherent statement law and philosophy, religion, and theology.

Composed of two components, a law code, the Mishnah, and a commentary to that code, the Gemara, the Talmud recorded a conception of constructing a coherent civilization based on reason and revealed truth. The rules for right and wrong, good and evil, formed a coherent statement based on cogent principles. The details all fit together, nothing was arbitrary, everything conformed with reason.

The Talmud began in the Mishnah as a utopian vision of how things ought to be. It continued in the Gemara with an exposition of many of the Mishnah's topics. But only centuries after the document came to closure did the world of Judaism begin to approximate the outlines of that vision, such as the memory of R. Huna embodied: the rational rule of sages guided by God.

The ancient Rabbis first produced the Mishnah, a law code laid out on topical lines and realizing philosophical modes of thought concerning concrete everyday affairs. A detailed vision of Israel the holy community in the age of restoration, the Mishnah was completed around 200 CE, about a century and a quarter after the destruction of the Second Temple of Jerusalem in 70 CE, and about three-quarters of a century after the defeat by the Romans of Bar Kokhba, who led a rebellion aimed at rebuilding the Temple in 132–135. The Mishnah from 200 onward served the Jewish communities of the Land of Israel and of Babylonia as the principal collection of laws governing the affairs of the two ancient communities of Judaism. Each community—the one in the Land of Israel in the Roman Empire, the other in Babylonia in the Iranian Empire—produced its own commentary, called the Gemara, to the Mishnah. Consequently there are two Talmuds: the Talmud of the Land of Israel and the Talmud of Babylonia, both of them built on the shared law code, the Mishnah. In due course we shall see how the two Talmuds, independent of one another, treat the same Mishnah passage. The more rigorous and perspicacious of the two commentaries to the Mishnah, the Talmud of Babylonia, through the ages took the paramount position in the formation of Judaic law and theology, and the Talmud of the Land of Israel suffered neglect until modern times.

The two Talmuds originated in stable, self-administering Jewish communities in the two dominant empires of the ancient world of Europe, North Africa, and the Near and Middle East. The Talmud of the Land of Israel, also known as the Yerushalmi (Jerusalem Talmud), derived from the originally pagan, then Christian, Roman Empire coming to closure around 400 CE, and the Talmud of Babylonia, also known as the Bavli, originated in Babylonia, a province corresponding to present-day central Iraq, in the Zoroastrian Iranian Empire, reaching a conclusion around 600 CE. The Mishnah and two Talmuds, accordingly, attest to the autonomy and freedom accorded to the Jewish community by the world empires in which that community was located. In late antiquity, for the first six centuries CE, the Land of Israel formed a small component of the Roman Empire, and Babylonia was a province of the Iranian Empire. Rome tolerated Israelite autonomy in religion and politics until Rome became Christian in the fourth century CE, and Iran, under the Arsacid Parthians from the third century BCE to the early third century CE and then under the Sasanian Persians to the seventh century, for all the four centuries of Parthian rule and for most of the following four centuries of Persian rule, did the same.

The dates for the closure of the two Talmuds, 400 CE for the Yerushalmi and 600 CE for the Bavli, are rough guesses. There are several firm dates as well. From 70 CE, when the Temple was destroyed, to the early fifth century, the Roman government recognized the Jews of the Land of Israel as a self-governing ethnic community. Their head, bearing the title of *nasi*, enjoyed Roman support, including the provision of troops of Goths to enforce his authority. The Roman Empire for three hundred years repressed Christianity, but in 312 the Roman emperor, Constantine, declared Christianity a licit religion, and in the next century Rome recognized Christianity as the religion of the state.

What then does the year 400 CE represent? It marks nearly the end of the first century after the legalization of Christianity by the Roman emperor Constantine. The Yerushalmi and other Rabbinic documents such as Genesis Rabbah, Leviticus Rabbah, and Pesiqta deRab Kahana, which came to closure in the same age, set forth a systematic response to the Christian challenge to Judaism. Within a quarter century after 400, the ethnic government of the Jewish community of the Land of Israel ceased to enjoy state recognition. But the laws and theology of an enduring community of Judaism in the crucible of Christianity were fully spelled out.

For Iran, 600 CE represents the end of the age of Iranian, Zoroastrian rule of Babylonia, among other regions, that closed with the advent of Islam in the early seventh century. The Iranian empire encompassed many languages and ethnic groups, among them a sizable Jewish community dating from the exile of the Judeans in 586 BCE by the Babylonian Empire. A half century later Babylonia was conquered by the Iranian empire under Cyrus the Great of Persia, a province within Iran. Cyrus restored exiled peoples to their lands, including Jews to the Land of Israel. While some went back, the greater part remained in Babylonia, where Jewish communities thrived for twenty-five centuries, till the advent of the State of Israel in 1948 CE. Shortly afterward, along with the other ancient Jewish communities of the Islamic world, Jews of Babylonia, now Iraq, were driven out and resettled in the State of Israel, France, Canada, or the United States.

Like their counterparts in Rome, the Jews in the Iranian Empire enjoyed the rights of a self-governing ethnic community, generally, though not always, able to practice its religion without interference on the part of the Iranian state and its Zoroastrian religion. A patriarch, or ruler of the ethnic community, called in Aramaic the *resh galuta*, the head of the exilic community, administered the affairs of that community, employing Rabbinic sages as judges, lawyers, and clerks in his government. In the early seventh century the prophet Muhammad proclaimed the Quran as God's writing, and Islam became the world-conquering religion, by the mid-seventh century overthrowing the rule of Zoroastrianism in Iran. The Jewish ethnic government continued under Islam, and over time the Rabbinic authorities established the Bavli as the constitution and bylaws of Judaism.

The Impact of the Destruction of the Temple in 70 CE and of the Failure of Efforts to Rebuild It

The Talmuds and compilations of Scriptural interpretation called Midrashim represent the destruction of the Temple in 70 as the result of the rule of zealots, who rejected the tolerant policies of Rome in favor of an independent Jewish state. Their implicit message was for Israel the holy community to keep the peace and not oppose the rule of Rome or Iran, a dominion executed through the state-supported and loyalist Jewish administrations of the local communities. Maintaining a free Jewish state mattered less than sustaining the service of God through Temple sacrifice and Torah study that the Rabbis affirmed. The exemplary

Rabbi was portrayed in the model of the prophet Jeremiah, who in about 600 BCE had favored conciliation with Nebuchadnezzar, the emperor of the Babylonian empire, and had opposed resistance in the years prior to the siege and destruction of the First Temple of Jerusalem by the Babylonians in 586 BCE. Thus the first great authority after 70 CE and teacher of the masters whose disciples produced the Mishnah, Rabban Yohanan ben Zakkai, is represented as guided by Jeremiah's prophecy.

In a document that came to closure in about 500 CE, a half millennium after the events are portrayed, the leading Rabbi of the day opposed the rebellion against Rome. He escaped from the besieged city and went to the Romans, who responded with clemency by giving him the right to study and practice the Torah in an academy in Yavneh, on the coast of the Land of Israel. Here is a picture that portrays in narrative form a fully realized Rabbinic vision.

The Fathers According to Rabbi Nathan IV:VI.1

Now when Vespasian came to destroy Jerusalem, he said to [the inhabitants of the city,] "Idiots! why do you want to destroy this city and burn the house of the sanctuary? For what do I want of you, except that you send me a bow or an arrow [as marks of submission to my rule], and I shall go on my way."

They said to him, "Just as we sallied out against the first two who came before you and killed them, so shall we sally out and kill you."

When Rabban Yohanan ben Zakkai heard, he proclaimed to the men of Jerusalem, saying to them, "My sons, why do you want to destroy this city and burn the house of the sanctuary? For what does he want of you, except that you send him a bow or an arrow, and he will go on his way."

They said to him, "Just as we sallied out against the first two who came before him and killed them, so shall we sally out and kill him."

Vespasian had stationed men near the walls of the city, and whatever they heard, they would write on an arrow and shoot out over the wall. [They reported] that Rabban Yohanan ben Zakkai was a loyalist of Caesar's.

After Rabban Yohanan ben Zakkai had spoken to them one day, a second, and a third, and the people did not accept his counsel, he sent and called his disciples, R. Eliezer and R. Joshua, saying to them, "My sons, go and get me out of here. Make me an ark and I shall go to sleep in it."

R. Eliezer took the head and R. Joshua the feet, and toward sunset they carried him until they came to the gates of Jerusalem.

The gatekeepers said to them, "Who is this?"

They said to him, "It is a corpse. Do you not know that a corpse is not kept overnight in Jerusalem?"

They said to them, "If it is a corpse, take him out," so they took him out and brought him out at sunset, until they came to Vespasian.

They opened the ark and he stood before him.

He said to him, "Are you Rabban Yohanan ben Zakkai? Indicate what I should give you."

He said to him, "I ask from you only Yavneh, to which I shall go, and where I shall teach my disciples, establish prayer [Goldin: a prayer house], and carry out all of the religious duties."

He said to him, "Go and do whatever you want."

He said to him, "Would you mind if I said something to you?"

He said to him, "Go ahead."

He said to him, "Lo, you are going to be made sovereign."

He said to him, "How do you know?"

He said to him, "It is a tradition of ours that the house of the sanctuary will be given over not into the power of a commoner but of a king, for it is said, 'And he shall cut down the thickets of the forest with iron, and Lebanon [which refers to the Temple] shall fall by a mighty one' (Is. 10:34)."

People say that not a day, two or three passed before a delegation came to him from his city indicating that the [former] Caesar had died and they had voted for him to ascend the throne.

They brought him a catapult and drew it up against the wall of Jerusalem.

They brought him cedar beams and put them into the catapult, and he struck them against the wall until a breach had been made in it. They brought the head of a pig and put it into the catapult and tossed it toward the limbs that were on the Temple altar.

At that moment Jerusalem was captured.

Rabban Yohanan ben Zakkai was in session and with trembling was looking outward, in the way that Eli had sat and waited: "Lo, Eli sat upon his seat by the wayside watching, for his heart trembled for the ark of God" (1 Sam. 4:13).

When Rabban Yohanan ben Zakkai heard that Jerusalem had been destroyed and the house of the sanctuary burned in flames, he tore his garments, and his disciples tore their garments, and they wept and cried and mourned.

Just as in the period from 610 BCE Jeremiah counseled passivity and obedience to the Babylonians and won the favor of Nebuchadnezzar the Babylonian ruler on that account, so Yohanan ben Zakkai advised Israel that the preservation of the Temple and its offerings takes priority over political aspirations of lesser, merely practical, consequence. His wisdom enabled him to save his life and the lives of his principal disciples.

Yohanan is represented as affirming Temple sacrifice and mourning its demise. But Rabbinic Judaism succeeded and replaced the Judaism of the Temple priests with its atonement rites. The act of mourning does not complete the story. The destruction of the Temple meant the end of its sacrifices of atonement. How was Israel the holy people going to replace those sacrifices? That question came from Yohanan's student, Joshua, some time after 70, again as portrayed half a millennium later:

THE FATHERS ACCORDING TO R. NATHAN IV:V.2

One time [after the destruction of the Temple] Rabban Yohanan ben Zakkai was going forth from Jerusalem, with R. Joshua following after him. He saw the house of the sanctuary lying in ruins.

R. Joshua said, "Woe is us for this place which lies in ruins, the place in which the sins of Israel used to come to atonement."

He said to him, "My son, do not be distressed. We have another mode of atonement, which is like [atonement through sacrifice], and what is that? It is deeds of loving kindness.

"For so it is said, 'For I desire mercy and not sacrifice, [and the knowledge of God rather than burnt offerings]' (Hos. 6:6)."

Clearly a Judaic system has taken shape in the model of Jeremiah's and, in 70 as in 586, in response to the destruction of the Temple and the cessation of the priestly government. Now there is a medium of atonement that takes the place of sacrifices, and it is self-sacrifice for the other person through deeds of loving kindness. And a means of proving that conviction derives from Scripture, which is interpreted to make that very point. So Yohanan ben Zakkai has made use of his learning in the Torah, here in the prophetic writing of Hosea as earlier in that of Jeremiah, to establish as integral to the Torah the revolutionary teaching that copes with the revolutionary situation facing the Israelites: "We have another mode of atonement, which is like [atonement through sacrifice], and what is that? It is deeds of loving kindness." What greater, more valued sacrifice than altruism!

The Rabbinic reading of the destruction competed with the aspirations of large numbers of Jews for the recovery of an independent Jewish state and the rebuilding of the Temple. In 132, roughly sixty years after the destruction in 70, a Jewish general, Bar Kokhba (aka Ben Koziba), led a great war against Rome. Most of the Rabbis of the age did not support the war, regarding it as an act of arrogance against Heaven. They nurtured an ethos of accommodation and reconciliation. Some of them recognized Bar Kokhba as the Messiah. In the following story, Aqiba, disciple of Yohanan ben Zakkai's disciples, Eliezer and Joshua, recognized the general Bar Kokhba as the Messiah and was rebuked by another Rabbi. Then the arrogance of the Jewish general is illustrated:

YERUSHALMI TAANIT 4:5 [VII:1]

When [Bar Kokhba] would go forth to battle, he would say, "Lord of the world! Do not help and do not hinder us! 'Hast thou not rejected us, O God? Thou dost not go forth, O God, with our armies'" (Ps. 60:10).

Three and a half years did Hadrian besiege Betar.

R. Eleazar of Modiin would sit on sack cloth and ashes and pray every day, saying, "Lord of the worlds! Do not sit in judgment today! Do not sit in judgment today!"

[The Roman general] Hadrian wanted to go to him. A Samaritan said to him, "Do not go to him until I see what he is doing, and so hand over the city [of Betar] to you. ['Make peace . . . for you.']"

He got into the city through a drain pipe. He went and found R. Eleazar of Modiin standing and praying. He pretended to whisper something into his ear.

The townspeople saw him do this and brought him to Ben Kozeba. They told him, "We saw this man having dealings with your uncle."

He said to him, "What did you say to him, and what did he say to you?"

He said to him, "If I tell you, then the king will kill me, and if I do not tell you, then you will kill me. It is better that the king kill me and not you."

He said to him, "He said to me, 'I shall hand over my city.' ['I shall make peace....']"

He went to R. Eleazar of Modiin. He said to him, "What did this Samaritan say to you?"

He replied, "Nothing."

He said to him, "What did you say to him?"

He said to him, "Nothing."

[Ben Kozeba] gave [Eleazar] one good kick and killed him.

Forthwith an echo came forth and proclaimed the following verse:

"Woe to my worthless shepherd, who deserts the flock! May the sword smite his arm and his right eye! Let his arm [69a] be wholly withered, his right eye utterly blinded!" (Zech. 11:17).

"You have murdered Eleazar of Modiin, the arm of all Israel and their right eye. Therefore may the right arm of that man wither, may his right eye be utterly blinded!"

Forthwith Betar was taken, and Ben Kozeba was killed.

The message is clear. Israelites are called upon to live lives of humility and self-abnegation, to make peace with Rome even in the Land of Israel. The war was lost because of the failings of morality and virtue exhibited by individual Israelites.

The defeat of Bar Kokhba was not the end of the story of futile efforts to restore the sacrificial rites. An opportunity to rebuild the Temple under the auspices of a pagan emperor presented itself. In 360–361, after Constantine's heirs had adopted Christianity as the state religion, an anti-Christian emperor, Julian, came to the throne of Rome and restored pagan worship and schools. To humiliate Christianity, he decreed that the Jews might rebuild Jerusalem's Temple. Julian died in battle against Iran shortly afterward, and nothing came of the project. The Rabbis' reading of Israel's condition won plausibility both through what happened, military disaster, and what did not happen, the restoration of the Temple, when Israel the holy community acted on its own.

The Formation of Judaism in a Voluntary Community, No Longer as a Political State

The crisis to which Talmudic Judaism responded transcended the replacement of a medium of atonement through animal sacrifice with a medium of atonement through knowledge of God and acts of mercy. The very social order of the Israelite community changed. The Israelites had constituted a political and corporate entity, a community subject to a politics of its own. The established institutions of government—king, priest, prophet—all focused on the conduct of corporate Israel as a unique moral entity. The sacrifices of atonement for all Israel, the daily whole offering morning and night, were paid for by a small offering collected from Israelites, so the rites were conducted in behalf of the community as a whole. From the times of Moses, then, the Temple rites had made of Israel a corporate moral entity, subject to collective sin and collective atonement. This is expressed in so many words in the account of the half-sheqel offering collected from all Israelite males for the support of the daily whole offering of atonement. This appears in the Tosefta, a collection of supplementary statements that accompany the Mishnah, circa 300 CE.

Tosefta Sheqalim 1:6

They exact pledges from Israelites for their *sheqels*, so that the public offerings might be made of their [funds].

This is like a man who got a sore on his foot, and the doctor had to force it and cut off his flesh so as to heal him. Thus did the Holy One, blessed be he, exact a pledge from Israelites for the payment of their *sheqels*, so that the public offerings might be made of their [funds].

For public offerings appease and effect atonement between Israel and their father in heaven.

Likewise we find of the heave offering of *sheqels* which the Israelites paid in the wilderness, as it is said, "And you shall take the atonement money from the people of Israel and shall appoint it for the service of the tent of meeting, that it may bring the people of Israel to remembrance before the Lord, so as to make atonement for yourselves" (Ex. 30:16).

Now with the destruction of the Temple and the cessation of the public offerings, Israelites persisted, but Israel as the corporate moral entity no longer found its natural venue in the realization of the Temple, which lay in ruins. For a generation or two, it was possible to preserve the memory of the Temple and conduct public life in its light:

Tosefta Shabbat 1:13

Said R. Ishmael, "One time I read by the light of a lamp, and [forgetfully,] I wanted to tilt it [to get more oil on the wick].

"I said, 'How great are the words of sages, who rule, "They do not read on Sabbath nights by the light of a lamp."'"

R. Nathan says, "He [Ishmael] most certainly did tilt it.

"And written on his notebook is the following: 'Ishmael b. Elisha tilted a lamp on the Sabbath.

"'"When the sanctuary will be rebuilt, he will bring a sin offering."'"

As the succession of generations lengthened without the restoration of the Temple, the expression of Israel as a corporate community lost its concreteness and became a theological abstraction. In this context we recall Yohanan's teaching of Joshua stressed individual conduct, atonement through the attitude and action of each private person. Israel no longer constituted a political state; it now was formed by the voluntary commitment of individuals.

Nowhere is that shift of Israel from a political entity to a voluntary community, a moral entity, more dramatically captured than in the teaching that redemption could be brought about only through the voluntary obedience of all Israelites *one by one*. Everything then depended on the conduct of individuals, and all of them mattered equally in the redemptive process. A single recusant could stop the redemption. That, more than any other shift, is what marks Israel as a voluntary community of faith, not a political state possessed of media of public and collective action. For in the end the state acts to coerce conformity, and the voluntary community at best persuades and cajoles. In the following story, we see how the Israelites are promised that their private, personal conduct is what will bring about the coming of the Messiah and the end of days and the resurrection of the dead—that and not the action of the Jewish state, which no longer exists, or the restoration of a Jewish government capable of resisting foreign rule and coercing local compliance. The Talmud would accomplish the transformation of Israel into a community of like-minded individuals, modeled on the Rabbi as exemplar of virtue and right thinking.

The composition that follows is in two parts. In the first part, the successive empires that exiled Israel from its homeland, the Land of Israel: Babylonia, Media (Persia), Greece, and finally, Rome, pass in succession. In each case God went with Israel into exile. Implicitly, God is seen to have left the Temple as well. In the second part attention shifts to the other half of Israel's story, its restoration to Jerusalem and the rebuilding of the Temple, all through the intervention of the Messiah. When will the age of redemption and restoration begin, and what does Israel have to do to bring it about? Here the answer contrasts with the conception of a corporate community symbolized by public offerings provided by a pittance from every Israelite. It now stresses the conduct of individuals, any one of whom suffices to prolong the exile through sinful conduct:

Yerushalmi Taanit 1:1 [II:5]

It has been taught by R. Simeon b. Yohai, "To every place to which the Israelites went into exile, the presence of God went with them into exile.

"They were sent into exile to Egypt, and the presence of God went into exile with them. What is the scriptural basis for this claim? '[And there came a man of God to Eli, and said to him, Thus the Lord has said], I revealed myself to the house of your father when they were in Egypt subject to the house of Pharaoh' (1 Sam. 2:27).

"They were sent into exile to Babylonia, and the presence of God went into exile with them. What is the scriptural basis for this claim? '[Thus says the Lord, your Redeemer, the Holy One of Israel]: For your sake I will send to Babylon [and break down all the bars, and the shouting of the Chaldeans will be turned to lamentations]' (Is. 43:14).

"They were sent into exile into Media, and the presence of God went into exile with them. What is the scriptural basis for this claim? 'And I will set my throne in Elam [and destroy their king and princes, says the Lord]' (Jer. 49:38). And Elam means only Media, as it is said, '[And I saw in the vision; and when I saw], I was in Susa the capital, which is in the province of Elam; [and I saw in the vision, and I was at the river Ulai]' (Dan. 8:2).

"They went into exile to Greece, and the presence of God went into exile with them. What is the scriptural basis for this claim? '[For I have bent Judah as my bow; I have made Ephraim its arrow]. I will brandish your sons, O Zion, over your sons, O Greece, [and wield you like a warrior's sword]' (Zech. 9:13).

"They went into exile to Rome, and the presence of God went into exile with them. What is the scriptural basis for this claim? '[The oracle concerning Dumah]. One is calling to me from Seir, "Watchman, what of the night? Watchman, what of the night?" (Is. 21:11).'"

Now the story of exile has been told. What of redemption? The Rabbis conceive that the prophets were Rabbis, and so they consult the prophetic writings for enlightenment on the requirement of restoration. Isaiah prophesied in the time of the Assyrian invasion, when the ten northern tribes of ancient Israel were taken into exile in the eighth century BCE.

YERUSHALMI TAANIT 1:1 [II:5]

The Israelites said to Isaiah, "O our Rabbi, Isaiah, What will come for us out of this night?"

He said to them, "Wait for me, until I can present the question."

Once he had asked the question, he came back to them.

They said to him, "Watchman, what of the night? What did the Guardian of the ages say [a play on 'of the night' and 'say']?"

He said to them, "The watchman says: 'Morning comes; and also the night. [If you will inquire, inquire; come back again]'" (Is. 21:12).

They said to him, "Also the night?"

He said to them, "It is not what you are thinking. But there will be morning for the righteous, and night for the wicked, morning for Israel, and night for idolaters."

They said to him, "When?"

He said to them, "Whenever you want, He too wants [it to be]—if you want it, he wants it."

They said to him, "What is standing in the way?"

He said to them, "Repentance: 'come back again'" (Is. 21:12).

R. Aha in the name of R. Tanhum b. R. Hiyya, "If Israel repents for one day, forthwith the son of David will come.

"What is the scriptural basis? 'O that today you would hearken to his voice!'" (Ps. 95:7).

Said R. Levi, "If Israel would keep a single Sabbath in the proper way, forthwith the son of David will come.

"What is the scriptural basis for this view? 'Moses said, Eat it today, for today is a Sabbath to the Lord; [today you will not find it in the field]' (Ex. 16:25).

"And it says, '[For thus said the Lord God, the Holy One of Israel], 'In returning and rest you shall be saved; [in quietness and in trust shall be your strength.' And you would not]'" (Is. 30:15). By means of returning and [Sabbath] rest you will be redeemed.

Now the Messiah, son of David, will come when all Israel concurs and acts, each individual in conformity with the Torah, to bring him. By means of repentance, a personal indeed subjective, action, and Sabbath observance, all Israel will be redeemed. The Sabbath figures because it was the first Sabbath, the eve of the seventh day of creation, that marked the advent of Adam and Eve in Eden. Israel's Eden is the Land of Israel. Israel is to repent, an act of individual regeneration. Israel is to enter into Sabbath rest, an act of home and family. When all Israel both repents and realizes the Sabbath rest, it will have restored the condition of Eden. Then Israel is redeemed, its own action having made the world ready for the Messiah's intervention.

The Talmud with its reasoned exposition of the law both enlightens Israelites as to their responsibilities and explains to them the reason why. The purpose of the Torah's law is to carry out the conditions of the covenant between God and Israel through the activity of each Israelite. Now we turn to the Talmud, the document itself and its traits, starting with the Mishnah.

2

What Is the Mishnah?

Israelite Law Codes before the Mishnah

The Talmud is made up of two parts, the Mishnah, a law code, of about 200 CE, and the Gemara, a commentary on the Mishnah and related legal traditions, which came to closure around 600 CE. The Mishnah, neatly organized by topics, is not the first law code produced in the Israelite setting. For example, Scripture contains several comparable collections of law, and the Dead Sea library has some more. But the Mishnah is the first that is laid out by subject matter, in topical expositions. Scripture's codes and those in the Dead Sea library tend not to be organized in topical expositions. But that formal trait is not the only thing that sets the Mishnah apart from all prior Israelite law codes. Assessed against comparable documents of Scripture and the Dead Sea library, the Mishnah shows itself as a triumph of imagination. Specifically, it exhibits remarkable capacity to think in new and astonishing ways about familiar things. That fact explains the success of the Mishnah and its companion, the Gemara—the Talmud all together.

How to define the Mishnah and show its traits? The true distinction of the Mishnah emerges only when we look backward from the Mishnah to prior Israelite models of how rules had earlier been collected and formed into law codes. The models supplied by Scripture encompass the Covenant Code (Ex. 20:22–23:33), the Priestly Code (Lev. 1–15), the Holiness Code (Lev. 17–26), and the Deuteronomic Code (Dt. 12–26). Other law codes are formed by other heirs of Scripture, those represented in the Dead Sea Scrolls by the Damascus Covenant and the Manual of Discipline of prior centuries. All define the context of comparison. The outcome is simply stated: There is no comparison. The Mishnah's intellectual vitality to imagine paths to truth none had trod before explains the difference. Therein also lies the power of the Talmud, as we shall see in chapter 3.

Scripture's law codes are not rigorously organized by topics, and the Mishnah's building blocks are defined by subject matter. How else might the laws have been organized? One way is by the name of a given authority, another is by the repetition of language formulas, a third is by a particular historical incident or setting, to mention three alternatives not followed by the Mishnah. The Mishnah's definitive conception—a law code standing on its own and systematically expounding the law in a topical program, lacking narrative and bearing no theological claims or implications—followed no parallel in Scripture and copied no precedent supplied by other Israelite religious communities besides that formed by the Rabbinic sages.

Comparing the Mishnah to the Covenant Code, Exodus 20:22–23:22

The Mishnah does not submit to the formal or topical program of Scripture but organizes matters in its own way. While they reverently recorded and expounded Scripture's laws, the sages did not simply recapitulate in their own wording the statements of Scripture. Nor, second, did they commonly follow the topical order and program of Scripture. In general what the Rabbinic sages did was to reorganize in their own framework Scripture's topics and to place them into the sages' own systematic context. And still more important, third, the Rabbinic sages brought to the exposition of topics shared with Scripture an analytical method and program unimagined by Scripture. It is there that we shall identify the qualities of the Mishnah that mark that code as unique.

These definitions tend to be abstract, and a concrete comparison will clarify matters. For that purpose we turn to the Book of the Covenant, Ex. 20:22–23:33, which will allow us to form an objective judgment on that matter of cogency and comprehensiveness. How does the program of the Book of the Covenant compare? The topical program of Ex. 20:22–23:33, rules and admonitions of the covenant, follows the following plan, according to Moshe Greenberg:

> These consist of cultic regulations, civil and criminal laws, and socio-moral exhortations, arranged as follows: (a) rules concerning access to God in worship (20:22–26), (b) the emancipation of Hebrew slaves (21:1–11); (c) homicide and assault (21:12–27); (d) the homicidal ox (21:28–32); (e) injury to property, i.e., to animals (including theft) (21:33–22:3); and to crops (22:4–5); the responsibility of bailees and borrowers (22:6–14); seduction (22:15–16) from the vantage point of the father's interest, i.e., the bride price; (f) a miscellany of religio-moral admonitions and commandments (22:17–23:13); (g) a cultic calendar (23:14–19).[1]

Greenberg comments, "A fairly clear principle of association and gradation is discernible from (c) through (e); the precedence given to (b) is conditioned by the situation—limitation of slavery among Hebrews being the chief boon that their liberator conferred upon them." Martin Noth sees the composition as originally an independent book of law:[2] "We have in Ex. 20:22–23:33 a collection of judgments of differing form and differing content which . . . are customarily described as the

'Book of the Covenant.' It is probable that this collection once formed an independent book of law that has been inserted into the Pentateuchal narrative as an already self-contained entity." The composition covers these topics:

Ex. 21:1–11: The law for slaves
Ex. 21:12–17: Offences punishable by death
Ex. 21:18–36: Bodily injury, cases that do or do not result in death
Ex. 22:1–17: Damage to property
Ex. 22:18–1: A long sequence of Apodictic laws
Ex. 23:1–9: Apodictic regulations for the conduct of cases at law
Ex. 23:10–13: Sabbath Year and Sabbath Day
Ex. 23:14–19: Special cultic regulations

The sequence 21:12–17, 21:18–36, and 22:1–17 coheres in the exposition of the laws of torts and damages, inclusive of the death penalty, but by the same criterion that classifies those passages as a systematic exposition, 21:18–23:9 form a miscellany:

21:1–11: The law for slaves
21:12–17: Offences punishable by death
21:18–36: Bodily injury, cases that do or do no result in death
22:1–17: Damage to property
22:18–31: A long sequence of apodictic laws
23:1–9: Apodictic regulations for the conduct of cases at law
23:10–13: Sabbath Year and Sabbath Day

We may judge the Book of the Covenant as cogent in some, though not all, of its parts, and surely not as a whole. That is because topical coherence characterizes some of the divisions but not others, for example, 22:18–31, a "sequence" that is hardly sequential in any but a formal sense. If topical cogency inures in 21:1–22:17, then by that criterion 22:18–31 and 23:1–9 are scattered and incoherent.

The laws of the Book of the Covenant demand explanation. More to the point, they are miscellaneous and so do not yield generalizations. They cover concrete cases. If there is a principle that particular cases illustrate, we are not told what it is. Cases do not yield principles and do not generate refinements. And that brings us to the Mishnah, which is topically organized and which does yield governing principles that can extend to new problems and even new topics. The character of Scripture's code of law underscores the reason that the Mishnah was required to complement Scripture.

We see the strength of the Mishnah in the comparison of the Book of the Covenant and Mishnah tractate Baba Qamma, which is devoted to torts and damages and goes over much of the same topical program as the Book of the Covenant, as we shall see. What we now see is that the Book of the Covenant presents information, while the Mishnah constructs information into patterns of knowledge subject to analysis. It not only seeks and transmits knowledge, it tests knowledge. We compare the presentation of that shared topic in Mishnah tractate Baba Qamma and Ex. 21–22.

What are we going to see? The Covenant Code cannot conceive a context beyond the data, and Mishnah tractate Baba Qamma exercises its gifts of generalization and analysis to open possibilities of extension and amplification. Above all, the Mishnah in treating the topic systematizes and organizes the data, inviting an analytical program of comparison and contrast that is unthinkable, indeed contextually incomprehensible, in Scripture.

Let us now refer to an exemplary passage, Ex. 21–22, where we may succinctly compare the presentation of the matter in the Book of the Covenant with Mishnah tractate Baba Qamma chapter 1. What we shall see is how the Covenant Code and the Mishnah present the same subject, and that will permit us immediately to grasp the contrast between Scripture's and the Mishnah's portrayal of the law. We begin with the pertinent statements of the Book of the Covenant, for reasons that quickly become self-evident. Here is Scripture.

Ox: "When one man's ox hurts another's, so that it dies, then they shall sell the live ox and divide the price of it; and the dead beast also they shall divide. Or if it is known that the ox has been accustomed to gore in the past, and its owner has not kept it in, he shall pay ox for ox, and the dead beast shall be his" (Ex. 21:35–36).

Pit: "When a man leaves a pit open or when a man digs up a pit and does not cover it, and an ox or an ass falls into it, the owner of the pit shall make it good; he shall give money to its owner and the dead beast shall be his" (Ex. 21:33).

Crop-destroying beast: "When a man causes a field or vineyard to be grazed over or lets his beast loose and it feeds in another man's field, he shall make restitution from the beast in his own field and in his own vineyard" (Ex. 22:5).

Fire: "When fire breaks out and catches in thorns so that the stacked grain or the standing grain or the field is consumed, he that kindled the fire shall make full restitution" (Ex. 22:6).

Ex. 21:35–36 yields two rules. First, in the case of an ox that gores, the surviving ox is sold and the proceeds divided; but that is where the owner of the goring ox could not have foreseen the possibility of goring. If the ox's history of goring shows that he should have made provision, the foreseeable incident has been caused by his negligence, with the stated outcome. Second, negligence involves inanimate as well as animate causes. The same principle operates for the third and the fourth rules. That sum and substance is the lesson of the four causes of damages to property: compensation gauged by culpability, the possibility of foreseeing damages and preventing them.

Now let us see how the Mishnah presents the same four matters in its opening statement on torts and damages. We shall observe how the four items of Scripture are formed into a single coherent statement. The payoff is that the Mishnah's topical exposition through cases yields a generalization rich in implications for further cases:

MISHNAH TRACTATE BABA QAMMA 1:1

[There are] four generative causes of damages: (1) ox [Ex. 21:35–36], (2) pit [Ex. 21:33], (3) crop-destroying beast [Ex. 22:4], and (4) conflagration [Ex. 22:5]. What they have in common is that they customarily do damage and taking care of them is your responsibility. And when one [of them] has caused damage, the [owner] of that which causes the damage is liable to pay compensation for damage out of the best of his land [Ex. 22:4].

MISHNAH TRACTATE BABA QAMMA 1:2

In the case of anything of which I am liable to take care, I am deemed to render possible whatever damage it may do. [If] I am deemed to have rendered possible part of the damage it may do, I am liable for compensation as if [I have] made possible all of the damage it may do.

Here, especially at M. B.Q. 1:2, is the Mishnah at its most elegant, a passage for reasons of taste and judgment often commencing the curriculum of Talmud study in the yeshiva world of contemporary Judaism, where the Talmud forms the center of the curriculum. What Mishnah tractate Baba Qamma 1:1 contributes is a systematic analysis of the category formation that covers the generative cases of damages. Mishnah tractate Baba Qamma 1:2 introduces the issue of responsibility and its gradations. If one is responsible, one is liable. If one is responsible in part, one is liable for the entire body of damages. These principles extend to an unlimited number of cases, the details of Scripture being reworked into an encompassing set of generalizing principles.

The Mishnah has treated the cases of Scripture as exemplary and generalized on them. It has spelled out the full range of responsibility. ("In the case of anything of which I am liable to take care, I am deemed to render possible whatever damage it may do. If I am deemed to have rendered possible part of the damage it may do, I am liable for compensation as if I have made possible all of the damage it may do.") It has defined the specifics required for applying Scripture's general rules ("a tooth is deemed an attested danger in regard to eating what is suitable for eating").

Let us turn to the comparison of Ex. 21:33, the pit, and Ex. 22:4, the crop-destroying beast, with the Mishnah's counterparts.

When a man leaves a pit open or when a man digs up a pit and does not cover it, and an ox or an ass falls into it, the owner of the pit shall make it good; he shall give money to its owner and the dead beast shall be his." (Ex. 21:33)

Scripture's message is that one is responsible for leaving a pit without making provision for the damage it may do. Now how does the Mishnah exposition proceed?

Damages Done by the Pit

MISHNAH TRACTATE BABA QAMMA 5:5

He who digs a pit in private domain and opens it into public domain, or in public domain and opens it into private domain, or in private domain and opens it into private domain belonging to someone else, is liable [for damage done by the pit]. He who digs a pit in public domain, and an ox or an ass fell into it and died, is liable. It is all the same whether one digs a pit, a trench, cavern, ditches, or channels: he is liable.

Scripture ignores the context of the pit, not distinguishing public domain, where one has no right to dig a pit, from private domain, where one does. It further extends the case of the pit to cover trenches, caverns, ditches, or channels. The former point is the more important. But the latter should not be missed. Scripture speaks of the pit and does not make provision for causes of damages that are analogous to the pit, trenches, caverns, ditches, or channels. By speaking in abstract generalizations, the Mishnah frames the law to cover a wide range of situations of the same sort. Let us proceed to the next way in which the Mishnah clarifies what Scripture has left unclear.

MISHNAH TRACTATE BABA QAMMA 5:6

A pit belonging to two partners—one of them passed by it and did not cover it, and the second one also did not cover it, the second one is liable. [If] the first one covered it up, and the second one came along and found it uncovered and did not cover it up, the second one is liable. [If] he covered it up in a proper way, and an ox or an ass fell into it and died, he is exempt. [If] he did not cover it up in the proper way and an ox or an ass fell into it and died, he is liable. [If] it fell forward [not into the pit] because of the sound of the digging, [the owner of the pit] is liable. [If] it fell backward [not into the pit] because of the sound of the digging, [the owner of the pit] is exempt. [If] an ox carrying its trappings fell into it and they were broken, an ass and its trappings and they were split, [the owner of the pit] is liable for the beast but exempt for the trappings. [If] an ox belonging to a deaf-mute, an idiot, or a minor fell into it, [the owner] is liable. [If] a little boy or girl, a slave boy or a slave girl [fell into it], he is exempt [from paying a ransom].

The matter of responsibility is refined. If there are two owners, they share liability. But that point is modified by the matter of responsibility. The partner who most recently has passed the pit is responsible for ensuing damage. One has to take action to cover the pit properly. Here is a principle that once more pertains to a wide variety of cases, not only the matter of the pit. Scripture's rule that the owner of the pit is responsible for damages is vastly extended beyond the limits of the case and the principle of culpability.

Mishnah Tractate Baba Qamma 5:7

All the same are an ox and all other beasts so far as (1) falling into a pit, (2) keeping apart from Mount Sinai [Ex. 19:12], (3) a double indemnity [Ex. 22:7], (4) the returning of that which is lost [Dt. 22:3; Ex. 23:4] (5), unloading [Ex. 23:51], (6) muzzling [Dt. 25:4], (7) hybridization [Lev. 19:19; Dt. 22:10], and the (8) Sabbath [Ex. 20:10; Dt. 5:14]. And so too are wild beasts and fowl subject to the same laws. If so, why is an ox or an ass specified? But Scripture spoken in terms of prevailing conditions.

Here the Mishnah explicitly acknowledges that Scripture's cases are exemplary, not particular. Here is an implicit judgment upon Scripture as formulated.

Damages Done by the Crop-Destroying Beast

When a man causes a field or vineyard to be grazed over or lets his beast loose and it feeds in another man's field, he shall make restitution from the beast in his own field and in his own vineyard (Ex. 22:5).

Damages done by one's property—herds or flocks here—to someone else's property must be compensated—so much for the Book of the Covenant, another simple and undeveloped declaration.

Mishnah Tractate Baba Qamma 6:1

He who brings a flock into a fold and shuts the gate before it as required, but [the flock] got out and did damage, is exempt. [If] he did not shut the gate before it as required, and [the flock] got out and did damage, he is liable. [If the fence] was broken down by night, or thugs broke it down, and [the flock] got out and did damage, he is exempt. [If] the thugs took [the flock] out, [and the flock did damage], the thugs are liable.

If one has taken appropriate precautions, he is not held responsible for unforeseeable accidents. If one has not carried out his responsibility to prevent damage, he is liable. If his precautions were rendered null by damages he could not foresee or prevent ("thugs broke it down"), he is not liable. If a third party caused his property to inflict damages, the third party is liable. Scripture's case now yields a governing rule that pertains to any number of cases, the rule is extended into an abstract law of responsibility.

Mishnah Tractate Baba Qamma 6:2

[If] he left it in the sun, [or if] he handed it over to a deaf-mute, idiot, or minor, and [the flock] got out and did damage, he is liable. [If] he handed it over to a shepherd, the shepherd takes the place of the owner [as to liability]. [If the flock] [accidentally] fell into a vegetable patch and derived benefit [from the produce], [the owner must] pay compensation [only] for the value of the benefit [derived by the flock]. [If the flock] went down in the normal way and did damage, [the owner must] pay compensation for the [actual] damage which [the flock] inflicted.

If the owner handed the flock out to an incompetent guardian, he is responsible, but if he employed a qualified shepherd, the shepherd assumes responsibility. If the flock accidentally did damage, the owner is liable only for the benefit enjoyed by the flock. But if this happened in an ordinary manner ("the normal way"), then the compensation must cover all damages. Here again the circumstances govern the compensation that is owing—a consideration not raised by Scripture.

Mishnah Tractate Baba Qamma 6:3
He who stacks sheaves in the field of his fellow without permission, and the beast of the owner of the field ate them up, [the owner of the field] is exempt. And [if] it was injured by them, the owner of the sheaves is liable. But if he had put his sheaves there with permission, the owner of the field is liable.

The owner of the field where one has stacked his sheaves without permission is not responsible to guard the interloper's crops from his own beasts. The interloper is responsible for damage done to the field owner's animals. But if the owner gave permission, he assumes full responsibility. That is a point that once more extends to a variety of cases. The exposition of the genus, damages done by fire, presents no surprises.

Damages Done by Fire

When fire breaks out and catches in thorns so that the stacked grain or the standing grain or the field is consumed, he that kindled the fire shall make full restitution (Ex. 22:6).

One who initially creates a cause of damages is responsible for the secondary damages that are done.

MISHNAH TRACTATE BABA QAMMA 6:4
He who causes a fire to break out through the action of a deaf-mute, idiot, or minor is exempt from punishment under the laws of man, but liable to punishment under the laws of heaven. [If] he did so through the action of a person of sound senses, the person of sound senses is liable. [If] one person brought the flame, then another person brought the wood, the one who brings the wood is liable. [If] one person brought the wood and the other person then brought the flame, the one who brought the flame is liable. [If] a third party came along and fanned the fire, the one who fanned the flame is liable. [If] the wind fanned the flame, all of them are exempt. He who causes a fire to break out, that consumed wood, stones, or dirt, is liable.

The one who acts through a third party is not responsible for the third party's actions. But if he acts through a party not responsible for his own actions, he bears no legal, actionable responsibility for that party's actions. The deaf-mute, idiot, or minor is not capable of culpable intentionality. But the one who is responsible for what they have done also is not liable in an earthly court for what they have done, but is answerable to Heaven. In a sequence of actions culminating in damages, the person who has completed the process bears responsibility. Thus if one person brought wood and then another flame, the latter is liable; if one person brought the flame and then another the wood, the latter is liable. If a third party fanned the flame, so increasing the damages, he is responsible. If the wind did so, all parties are exempt. The final statement recapitulates Scripture's principle, pure and simple. The upshot is that the case of Scripture is not only turned into an exemplification of a transaction not limited to the case at hand, it also is made to yield abstract principles of culpability that vastly transcend the issue of property damage.

Mishnah Tractate Baba Qamma 6:6

A spark which flew out from under the hammer and did damage—[the smith] is liable. A camel which was carrying flax and passed by in the public way, and the flax it was carrying got poked into a store and caught fire from the lamp of the storekeeper and set fire to the building—the owner of the camel is liable.

One is responsible for the foreseeable damage that he has done, an obvious point that serves to set the stage for what is not self-evident, the matter of the camel. If the animal has caused foreseeable damages—its flax poked into the stores along the sides and caught fire—the owner of the camel is liable; the storekeeper has done nothing that requires compensation; he is not responsible for damages.

The details of the laws must not be permitted to obscure the character of the Mishnah's exposition of the law. The syllogistic character of the Mishnah contrasts with the episodic formulation of the Book of the Covenant. At every point at which Scripture and the Mishnah take up the same subject, the Book of the Covenant sets forth a governing rule for a case, while Mishnah tractate Baba Qamma finds a way of *exemplifying* a governing rule. That is because an analytical program animates the Mishnah's presentation of the law. It is not simply the Mishnah's capacity to present the rules as exemplary. It is also, and especially, the Mishnah's implicit theoretical framework that generates syllogisms extending far beyond the case at hand.

The Mishnah's judgment of the counterpart passages of Scripture comes to realization in the exemplary passages just now surveyed. The Mishnah has revolutionized the presentation of the topics that are shared with Scripture. That is in two aspects. First, Scripture's cases—ox, pit, crop-destroying beast, fire—are turned into exemplifications of types of damage, animate and inanimate, active and passive, for example. These cases furthermore illustrate the types of responsibility assigned for damages and contain a deeper analysis of types of causes, all in the manner of natural philosophy. The cases then yield rules. Each is treated as a genus, capable of speciation, and in due course the Talmud would compare and contrast the four basic categories or types of causes of damages and refine matters. But the analytical work of types of generative causes of damages is done in the Mishnah.

Second, and more important, the rules that are so worded as to exemplify and pertain to agricultural circumstances are translated into generalizations that govern all manner of transactions, a wide variety of topics. The basic issue concerns responsibility. Responsibility is framed in eloquent language: "In the case of anything of which I am liable to take care, I am deemed to render possible whatever damage it may do. If I am deemed to have rendered possible part of the damage it may do, I am liable for compensation as if I have made possible all of the damage it may do." That formulation transcends the cases and the classifications yielded by the cases and turns the law into jurisprudence.

By the criterion of formulating the law with the power to extend and amplify itself beyond the case at hand and even past the limits of the transaction that the law explicitly describes, one must judge as unique the Mishnah's counterpart to passages in the Book of the Covenant that are explicitly encompassed by the Mishnah. The intellectual ambition that culminated in the hierarchization of degrees of responsibility marks the Mishnah as the outcome of a remarkable imagination.

What Marks the Mishnah as a Unique Code of the Law of Judaism?

Let us generalize these results so that we may appreciate the unique standing of the Mishnah in the history of Judaism. A law code, a collection of norms or rules, is measured by three criteria: by (1) its comprehensiveness in coverage of its topics, (2) its cogency, and (3) its capacity for extension to cases and circumstances not explicitly addressed by the code itself. A collection of laws that covers a topic in a comprehensive way is different from one that covers that same topic in a superficial way. One that is cogent in its topical expositions is different from one that is incoherent. One that can set forth cases that exemplify principles subject to generalization is different from one that supplies ad hoc, case-by-case inert information.

The Mishnah struck out in new paths altogether from those set forth by Scripture's codes and those that imitated them. The capacity to think in fresh ways about Scripture's own imperatives and their implications attests to the validity of Rabbinic imagination that reaches concrete expression in the Mishnah, a triumph of reconstruction and creative recapitulation. Some of the prior codes compete in comprehensiveness—the Covenant Code of Exodus, which we examined, is one example—some in cogency, but none in capacity for extension and amplification, in syllogistic character, as I shall explain. And that is where I identify the marks of imaginative vitality. Those that compete in cogency do not attempt a comprehensive topical exposition, and those that undertake a comprehensive presentation do not exhibit an obvious principle of cogency.

The Mishnah is distinctive in one aspect and unique in another. It is singular, first, in combining cogency and comprehensiveness. But in the Israelite context it is absolutely unique, second, in undertaking syllogistic discourse. That is to say, the Mishnah has the power to turn facts into examples, cases into facts illustrative of comprehensive principles affecting a variety of types of circumstances or transactions. Above all, the imaginative code will present rules in patterns susceptible to development and so yield further analytical propositions and secondary syllogisms. That marks the document as remarkable for its cogency, comprehensiveness, capacity for extension. It will impose patterns upon bits and pieces of data (cogency). It will address the widest program of topics (comprehensiveness). It will construct a syllogistic discourse, signaling problems of a theoretical character that invite further analysis (capacity for extension), moving from "two apples and two apples equal four apples" to "two and two are four" (anythings).

The Mishnah's Indicative Traits: Topical Cogency and Comprehensiveness

Now to describe the Mishnah in its own terms, not only in comparison with law codes in Scripture and the Dead Sea Scrolls. The Mishnah is a philosophical law code, with the analysis formed by applied logic and practical reason expounding topics of both a theoretical and practical character. The Mishnah contains expositions of laws that at the time of its closure in 200 CE, more than a century after the destruction of the Temple in 70, could not apply. It sets forth elaborate expositions, for example, of laws governing the Temple rites, though the Temple was in ruins when the document was produced. It also presents laws that did pertain, dealing with family affairs, the Sabbath and festivals, torts and damages, and many other practical matters. No distinction of form or analytical program separates the one from the other.

If I had to say in a single sentence what the Mishnah does with the topics it treats, it would be something like the following: The Mishnah forms of details a coherent construction, so that each piece of information joins with others to make a cogent statement bearing broad implications.

The synergy of the parts yields a whole greater than the sum of those parts. Taken all together, the tractates—topical expositions—of the entire Mishnah join together to form of the individual messages a system capable of endless elaboration and extension, able to take up topics and transactions unimagined in the Mishnah at all.

Who wrote the Mishnah? No one person—it is a public document, rarely admitting the traits of style that mark a passage as the work of a singular author. The Mishnah as a whole is anonymous and contains no internal evidence as to its ultimate sponsorship or authorship. But the Mishnah, like the other documents of Rabbinic Judaism in the formative age, persistently cites named Rabbinic sages and attributes rulings to them. Thus few chapters lack rulings attributed to named authorities, often in conflict on details of the law, occasionally on matters of principle. Most of the named authorities flourished in the first and second centuries CE. That is why we think that the document was produced at about 200 CE. It was under the sponsorship of Judah, Patriarch (*nasi*) or ethnic ruler of the Jews of the Land of Israel.

In detail, the document comprises sixty-three tractates, sixty-one of them organized as topical expositions, one tractate organized by the names of authorities, called Eduyyot, testimonies, and a collection of wise sayings, tractate Abot, the Fathers. The other Israelite codes—whether in Scripture, whether in the Qumran library—do not come close to the comprehensive coverage of areas of the social order that is attained by the Mishnah. The ambition of the compilers of the Mishnah to create an account of the Israelite social order finds no match in any other Israelite code, all of the competition being partial and fragmentary. And the Mishnah's topical program governed the exposition of the law of Judaism for the next thousand years, until Maimonides in his law code, the *Mishneh Torah*, recast the topical program in a still more logical pattern than did the Rabbinic sages who produced the Mishnah.

The Contents of the Mishnah and of the Halakhah

What exactly does the Mishnah subject to legal organization and presentation? The topics within the six divisions are arranged by volume, the largest set of rules coming first, the next largest second, and so throughout, with some variation. The topical tractates, in the six divisions into which the Mishnah is divided, with their Hebrew titles and the English translation of those titles, are as follows:

1. *Agriculture* (Zera'im): Berakhot (Blessings); Pe'ah (the corner of the field); Dema'i (doubtfully tithed produce); Kilayim (mixed seeds); Shebi'it (the seventh year); Terumot (heave offering or priestly rations); Ma'aserot (tithes); Ma'aser Sheni (second tithe); Hallah (dough offering); 'Orlah (produce of trees in the first three years after planting, which is prohibited for use); and Bikkurim (first fruits).

2. *Appointed Times* (Mo'ed): Shabbat (the Sabbath); 'Erubin (the fictive fusion meal or boundary for Sabbath fusion of private domains into a single tract for purposes of carrying); Pesahim (Passover); Sheqalim (the Temple tax); Yoma (the Day of Atonement); Sukkah (the festival of Tabernacles); Besah (the preparation of food on the festivals); Rosh Hashanah (the New Year); Ta'anit (fast days); Megillah (Purim); Mo'ed Qatan (the intermediate days of the festivals of Passover and Tabernacles); Hagigah (the festal offering).

3. *Women* (Nashim): Yebamot (the levirate widow); Ketubot (the marriage contract); Nedarim (vows); Nazir (the special vow of the Nazirite); Sotah (the wife accused of adultery); Gittin (writs of divorce); Qiddushin (betrothal).

4. *Damages* or civil law (Neziqin): Baba Qamma (the first gate), Baba Mesi'a (the middle gate), Baba Batra (the final gate) (civil law, covering damages and torts, then correct conduct of business, labor, and real estate transactions); Sanhedrin (institutions of government; criminal penalties); Makkot (flogging);

Shabu'ot (oaths); 'Eduyyot (a collection arranged on other than topical lines); Horayot (rules governing improper conduct of civil authorities).

5. *Holy Things* (Qodoshim): Zebahim (everyday animal offerings); Menahot (everyday meal offerings); Hullin (animals slaughtered for secular purposes not in the Temple in Jerusalem); Bekhorot (firstlings); 'Arakhin (vows of valuation); Temurah (vows of exchange of a beast for an already consecrated beast); Keritot (penalty of extirpation or premature death); Me'ilah (sacrilege); Tamid (the daily whole offering); Middot (the layout of the Temple building); Qinnim (how to deal with bird offerings designated for a given purpose and then mixed up with birds designated for some other purpose, e.g., purification offering versus offering of well-being).

6. *Purity* (Tohorot): Kelim (susceptibility of utensils to uncleanness); Ohalot (transmission of corpse uncleanness in the tent of a corpse); Nega'im (the uncleanness described at Lev. 13–14); Parah (the preparation of purification water); Tohorot (problems of doubt in connection with matters of cleanness); Miqva'ot (immersion pools); Niddah (menstrual uncleanness); Makhshirin (rendering susceptible to uncleanness produce that is dry and so not susceptible); Zabim (the uncleanness covered at Lev. 15); Tebul-Yom (the uncleanness of one who has immersed on that self-same day and awaits sunset for completion of the purification rites); Yadayim (the uncleanness of hands); 'Uqsin (the uncleanness transmitted through what is connected to unclean produce).

Of these tractates, only 'Eduyyot is organized along other than topical lines, rather collecting sayings on diverse subjects attributed to particular authorities. The Mishnah as printed today always includes tractate Abot (sayings of the sages), but that document reached closure about a generation later than the Mishnah. While it serves to explain the origin of the Mishnah and cites authorities who occur in the Mishnah, it does not conform to the formal, rhetorical, or logical traits characteristic of the Mishnah overall.

The Mishnah's topical program emphasizes priestly interests. In volume, the sixth division with its interest in cultic purity (Temple and home alike) covers approximately a quarter of the entire document. Topics of interest to the priesthood and the Temple, such as priestly fees, conduct of the cult on holy days, conduct of the cult on ordinary days, and management and upkeep of the Temple, and the rules of cultic cleanness predominate in the first, second, fifth, and sixth divisions. Rules governing the social order form the bulk of the third and fourth.

The stress of the Mishnah throughout on the priestly caste and the Temple cult points to the document's principal concern. That is centered upon sanctification, understood as the correct arrangement of all things, each in its proper category, each called by its rightful name, just as at the creation as portrayed in the Priestly Creation Narrative (Gen. 1:1ff.).

The Mishnah's Philosophy of Israel's Social Order

Let us now consider the Mishnah as a whole and characterize its program, its philosophy for the regulation of Israel's social order. First we take a reading of the Mishnah in history, in concrete time. It is a document of restoration and reconstruction. In the aftermath of the two great wars against Rome and the desolation of the land of Judea in consequence, the Mishnah's legal system provides for the stabilization of the social order and the restoration of the Israelite polity.

The system of philosophy expressed through concrete and detailed law presented by the Mishnah consists of a coherent logic and topic, a cogent worldview and comprehensive way of living. It is a worldview that speaks of transcendent things, a way of life in response to the supernatural meaning of what is done, a heightened and deepened perception of the sanctification of Israel in deed and in deliberation. Sanctification thus means two things: what is unique and what is dependable. Thus the holiness to which the Mishnah is devoted aims, first, at distinguishing Israel in all its dimensions from the world in all its ways. Second, the Mishnah attains sanctification for Israel by establishing the stability, order, regularity, predictability, and reliability of Israel in particular at moments and in contexts of danger. Danger means instability, disorder, irregularity, uncertainty, and betrayal. Each topic of the system as a whole takes up a critical and indispensable moment or context of social being. Through what is said in regard to each of the Mishnah's principal topics, the Mishnah makes its broad, general statement as a whole. Yet if the parts severally and jointly give the message of the whole, the whole cannot exist without all of the parts, so well joined and carefully crafted are they all. The details become clear in our survey of the document's topical program.

To understand the complete system set forth by the Mishnah, we review the six divisions as coherent statements.

The Division of Agriculture treats two topics—first, producing crops in accord with the scriptural rules on the subject, second, paying the required offerings and tithes to the priests, Levites, and poor. The principal point of the division is that the land is holy, because God has a claim both on it and on what it produces. God's claim must be honored by the setting aside of a portion of the produce for those for whom God has designated it. God's ownership must be acknowledged by observance of the rules God has laid down for use of the land. In the temporal context in which the Mishnah was produced, some generations after the disastrous defeat by the Romans of Bar Kokhba and the permanent closure of Jerusalem to Jews' access, the stress of the division brought assurance that those aspects of the sanctification of Israel—Land of Israel, Israel itself, and its social order, the holy cycle of time— that survived also remained holy and subject to the rules of Heaven.

The Division of Appointed Times carried forward the same emphasis upon sanctification, now of the high points of the lunar-solar calendar of Israel. The law tells time by the six days of Creation followed by the Seventh Day, the Sabbath of sacred repose for God and man alike. The law also tells time by appeal to the movement of the moon, with the lunar months correlated with the solar seasons. The key to the lunar-solar calendar is the vernal equinox, March 21, and the autumnal equinox, September 21. The first full moon after March 21 is Passover, and the first full moon after September 21 is Tabernacles. How does the division of time into sacred and profane work? The second division forms a system in which the advent of a holy day, like the Sabbath of creation, sanctifies the life of the Israelite village through imposing on the village rules on the model of those of the Temple. The purpose of the system, therefore, is to bring into alignment the moment of sanctification of the village and the life of the home with the moment of sanctification of the Temple on those same occasions of appointed times. Together the village and the Temple on the occasion of the holy day form a single continuum, a completed creation.

The Division of Women: Women acquire definition in relationship to men. The status of women is affected through both supernatural and natural, this-worldly action. Women formed a critical systemic component, because the proper regulation of women—subject to the father, then the husband—was deemed a central concern of Heaven, so that a betrothal would be subject to Heaven's supervision (Qiddushin, sanctification, being the pertinent tractate); documents, such as the marriage contract or the writ of divorce, drawn up on earth stand also for Heaven's concern with the sanctity of women in their marital relationship; so too, Heaven may through levirate marriage dictate whom a woman marries. That is the marriage between a widow and her deceased childless husband's brother that is required by Dt. 25:5–10. What man and woman do on earth accordingly provokes a response in Heaven, and the correspondences are perfect. So women are defined and secured both in Heaven and here on earth, and that position is always and invariably relative to men.

The principal interest for the Mishnah is the point at which a woman becomes, and ceases to be, holy to a particular man, that is, enters and leaves the marital union. These transfers of women are the dangerous and disorderly points in the relationship of woman to man, and therefore, the Mishnah states, to society as well. The Mishnah's law stresses the preservation of order in transactions involving women and (other) property. Mishnah tractate Yebamot states that Heaven sanctifies a woman to a man (under the conditions of the levirate connection). What it says by indirection is that man sanctifies too: man, like God, can sanctify that relationship between a man and a woman and can also effect the cessation of the sanctity of that same relationship.

Five of the seven tractates of the Division of Women are devoted to the formation and dissolution of the marital bond. Of them, three treat what is done by man here on earth, that is, formation of a marital bond through betrothal and marriage contract and dissolution through divorce and its consequences. The division and its system therefore delineate the natural and supernatural character of the woman's role in the social economy framed by man: the beginning, end, and middle of the relationship. The whole constitutes a significant part of the Mishnah's encompassing system of sanctification, for the reason that Heaven confirms what men do on earth.

A correctly prepared writ of divorce on earth changes the status of the woman to whom it is given, so that in Heaven she is available for sanctification to some other man, while, without that same writ, in Heaven's view, should she go to some other man, she would be liable to be put to death.

The Division of Damages comprises two subsystems, which fit together in a logical way. One part presents rules for the normal conduct of civil society. These cover commerce, trade, real estate, and other matters of everyday intercourse, as well as mishaps, such as damages by chattels and persons, fraud, overcharge, interest, and the like, in that same context of everyday social life. The other part describes the institutions governing the normal conduct of civil society, that is, courts of administration, and the penalties at the disposal of the government for the enforcement of the law. The two subjects form a single tight and systematic dissertation on the nature of Israelite society and its economic, social, and political relationships, as the Mishnah envisages them.

The main point of the first of the two parts of the division is that the task of society is to maintain perfect stasis, to preserve the prevailing situation, and to secure the stability of all relationships. To this end, in the interchanges of buying and selling, giving and taking, borrowing and lending, it is important that there be an essential equality of interchange. No party in the end should have more than what he had at the outset, and none should be the victim of a sizable shift in fortune and circumstance. All parties' rights to, and in, this stable and unchanging economy of society are to be preserved. When the condition of a person is violated, so far as possible the law will secure the restoration of the antecedent status.

The goal of the system of civil law is the recovery of the prevailing order and balance, the preservation of the established wholeness of the social economy. This idea is powerfully expressed in the organization of the three tractates that make up the civil law, which treat first abnormal and then normal transactions. The framers deal with damages done by chattels and by human beings, thefts and other sorts of malfeasance against the property of others. The civil law in both aspects pays closest attention to how the property and person of the injured party so far as possible are restored to their prior condition, that is, a state of normality. So attention to torts focuses upon penalties paid by the malefactor to the victim, rather than upon penalties inflicted by the court on the malefactor for what he has done. When speaking of damages, the Mishnah thus takes as its principal concern the restoration of the fortune of victims of assault or robbery. Then the framers take up the complementary and corresponding set of topics, the regulation of normal transactions. When we rapidly survey the kinds of transactions of special interest, we see from the topics selected for discussion what we have already uncovered in the deepest structure of organization and articulation of the basic theme.

The other half of this same unit of three Baba tractates presents laws governing normal and routine transactions, many of them of the same sort as those dealt with in the first half. At issue are deposits of goods or possessions that one person leaves in safekeeping with another. For example, cases of such transactions, called bailments, occur in both wings of the triple tractate—first, bailments subjected to misappropriation, or accusation thereof, by the bailiff, then bailments transacted under normal circumstances. Under the rubric of routine transactions are those of workers and householders, that is, the purchase and sale of labor, rentals and bailments, real estate transactions, and inheritances and estates. Of the lot, the one involving real estate transactions is the most fully articulated and covers the widest range of problems and topics. The three tractates of the civil law all together thus provide a complete account of the orderly governance of balanced transactions and unchanging civil relationships within Israelite society under ordinary conditions.

The character and interests of the Division of Damages present probative evidence of the larger program of the philosophers of the Mishnah. Their intention is to create nothing less than a full-scale Israelite government, subject to the administration of sages. This government is fully supplied with a constitution and bylaws. It makes provision for a court system and procedures, as well as a full set of laws governing civil society and criminal justice. This government, moreover, mediates between its own community and the outside ("pagan") world. Through its system of laws it expresses its judgment of the others and at the same time defines, protects, and defends its own society and social frontiers. It even makes provision for procedures of remission, to expiate its own errors. The Israelite government imagined by the second-century philosophers centers upon the Temple that they imagined, and the (then forbidden) city, Jerusalem. For the Temple is one principal focus. There the highest court is in session; there the high priest reigns.

The penalties for law infringement are of three kinds, one of which involves sacrifice in the Temple. (The others are compensation, physical punishment, and death.) The basic conception of punishment, moreover, is that unintentional infringement of the rules of society is not penalized but rather atoned for through an offering in the Temple. If a member of the people of Israel intentionally infringes against the law, to be sure, that one must be removed from society and is put to death. And if there is a claim of one member of the people against another, that must be righted, so that the prior, prevailing status may be restored. So offerings in the Temple are given up to appease Heaven and restore a whole bond between Heaven and Israel, specifically on those occasions on which without malice or ill will an Israelite has disturbed the relationship. Israelite civil society without a Temple is not stable or normal, and not to be imagined.

The plan for the government involves a clear-cut philosophy of society, a philosophy that defines the purpose of the government and ensures that its task is not merely to perpetuate its own power. What the Israelite government is supposed to do is to preserve a perfect, steady-state society. That state of perfection that, within the same fantasy, the society to begin with everywhere attains and expresses forms the goal of the system throughout: no change anywhere from a perfect balance, proportion, and arrangement of the social order, its goods and services, responsibilities and benefits. This is in at least five aspects:

First of all, one of the ongoing principles of the law, expressed in one tractate after another, is that people are to follow and maintain the prevailing practice of their locale.

Second, the purpose of civil penalties is to restore the injured party to his or her prior condition, so far as this is possible, rather than merely to penalize the aggressor.

Third, there is the conception of true value, meaning that a given object has an intrinsic worth, which, in the course of a transaction, must be paid. In this way the seller does not leave the transaction any richer than when he entered it, or the buyer any poorer (parallel to penalties for damages).

Fourth, there can be no usury, a biblical prohibition adopted and vastly enriched in the Mishnaic thought, for money ("coins") is what it is. Any pretense that it has become more than what it was violates, in its way, the conception of true value.

Fifth, when real estate is divided, it must be done with full attention to the rights of all concerned, so that, once more, one party does not gain at the expense of the other.

In these and many other aspects the law expresses its obsession with the perfect stasis of Israelite society. Its paramount purpose is in preserving and ensuring that that perfection of the division of this world is kept inviolate or restored to its true status when violated.

The Division of Holy Things presents a system of sacrifice and sanctuary. As in the other divisions, abstract principles, for example, those concerning the correct intentionality and actions that realize that intentionality, are expressed in concrete, topical cases. The division centers upon the everyday and rules always applicable to the cult: the daily whole offering, the sin offering and guilt offering that one may bring any time under ordinary circumstances; the right sequence of diverse offerings; the way in which the rites of the whole, sin, and guilt offerings are carried out; what sorts of animals are acceptable; the accompanying cereal offerings; the support and provision of animals for the cult and of meat for the priesthood; the support and material maintenance of the cult and its building. We have a system before us: the system of the cult of the Jerusalem Temple, seen as an ordinary and everyday affair, a continuing and routine operation. That is why special rules for the cult, both in respect to the altar and in regard to the maintenance of the buildings, personnel, and even the whole city, will be elsewhere—in Appointed Times and Agriculture. But from the perspective of Holy Things, those divisions intersect by supplying special rules and raising extraordinary (Agriculture: land-bound; Appointed Times: time-bound) considerations for that theme that Holy Things claims to set forth in its most general and unexceptional way: the cult as something permanent and everyday.

The Division of Purities presents a very simple system of three principal parts: sources of uncleanness, objects and substances susceptible to uncleanness, and modes of purification from uncleanness. So it tells the story of what makes a given sort of object unclean and what makes it clean. Viewed as a whole, the Division of Purities treats the interplay of persons, food, and liquids. Dry inanimate objects or food are not susceptible to uncleanness, in line with Lev. 11:34, 37. What is wet is susceptible. So liquids activate the system. What is unclean, moreover, emerges from uncleanness through the operation of liquids, specifically, through immersion in fit water of requisite volume and in natural condition. Liquids thus deactivate the system. Thus, water in its natural condition is what concludes the process by removing uncleanness. Water in its unnatural condition, that is, deliberately affected by human agency, is what imparts susceptibility to uncleanness to begin with. The uncleanness of persons, furthermore, is signified by body liquids or flux in the case of the menstruating woman and the *zab* (the person suffering from the form of uncleanness described at Lev. 15:1ff.). Corpse uncleanness is conceived to be a kind of effluent, a viscous gas that flows like liquid. Utensils for their part receive uncleanness when they form receptacles able to contain liquid.

In sum, we have a system in which the invisible flow of fluidlike substances or powers serves to put food, drink, and receptacles into the status of uncleanness and to remove those things from that status. Whether or not we call the system "metaphysical," it certainly has no material base but is conditioned upon highly abstract notions. Thus in material terms, the effect of liquid is upon food, drink, utensils, and man. The consequence has to do with who may eat and drink what food and liquid, and what food and drink may be consumed in which pots and pans. These are specified by tractates on utensils and on food and drink.

The human being is ambivalent. Persons fall in the middle, between sources and loci of uncleanness. They serve as sources of uncleanness. They also become unclean. But being unclean, they fall within the system's program of consequences. So they make other things unclean and are subject to penalties because they are unclean. Unambiguous sources of uncleanness always are unclean and never can become clean: the corpse, the dead creeping thing, and things like them. Inanimate sources of uncleanness and inanimate objects convey uncleanness *ex opere operato*; their status of being unclean never changes; they present no ambiguity. Systemically unique, man and liquids have the capacity to inaugurate the processes of uncleanness (as sources) and also are subject to those same processes (as objects of uncleanness).

Emphases and Silences: Omitted Divisions and Topics

When we listen to the silences of the system of the Mishnah, as much as to its points of stress, we hear a single message. It is a message of a system that answered a single encompassing question, and the question formed a stunning counterpart to that set forth in the Torah. At stake was how Israel as defined by that system related to its land, represented by its Temple, and the message may be simply stated: What appears to be the given is in fact a gift, subject to stipulations. That formed the lesson of 586 BCE that the Pentateuch set forth. And the precipitating event for the Mishnaic system was the destruction of the Jerusalem Temple in 70

CE. Then the question turned obsession with the defeat of Bar Kokhba in 135 and the closure of Jerusalem to Jews. The urgent issue taken up by the Mishnah in the aftermath of the massive defeats of 70 and 135 was, specifically, what, in the aftermath of the destruction of the holy place and holy cult, remained of the sanctity of the holy caste, the priesthood, the holy land, the Land of Israel and, above all, the holy people, the people of Israel, and its holy way of life?

The answer was that sanctity persists, indelibly, in Israel, the people, in its way of life, in its land, in its priesthood, in its food, in its mode of sustaining life, in its manner of procreating and so sustaining the nation. That judgment is expressed in the Halakhah in the flagship tractate of the Mishnah, tractate Hullin, at Mishnah Hullin 5:1, 6:1, 7:1, 10:1, 11:1, and 12:1. That is, the Mishnah's legislation recognizes that the destruction of the Temple in 70, as in 586, marked a change in Israel's holy life. But the sanctity of Israel, expressed in the Halakhic system, endures beyond the loss of the holy city, the holy Temple, and, ultimately, the holy land. The events of 132–135 registered in the same context. But for the law of the Mishnah the destruction of the Temple formed an established fact bearing obvious liturgical consequences, not the paramount proposition of the Mishnah's Halakhic program throughout.

Mishnah Hullin 5:1

[The prohibition against slaughtering on the same day] it and its young [Lev. 22:28] applies (1) in the Land and outside the Land, (2) in the time of the Temple and not in the time of the Temple, (3) in the case of unconsecrated beasts and in the case of consecrated beasts.

Mishnah Hullin 6:1

[The requirement to] cover up the blood applies in the Land and abroad, (2) in the time of the Temple and not in the time of the Temple, (3) in the case of unconsecrated beasts, but not in the case of Holy Things.

Mishnah Hullin 7:1

[The prohibition of] the sinew of the hip [sciatic nerve, Gen. 32:32] applies (1) in the Land and outside of the Land, (2) in the time of the Temple and not in the time of the Temple, (3) to unconsecrated animals and to Holy Things.

Mishnah Hullin 10:1

[The requirement to give to the priests] the shoulder, the two cheeks, and the maw [Dt. 18:3] applies (1) in the Land and outside of the Land, (2) in the time of the Temple and not in the time of the Temple, (3) to unconsecrated beasts, but not to consecrated beasts.

Mishnah Hullin 11:1

[The requirement to give to the priest] the first of the fleece [Dt. 18:41] applies (1) in the Land and outside of the Land, (2) in the time of the Temple and not in the time of the Temple, (3) to unconsecrated beasts but not to consecrated beasts.

MISHNAH HULLIN 12:1

[The requirement to] let [the dam] go from the nest [Dt. 22:6–7] applies (1) in the Land and outside of the Land, (2) in the time of the Temple and not in the time of the Temple, (3) to unconsecrated [birds] but not to consecrated ones.

The tripartite formulation, "time of the Temple/not in the time of the Temple" or "in the Land/outside of the Land" or in the case of what is unconsecrated as much as in the case of what is consecrated, explicitly recognizes that the destruction of the Temple marked a boundary in the situation of Israel. The limits of the land marked another. The status as to sanctification recorded a third. The question then was, do these marks of sanctification—Temple, land, consecration—apply now that the Temple and priesthood have ceased to function. But the point is that the liturgical changes can accommodate the new situation; it is not a caesura in time or a new age of history. The question is, do the specified rites pertain in the present age, when the Temple lies in ruins, and in the present situation, when Israel is located outside of the Holy Land. The issue then is, what is the status as to sanctification of the food that Israel eats (Mishnah tractate Hul. 5:1, 6:1, 7:1, 12:1) or hands over to the priesthood as part of its rations (Mishnah tractate Hul. 10:1, 11:1). Israel the holy people remains holy and subject to the disciplines of sanctification, and the priesthood remains holy and worthy of receiving its rations, which form part of the disciplines of sanctification of the produce and the yield of the land.

The Mishnah's system therefore focused upon the holiness of the life of Israel, the people, a holiness that had formerly centered on the Temple. The logically consequent question was, what is the meaning of sanctity, and how shall Israel attain, or give evidence of, sanctification? For the meaning of sanctity the framers therefore turned to that first act of sanctification, the one in creation. It came about when, all things in array, in place, each with its proper name, God blessed and sanctified the seventh day on the eve of the first Sabbath. Creation was made ready for the blessing and the sanctification when all things were very good, that is to say, in their rightful order, called by their rightful name.

An orderly nature was a sanctified and blessed nature, so dictated Scripture in the name of the Supernatural. So to receive the blessing and to be made holy, all things in nature and society were to be set in right array. Given the condition of Israel, the people, in its land, in the aftermath of the catastrophic war against Rome led by Bar Kokhba in 132–135, putting things in order was no easy task. But that is why, after all, the question pressed, the answer proving inexorable and obvious. The condition of society corresponded to the critical question that obsessed the system builders.

Extension, Amplification, and Syllogistic Character: [1] From Cases to Rules

To conclude this exposition of the Mishnah we turn from the comparison of the Mishnah and other Israelite law codes and the topical description of the

Mishnah to consider the Mishnah's modes of thought. These exercised a profound influence in the shaping of the intellect of the Talmud, which we meet in chapter 3.

The Talmud—both Talmuds—conducted a massive and systematic exegesis—systematic, principled interpretation—of tractates of the Mishnah. The Bavli deals with thirty-seven of the Mishnah's sixty-two topical tractates, and the Yerushalmi with thirty-nine, as we shall see. How does the Mishnah precipitate the program of the Talmud? The Mishnah presents information in such a way that the facts of a case point to rules of a general character. The details are so shaped as to form a demonstration of a comprehensive principle, and the formalization of the prose participates in the shaping. The Talmuds then respond to the implicit program of the Mishnah and articulate the logical consequences of its presentation. They carry forward the message of the Mishnah's cases, articulating the generalization contained in the Mishnah's cases and introducing refinements and amplifications of that generalization.

How this is done is best conveyed through an illustration. In the following passage, drawn from Mishnah tractate Sanhedrin chapter 2 (2:1–5), the authorship wishes to say that Israel has two heads, one of state, the other of cult, the king and the high priest, respectively, and that these two offices are nearly wholly congruent with one another, with a few differences based on the particular traits of each. The genus is head of holy Israel. The species are king and high priest. Here are the traits in common and those not shared, and the exercise is fully exposed for what it is, an inquiry into the rules that govern, the points of regularity and order, in this minor matter, of political structure. The exercise is one of analogical-contrastive reasoning, that is, comparison and contrast.

My simple outline, indicated by the top-level topics I and II, makes the point important in this setting. Each item is singled out with a letter, A, B, C, so we see the match and the pattern of comparison and contrast. In this way we see how the facts that pertain to the high priest and the king yield a generalization that transcends the details. At issue is the question, which classification of national leader, king or high priest, is more exalted than the other?

I. The rules of the high priest: subject to the law, marital rites, conduct in bereavement (Mishnah Sanhedrin 2:1)

    A. A high priest judges, and [others] judge him;

    B. gives testimony, and [others] give testimony about him;

    C. performs the rite of removing the shoe [Dt. 25:7–9], and [others] perform the rite of removing the shoe with his wife.

    D. [Others] enter levirate marriage with his wife, but he does not enter into levirate marriage,

    E. because he is prohibited to marry a widow.

    F. [If] he suffers a death [in his family], he does not follow the bier.

II. The rules of the king: not subject to the law, marital rites, conduct in bereavement (Mishnah Sanhedrin 2:2)

A. The king does not judge, and [others] do not judge him;
B. does not give testimony, and [others] do not give testimony about him;
C. does not perform the rite of removing the shoe, and others do not perform the rite of removing the shoe with his wife;
D. does not enter into levirate marriage, nor [does his brother] enter levirate marriage with his wife.
E. [Others] do not marry his widow.

The subordination of Scripture to the classification scheme is self-evident. Scripture supplies facts. The traits of things—kings, high priests—dictate classification categories on their own, without Scripture's dictate. How do the data yield a proposition, a syllogism, in the comparison of the king and the high priest?

The philosophical cast of mind, which organizes information into constructions of useful knowledge, is amply revealed in this little essay, which in concrete terms effects a taxonomy, a classification that yields a study of the genus, national leader, and its two species, (I) high priest, (II) king. The assembled facts show how they are alike, how they are not alike, and what accounts for the differences. The premise is that national leaders are alike and follow the same rule, except where they differ and follow the opposite rule from one another. But that premise also is subject to the proof effected by the survey of the data consisting of concrete rules, those systemically inert facts that here come to life for the purposes of establishing a proposition. By itself, the fact that, for example, others may not ride on his horse bears the burden of no systemic proposition. In the context of an argument constructed for taxonomic purposes, the same fact is active and weighty.

The whole depends upon three premises: (1) the importance of comparison and contrast, with the supposition that (2) like follows like, and the unlike follows the opposite, rule; and (3) when we classify, we also hierarchize, which yields the argument from hierarchical classification: if this, which is the lesser, follows rule X, then that, which is the greater, surely should follow rule X. And that is the whole sum and substance of the logic of *list making* as the Mishnah applies that logic in a practical way.

If I had to specify a single mode of thought that established connections between one fact and another, it is in the search for points in common and therefore also points of contrast. We seek connection between fact and fact, sentence and sentence in the subtle and balanced rhetoric of the Mishnah, by comparing and contrasting two things that are alike and not alike. At the logical level, too, the Mishnah falls into the category of familiar philosophical thought. Once we seek regularities, we propose rules. What is like another thing falls under its rule, and what is not like the other falls under the opposite rule.

Accordingly, as to the species of the genus, so far as they are alike, they share the same rule. So far as they are not alike, each follows a rule contrary to that governing the other. So the work of analysis is what produces connection, and therefore the drawing of conclusions derives from comparison and contrast: the *and,* the *equal.* The proposition then that forms the conclusion concerns the essential likeness of the two offices, except where they are different, but the subterranean premise is that we can explain both likeness and difference by appeal to a principle of fundamental order and unity. So the point is obvious. The high priest and king fall into a single genus, but speciation, based on traits particular to the king, then distinguishes the one from the other. All of this exercise is conducted essentially independently of Scripture; the classifications derive from the system, are viewed as autonomous constructs; traits of things define classifications and dictate what is like and what is unlike.

Extension, Amplification, and Syllogistic Character [2]: From Rules to Generalizations

A paramount problematic occurring in a variety of topical expositions concerns the relationship of intentionality and actuality, and it suffices to show the other side of the Mishnah's syllogistic character, its power to encapsulate weighty principles in minor details of law, properly set forth. A single example serves. It shows how the analytical program of the Mishnah comes to expression in matters of small detail.

The case that illustrates the relationship between intent and act concerns the laws of cultic cleanness. The details capture the issue and must be grasped to make sense of the matter. Scripture states that what is dry is insusceptible to uncleanness. What is deliberately wet down is susceptible, and if it is touched by a source of uncleanness, for instance a dead creeping thing, then the produce becomes unclean. Now liquid imparts uncleanness or becomes susceptible to uncleanness when it is subject to the will or intentionality of a human actor ("deliberately wet down" treated as an instance of a generalization). Thus we must identify the point at which liquid is deemed subject to a person's will and intention, serving his purpose. Then and only then the liquid enters the status of susceptibility to uncleanness, in line with Lev. 11:34, 37. The case involves honeycombs. These are approached in two stages for the removal of the honey. First, the bees are smoked out. Then the beekeeper has to break the combs to get at the honey. At what point does the liquid become subject to the beekeeper's intentionality, for example, his desire to make use of the honey?

MISHNAH TRACTATE UQSIN 3:11

Honeycombs: from what point are they susceptible to uncleanness [in the status of liquid]?

The House of Shammai say, "When one smokes out [the bees from the combs so that one can potentially get at the honey]."

The House of Hillel say, "When one will [actually] have broken up [the honeycombs to remove the honey]."

One party maintains that the liquid of honeycombs is susceptible to uncleanness when one has smoked out the bees, the other, when one has broken the honeycombs. Clearly, therefore, when I have access to the honey, so that I may make use of it, the honey is susceptible; hence liquid that is not accessible to human use (in this context) is deemed insusceptible; Lev. 11:34, 37 are read to make that point. So much for the concrete issue.

But what is the principle at hand? I have interpolated some words to make clear in context the issue of whether what is potential is real. That is to say, do I take account of what potentially may happen? Or do I treat as fact only what has happened? The House of Shammai say that once you have smoked out the bees, you have access to the honey. What is potential is treated as equivalent to what is actual. Since you can get at the honey, the honey can be useful to you and so is susceptible. The House of Hillel say that only when you actually have broken the honeycombs by a concrete deed is the honey susceptible. What is potential is not taken into account, only what is actual.

So at stake is the old philosophical problem of the acorn and the oak, the egg and the chicken, the potential and the actual. In other disputes, what is at stake is how to correctly classify things, so as to discover the single rule that governs a number of diverse cases. Elsewhere, the subterranean principle concerns intention and how we assess what a person plans to do: as if it is done, as if it might be done, as if it is null until some action confirms the intention, and so on. We have chapters of the Mishnah in which these are the stakes.

More broadly speaking, through the cases and laws they yield, the framers of the Mishnah address profound issues of theology, for instance, the relationship among God, Israel, and the Land of Israel; of philosophy, for example, classification, intention, and mixtures (today a matter of physics, but then a matter of philosophy); and social policy, for instance, the standing of women, the meaning of wealth, the right conduct of the market, and the like. The Talmud—both Talmuds—took as its task the analysis of these cases and laws with the goal of showing the comprehensive system of thought that inhered in them. To that natural next step in the formation of the oral Torah we turn in chapter 3.

ENDNOTES

1. Moshe Greenberg, "Exodus, book of," *Encyclopaedia Judaica* (Jerusalem: 1971), 6:1050ff. Passage cited: cols. 1056–57. I also consulted Jeffrey H. Tigay, "Exodus. Introduction and Annotations," in Adele Berlin and Marc Zvi Brettler, *The Jewish Study Bible* (New York: Oxford University Press, 2002), 102–202.
2. Martin Noth, *Exodus, A commentary* (London: SCM Press, 1962), 173.
4. These are directed toward all free Israelites who had to discuss and decide together in the local legal assembly. The principal aim of these requirements is to protect the poor and the weak against a partial judgment in favor of the rich and the powerful (Noth, p. 188).

3

What Is the Gemara?

Dispute, Debate, Argument: The Unique Trait of the Gemara

The Gemara ("learning") forms a commentary to the Mishnah, line by line. The Mishnah is about life, the Gemara is about the Mishnah. But that simple observation does not capture what is unique in the Gemara as in the Mishnah. What marks Rabbinic literature off from all other legal and theological bodies of writing in the Israelite setting is this: Disputes matter. Differences of opinion on a single matter are recorded and set forth in a rational manner. The Gemara is the most contentious piece of writing in the entire literature of Judaism. It also is the most energetic and exacting.

Persistent dispute forms the heart of the matter, marking a Rabbinic text off from all other texts of Judaism. We look in vain in Scripture for a legitimate hearing accorded to two conflicting positions. There is heresy and orthodoxy, conflict and consensus. But heresy gets no hearing, and orthodoxy prevails in the very representation of the Scripture's rules. And Scripture is not alone in eschewing contention. We look in vain in Judaic writings beyond the limits of Scripture for conflicting opinions, side by side, attributed to named authorities. By contrast, the provision of disputes about the law, debates about the resolution of difference, and arguments based on reason and evidence define the dominant trait of the Rabbinic canon, especially of the Mishnah and the Gemara.

A quick comparison distinguishes the Talmud from the Damascus Covenant, a law code found among the Dead Sea Scrolls. For that purpose we consider how the laws of the Sabbath are set forth in the Damascus Covenant with reference to a single item, making plans on the Sabbath for work to be done after the Sabbath. May one give thought on the holy day of rest to activities to be undertaken after the Sabbath repose has come to an end? Is this a form of prohibited labor, a violation of the Sabbath? Both law codes prohibit doing so, but the way in which the Mishnah and the Gemara set forth the law markedly comprehends conflicting opinion. First is the formulation of the Damascus Covenant:

Let him not speak [on the Sabbath] of matters of labor and work to be done on the morrow. . . . Let no man walk about in the field on the Sabbath in order to do the work he requires after the Sabbath ends." (Rabin, *The Zadokite Fragments*, p. 52)

The point of the law is simple: One may not discuss on the Sabbath day plans for after-the-Sabbath labor. He may not hire workers on the Sabbath in the context of work to be done afterward. Where the presentation of the law by the Mishnah and the Gemara emerges as unique becomes clear in the contrast between the foregoing presentation of rules and the Mishnah's and Gemara's counterpart:

MISHNAH TRACTATE SHABBAT 23:3
A man should not hire workers on the Sabbath.
And a man should not ask his fellow to hire workers for him.

What is important in what follows is the critical questioning that animates the commentary of the Talmud:

BAVLI TO MISHNAH TRACTATE SHABBAT 23:3 I.1
[And a man should not ask his fellow to hire workers for him:] Well, what might be the difference between the man and his neighbor [that we have to be told he may not ask the fellow to hire for him, since he cannot hire for himself]?

Said R. Pappa, "Reference is made to a gentile friend."

Objected R. Ashi, "Making such a statement to a gentile would constitute a violation of the general principle of Sabbath rest!"

Rather, said R. Ashi, "You may even say that it is an Israelite fellow. So we are informed that, while a man should not ask his fellow to hire workers for him, he may say to him, 'Let's see whether you stand with me this evening.' [Both understand the sense of the statement, but there is no violation of the law.]"

And who then stands behind the Mishnah rule? It is R. Joshua b. Qorhah, for it has been taught on Tannaite authority: A man may not say to his fellow, "Well, we shall see whether you will join me to work for me in the evening."

R. Joshua b. Qorhah said, "A man may say to his fellow, 'Well, we shall see whether you will join me to work for me in the evening'" [T. Shab. 17:11].

Said Rabbah bar Hannah said R. Yohanan, "The decided law accords with R. Joshua b. Qorhah."

And said Rabbah bar Hannah said R. Yohanan, "What is the scriptural basis for the position of R. Joshua b. Qorhah? 'Not finding your own pleasure nor speaking your own words' (Is. 58:13). An act of speech is forbidden, but expressing an unarticulated thought is permitted."

We look in vain in Scripture's law codes and in those found in the Dead Sea library for three traits absolutely routine in the Mishnah and the Gemara, that is in the Talmud.

First, the Mishnah and the Gemara cite conflicting opinion in the name of specific authorities, all of them equally reliable in general. Each authority possesses his traditions and his reasons. The Talmud preserves not consensus but contention.

Second, the Gemara undertakes a critical analysis of the Mishnah—a matter we shall examine in detail later on. Here it suffices to notice how the Talmud asks questions about the Mishnah, as though finding fault.

Third, the Gemara records not only rulings but reasons for them and investigates the general principles that govern. The Talmud then forms the record of not only the decisions and rules, but also the deliberations and disputes. The contours of consensus do not form the outer boundaries of the law. Not only that, but disputes are accompanied by debates, and both (or all) parties enjoy a hearing and participate in fair contention.

The Balanced, Fair Argument: Both Sides Address a Single Issue in Common and Each Gets Its Say

While the Talmud presents a vast corpus of debates about disputed laws, the clearest characterization of how these debates are carried on comes to us from the Tosefta, a collection of rules that supplement or complement those of the Mishnah, produced by circa 300 CE, about a century after the completion of the Mishnah. So for our example of how Talmudic disputes give way to debates, we turn to that document.

What is subject to dispute and debate? To understand the answer, we have to keep in mind that where the ruling for a case is unknown, the sages look for a comparable or parallel case. The known, the comparable case, then supplies the rule for the unknown, the case requiring a decision. That is because the mode of thought at hand maintains that things are alike, so the same rule applies, or that they are not alike, so the opposite rule pertains. This is called analogical-contrastive reasoning—reasoning by analogy, reasoning by appeal to opposites or contrasts. (In a moment we shall see how this works, in a case that is not complicated.) That explains why what is at stake in the dispute is the identification of the governing analogy. In the system of analogical-contrastive thinking that the Mishnah put forth, what settles an argument is the principle governing the case corresponding to the issue at hand.

A concrete example of analogical-contrastive reasoning will make matters entirely clear. The Tosefta presents us with a striking case in which the governing analogy is introduced in an explicit manner. At issue is identifying the governing analogy: To what known situation does the case requiring a ruling pertain? If it is like situation A, it follows the rule of A, and if it is like situation B, it follows the rule of B. Here we see how argument by analogy and contrast works in the Mishnah, Tosefta, and Talmuds. The case concerns the disposition of what is subject to doubt—a favorite theme of the framers of the Mishnah and a paramount problem for the Gemara, too. Two positions are outlined, each deriving from the governing analogy chosen by a contending party.

To understand the problem before us, we need a few facts. First, the book of Leviticus in chapters 11 through 15 lists various sources of uncleanness, which render a person unfit to enter the Temple and to participate in its rites. If someone has contracted uncleanness, he is unfit for the holy place. If an object has become unclean, it is not to be used for the divine service. But there is a way of removing uncleanness. That involves immersing the unclean person or object in a pool of water that has collected naturally, not through human intervention, for example, collecting and transporting the water. This is called an immersion pool, in Hebrew, *miqveh*. Such a pool must contain a given volume of suitable water, enough water to cover an average human being, about forty *seahs*. Now, if it does, then objects immersed therein are deemed at sunset to have been cleansed of the uncleanness they have contracted from sources of uncleanness.

In the following case, what we do not know is the status of objects immersed in an immersion pool—does it contain the required volume of suitable water? The problem is that the pool had been assumed valid but that, at a given point in time, is found to be lacking in the requisite volume of water and so is unable to effect the purification of what is immersed. Specifically, how do we dispose of those objects immersed in the time from the last point at which it was known that the pool had a valid volume of water to the present time? The style of writing is familiar from the Mishnah: statement of the facts of the case and the ruling of the Rabbinic authority.

Tosefta Miqvaot 1:16–19

An immersion pool which was measured and found lacking—all the acts requiring cleanness which were carried out depending upon it

whether this immersion pool is in the private domain, or whether this immersion pool is in the public domain—[Supply:] objects that have been immersed are unclean.

R. Simeon says, "In the private domain, it is unclean. In the public domain, it is clean."

Simeon invokes the rule that cases of doubt in the private domain are resolved in a strict manner and classified as unclean and in public domain are resolved in a lenient manner and are classified as clean. But that is not the focus of the dispute. Thus far we have the statement of the case that embodies the dispute at hand:

Said R. Simeon, "There was the case of the water reservoir of Disqus in Yabneh was measured and found lacking.

"And R. Tarfon did declare clean, and R. Aqiba unclean."

Thus far we have the two positions on the outcome of the case at hand, two rulings lacking reasons. The narrator now introduces the governing consideration, identical for both parties to the dispute.

"Said R. Tarfon, 'Since this immersion pool is in the assumption of being clean, it remains perpetually in this presumption of cleanness until it will be known for sure that it is made unclean.'

"Said R. Aqiba, 'Since this immersion pool is in the assumption of being unclean, it perpetually remains in the presumption of uncleanness until it will be known for sure that it is clean.'"

The principle is, do we focus upon the prevailing assumption as to the status of the pool, and confirm that status? We assumed the pool was valid; why change now? Or do we declare the governing analogy to be the status of the unclean object that was immersed in the pool and confirm that status? We assumed the object was unclean; why change now? The former status is confirmed as valid, since we have assumed the pool was valid until we discovered that it was lacking in the requisite volume of valid water; the latter status is confirmed as unclean, since we assume objects that have been declared unclean remain so until they are validly purified.

But the importance of the item for our purpose has not yet emerged. It becomes apparent when we come to the debate that accompanies the dispute. Each party has a valid argument. Now at stake is, which is the governing analogy?

"Said R. Tarfon, 'To what is the matter to be likened? To one who was standing and offering [a sacrifice] at the altar, and it became known that he is a son of a divorcee or the son of a woman who has undergone the rite of removing the shoe,
"'for his service is valid.'
"Said R. Aqiba, 'To what is the matter to be likened?
"'To one who was standing and offering [a sacrifice] at the altar, and it became known that he is disqualified by reason of a blemish—
"'for his service is invalid.'"

Thus far we have the conflict between relevant analogies. Now how is the argument articulated? It is through the challenge of each party to the pertinence of the analogy introduced by the other:

"Said R. Tarfon to him, 'You draw an analogy to one who is blemished. I draw an analogy to the son of a divorcee or to the son of a woman who has undergone the rite of removing the shoe [and is invalid for marriage into the priesthood].
"'Let us now see to what the matter is appropriately likened.
"'If it is analogous to a blemished priest, let us learn the law from the case of the blemished priest. If it is analogous to the son of a divorcee or to the son of a woman who has undergone the rite of removing the shoe, let us learn the law from the case of the son of the divorcee or the son of a woman who has undergone the rite of removing the shoe.'"

In fact, as we shall now see, Tarfon's statement of the issue of which analogy governs proves to set matters up to allow Aqiba to settle the question. He does so by differentiating the analogical cases, showing where the true point of similarity—now, he insists, not mere similarity but identity!—is to be located:

"R. Aqiba says, 'The unfitness affecting an immersion pool affects the immersion pool itself, and the unfit aspect of the blemished priest affects the blemished priest himself.

"'But let not the case of the son of a divorcee or the son of a woman who has undergone the rite of removing the shoe prove the matter, for his matter of unfitness depends upon others.

"'A ritual pool's unfitness [depends] on one only, and the unfitness of a blemished priest [depends] on an individual only, but let not the son of a divorcee or the son of a woman who has undergone the rite of removing the shoe will prove the matter, for the unfitness of this one depends upon ancestry.'

"They took a vote concerning the case and declared it unclean."

"Said R. Tarfon to R. Aqiba, 'He who departs from you is like one who perishes.'"

This is what is meant by an analogical-contrastive argument: What is the governing analogy is at issue. All parties agree that things may *look* alike but not *be* alike. We must not confuse verisimilitude with identity. That is why the players are quick to differentiate between similarity and identity.

Tarfon argues that the similarity governs. Aqiba's task is to find difference where Tarfon perceives similarity. Aqiba finds no difficulty in acknowledging the similarity, but he criticizes the use of the analogy by differentiating between similarity and identity. Things that look alike are not necessarily alike at all.

How to show this? Aqiba is able to differentiate ("divide") the analogy into its operative components, and in doing so, he shows that the analogy as he proposes to apply it sustains his position. What we have seen is the power of the dispute and accompanying debate to reach the deepest layers of thought and expose them. Every page of the Talmud contains disputes, and many add debates such as we have seen just now. These modes of thought and expression mark the Talmud as rare indeed in the history of humanity's intellectual life. But there is something that marks the Talmud as unique, the dialectical argument.

The Moving, or Dialectical, Argument of the Bavli

So far we have seen the dispute, the debate, and the formal argument. But these set-piece recitations form scripts for the recapitulation of ritual arguments; even the language of the one authority matches that of the other. This rarely reflects the reality of ordinary folk engaged in the urgent exchange of reasons for their views. So these are highly stylized exercises, not records of things really said in the heat of argument. But the Talmud also contains the kind of meandering, tit-for-tat argument that takes place in everyday life: the exchange between real people thinking on the spot. That is the moving or dialectical argument.

Particular to the Gemara of the Talmud of Babylonia is an argument that moves from point to point and that covers ground not indicated in the opening of the debate at all. That is the mark of movement. For the Bavli's purpose argument demanded not merely the static presentation of propositions, pro and con, but the dynamic, unfolding challenge and response, analytical reasoning on the spot—

dialectical argument. Well-reasoned demonstration did not suffice. Only rigorous dispute, moving from point to point, between responsive, reasonable players served.

We begin with a brief account of dialectics as defined by philosophy in the world in which the Talmud took shape, the world of Socrates, Plato, and especially Aristotle. That is where the Rabbinic sages find their place, in the world of reasoned exchanges of ideas. And then we turn to cases that set forth the Bavli's version of the same mode of argument. To begin with a simple definition, Robin Smith provides the following:

> Generally speaking, the practice of arguing with others on the basis of their own opinions and securing premises by asking questions may be described as "dialectical argument. . . . I would propose . . . as a definition of dialectical argument in its most general sense, *argument directed at another person which proceeds by asking questions.*[1]

The Talmud bears a massive collection of arguments directed at another person that proceed by asking questions—and provoking answers, then asking questions of the answers, then answering those questions and generating new questions.

There is an important distinction between a dispute composed of set-piece arguments and a dialectical argument. In the dialectical argument each party addresses the position of the other. Exchanges of reasoning, evidence, and argument, not merely presentation of static positions, define the course of discussion. In a dialectical argument the purpose is to persuade the other party that he is wrong, not merely to inform him of your views and the reasons for them: to challenge and elicit response. Accordingly, a dialectical argument is an exchange of conflicting opinion that moves from point to point, not remaining bound to the initial proposition but pursuing the consequences of practical reason and applied logic wherever they direct the flow of argument.

Where in the canon of Rabbinic Judaism that took shape from the completion of the Mishnah circa 200 CE to the closure of the Talmud of Babylonia circa 600 CE do we find dialectical argument? As a matter of fact the movement of thought through contentious challenge and passionate response, initiative, ploy and counterploy characterizes the Bavli in particular.[2]

The dialectical argument imparts flavor to the whole Bavli by imposing tension and supplying energy, focus, and purpose. By its movement, from question to answer, point to point, problem to problem, case to case, the dialectical argument also makes the Bavli an exciting writing. The rigor required to participate in a challenging exchange defines the intellectual quality of the whole document, even though most of the sustained discussions prove merely illuminating, not contentious. For its part the dialectical argument asks for not merely information but analysis, not merely acute reading of existing language but formulation of new points of interest altogether.

In the Bavli a dialectical argument is a systematic exposition, through give and take, moving from point to point. It does not run in a straight line but veers this way and that. The argument is the thing, since the dialectical argument strays from its original, precipitating point and therefore does not ordinarily undertake the demonstration, but rather the *exploration*, of a fixed proposition. Argument moves along, developing an idea through questions and answers, sometimes implicit, but more commonly explicit. That mode of analysis through media of question-answer and contentious argument imparts to the Bavli its distinctive, and I should claim, unique characteristics of thought.[3] Called in the language of the Bavli *shaqla vetarya,* give and take, dialectics requires definition in neutral terms.

Thus a "moving argument" is one that transcends the set-piece juxtaposition of propositions, arguments, and evidence, such as we saw in the Tosefta's dispute and debate about the faulty immersion pool and its consequences. This transcendence of set-piece exchanges is accomplished by treating propositions, arguments, and evidence to a process of interchange and challenge. It is realized by composing out of the pronouncement of differences of opinion an ongoing, unfolding argument, that is, one in which one point is countered by another that intersects, so that what then follows is not a recapitulation of what has been said but an unfolding, developing interchange of reason and argument.

The ticket of admission to the argument is the power to listen carefully and concentrate. Then because the players listen thoughtfully to one another and respond to the point, the "moving argument" may, and should, change course. This is always in response to the arguments that are set forth, the obstacles placed in the original path of thought. The purpose of the dialectical argument is not to advocate but to explore, not to demonstrate truth but to discover truth out of a process of contention and confrontation. The successful argument formed dialectically will deal with all possibilities and reach not a climax but a calm, anticlimactic conclusion: All things having been said, we end up here, rather than somewhere else.

Let me review this somewhat unfamiliar yet critical matter. The Rabbinic dialectical argument—the protracted, sometimes meandering, always moving flow of contentious thought—raises a question and answers it, then raises a question about the answer, and, having raised another question, then gives an answer to that question and continues in the same fashion until a variety of issues have been sorted out. So it moves hither and yon; it is always one and coherent, but it is never the same, and it flows across the surface of the document at hand. The dialectical character derives not from the mere rhetorical device of question and answer, but from the pursuit of an argument, in a single line, but in many and diverse directions. And the power of the dialectical argument flows from that continuity. We find the source of continuity in the author's capacity to show connections through the momentum of rigorous analysis on the one side and free-ranging curiosity on the other.

Those second and third and fourth turnings therefore differentiate a dialectical argument from a static dispute and debate, much as the bubbles tell the difference between still and sparkling wine. The always sparkling dialectical argument is one principal means by which the Bavli or some other Rabbinic writing accomplishes its goal of showing the connections between this and that, ultimately demonstrating the unity of many "thises and thats."

These efforts at describing the argument serve precisely as well as program notes to a piece of music: They tell us what we are going to hear; they cannot play the music. What "moves" therefore is the flow of argument and thought, and that is—by definition—from problem to problem. The movement is generated specifically by the raising of contrary questions and theses. What characterizes the dialectical argument in Rabbinic literature is its moving hither and yon. It is not a direct or straight-line movement, for example, the dialectical argument with which we are familiar in the modern West, thesis, antithesis, synthesis.

Why Dialectics Was the Chosen Medium of Thought and Expression for the Mishnah's Heirs and Continuators in the Gemara

Why does the Gemara take the form of ever-flowing argument? To understand the answer, we have to take note of the Talmud's task. To begin with, Scripture and the Mishnah did not form the sole sources of laws that the Rabbis of the Talmud addressed. The Tosefta, which we met as a supplement to the Mishnah, contained other traditions. And a sizable corpus of legal traditions enriched the heritage. These traditions contained valued norms but also conflicts and contradictions. But the Rabbis were engaged in setting forth a coherent, logical, cogent corpus of rules and principles. How to cover the massive body of diverse rulings and transform the whole into the work of reason and rationality? How better than through arguments that encompassed a wide range of cases subject to a common principle and rule?

The Mishnah collected only a small portion of the law that had come into being before and in the first and second centuries. A sizable corpus of opinion, rulings, cases, and disputes circulated from the period in which the Mishnah emerged but found (or was given) no place within the Mishnah. Some of these materials came to rest in the compilation of supplements to the Mishnah called the Tosefta, as we have seen in passing. Corresponding to the Mishnah in its topical organization and program, the Tosefta exceeded the Mishnah in sheer volume by at least four times—perhaps more. Other laws were formulated along with attributions to the same authorities, called Tannaite sages, who occur in the Mishnah. These laws scarcely differentiated themselves from those in the Mishnah, except in contents. Still more laws circulated, whether or not attributed to the names of authorities who occur also in the Mishnah, bearing the mark TNY—yielding "it was formulated for repetition as a Tannaite rule"[4]—and these too enjoyed the same standing and authority as Tannaite sayings collected in the Mishnah or the Tosefta.

How were all these laws, deriving from diverse authorities and collected in varied ways, to hold together? Points of contradiction would have to be sorted out. Harmony between and among diverse laws would have to be established. The kind of analysis of the difference between likeness or similarity and identity or sameness presents an example of what was required. Here is where the dialectical, unfolding, analytical argument comes to the fore. How better to accomplish the task than through the analysis of sayings? So the Rabbinic sages undertook the formulation and testing of generalizations, above all, the discovery of the principles embedded in the normative rules governing discrete cases.

That is why the Bavli resorted to the dialectal argument. The Mishnah made lists and compared them, so we saw in the presentation of the king and the high priest. But further steps were required, steps that would make possible the transformation of the Mishnah's lists, limited by their nature to data of a single kind, on a single subject (in the case we examined: the king, the high priest, and how they compare) into the starting points for series—consideration of diverse topics that adhere to the same rule. This I shall illustrate and explain in due course.

The implications of the character of the heritage of norms that the Rabbinic sages addressed with the Mishnah in hand prove self-evident. Specifically, had the Rabbinic sages received only the Mishnah, the character of that document would have imposed a labor of mere amplification of a well-crafted document and application of a uniform law. That is not only because of the exquisite quality of the craftsmanship exhibited in the Mishnah's composition, but also because of the pristine clarity of its laws themselves. Where there is a difference of opinion, it is labeled by assigning to the minority view a name, with the majority, and normative, position given anonymously. So was schism signaled clearly if tacitly. Hence applying the law would have imposed no formidable burdens. And had the Babylonian sages of the third through seventh centuries received only a mass of laws, deriving from hither and yon, the primary work of selection and organization, not analysis and theoretical synthesis, would have occupied their best energies. But that is not how matters worked out.

The Mishnah imposed structure and order. The boundaries of discourse therefore were laid out. But the Mishnah's selectivity defined the issues for further inquiry. Accordingly, the Rabbinic sages addressed a dual challenge, both subjecting a well-crafted document to exegesis, amplification, and theoretical inquiry, and also sorting out conflicting data on the same matters that said document took up. To amplify this point, which is crucial to all that follows, the intellectual tasks confronting the heirs of the Mishnah were made complicated by the conflict between the status of the Mishnah and the sizable legacy of authoritative legal data transmitted along with the Mishnah. The Mishnah enjoyed privileged status. All other compositions and composites received the form of commentary to the Mishnah. But the exegesis of the Mishnah did not then define the sole intellectual labor at hand. For the privileging of the Mishnah proved incomplete, with a huge corpus of other rulings on the same agenda compiled in the Tosefta, with other corpora of rulings on elements of the same agenda compiled alongside the Tosefta ("our Rabbis have taught on Tannaite authority" of my translations), and with still other free-floating sayings endowed with Tannaite status to cope with as well. Mishnah exegesis—words, phrases, sources in Scripture—then would ordinarily enjoy pride of position, at the head of any sustained composite. But following that work, next in line would come the challenge of conflicting opinion on the Mishnah's topics and rulings. Not only that, but the privileging of the Mishnah would remain a mere formality, without a direct confrontation with the conflicting opinions preserved along with the Mishnah. The Mishnah had to be shown perfect in form, harmonious in contents, dominant in norm setting, if that initial act of privileging were to signal long-term status as the authoritative statement.

The Mishnah's character as a mass of petty rulings defined a third task, one that was natural to the rigorous intellects that composed the cadre of the Rabbinic sages. That was to require the quest for not only harmony but also generalization, the encompassing principle, the prevailing rule emerging from concrete data. For intellectuals of the sages' sort sought not only information about details, but also guidance on the main lines of thought. Not only this, but engaged as they were in the administration of the life of the Jewish communities of Babylonia, theirs proved to be a practical reason and applied logic. They had to rule not only on cases covered by the Mishnah—and laws of its standing in addition—but also on cases not envisaged at all within the framework of the Mishnah. These cases of new kinds altogether, involving not only application of the law but penetration into the principles behind the law that could be made to cover new cases, demanded the formation of an analytical logic capable of generating principles to produce new laws.

An Example of a Dialectical Argument

These broadly theoretical remarks prepare the way for a particular example of a dialectical argument. The exemplary passage that we consider occurs at the Bavli Baba Mesia 5B–6A, the Talmud to Mishnah Baba Mesia 1:1–2. Our interest is in the twists and turns of the argument. We have now to discern what is at stake in the formation of a continuous and unfolding composition.

The law of the Mishnah concerns conflicting claims to an object, a cloak that two persons claim to have found and to own. How does the court settle the dispute? The Mishnah deals with a concrete case and imposes a fixed procedure: Each party takes an oath and the cloak is divided. To show the various voices that come together, I use different typefaces. Boldface type signals the Mishnah's presence. Regular type is the Talmud's voice. The Talmud is a multilingual document, citing Scripture in biblical Hebrew, the Mishnah and related writings in Middle or Mishnaic Hebrew, and Aramaic, the international language of the time equivalent to English today, as well. When the Talmud cites legal formulations, it is in Hebrew. But the recorded dialogue, the voices of the various parties to an argument, are given in Aramaic. I show what is in Aramaic in italics. The discussion emerges, then, as a drama, with different voices speaking different parts. We are invited to reconstruct the processes of reasoning, the arguments as they unfold, and because reason governs throughout, we are asked to participate in the argument. We are given a part in the play.

I have inserted point-by-point explanations to guide the reader through the argument.

To begin with, the Mishnah speaks:

MISHNAH TRACTATE BABA MESIA 1:1–2

1:1

Two lay hold of a cloak—
this one says, "I found it!"—
and that one says, "I found it!"—
this one says, "It's all mine!"—
and that one says, "It's all mine!"—
this one takes an oath that he possesses no less a share of it than half,
and that one takes an oath that he possesses no less a share of it than half,
and they divide it up.
This one says, "It's all mine!"—
and that one says, "Half of it is mine!"
the one who says, "It's all mine!" takes an oath that he possesses no less of a
share of it than three parts,
and the one who says, "Half of it is mine!," takes an oath that he possesses no
less a share of it than a fourth part.
This one then takes three shares, and that one takes the fourth.

1:2

Two were riding on a beast,
or one was riding and one was leading it—
this one says, "It's all mine!"—
and that one says, "It's all mine!"—
this one takes an oath that he possesses no less a share of it than half,
and that one takes an oath that he possesses no less a share of it than half.
And they divide it.
But when they concede [that they found it together] or have witnesses to
prove it, they divide [the beast's value] without taking an oath.

So much for the Mishnah's rule. What does the Talmud want to know? Now the Gemara raises the obvious question: concerning *what* does the claimant take the oath? The Talmud begins by citing the Mishnah's rule.

M. B.M. 1:1–2 **IV.1.**

    A. [5B] This one takes an oath that he possesses no less a share of
           it than half, [and that one takes an oath that he possesses no
           less a share of it than half, and they divide it up]:

The rule of the Mishnah, which is cited at the head of the sustained discussion, concerns the case of two persons who find a garment. We settle their conflicting claim by requiring each to take an oath that he or she owns title to no less than half of the garment, and then we split the garment between them.

Our first question is one of text criticism: analysis of the Mishnah paragraph's word choice. We say that the oath concerns the portion that the claimant alleges he possesses. But the oath really affects the portion that he does not have in hand at all:

> B. *Is it concerning the portion that he claims he possesses that he takes the oath, or concerning the portion that he does not claim to possess?* ["The implication is that the terms of the oath are ambiguous. By swearing that his share in it is not 'less than half,' the claimant might mean that it is not even a third or a fourth (which is 'less than half'), and the negative way of putting it would justify such an interpretation. He could therefore take this oath even if he knew that he had no share in the garment at all, while he would be swearing falsely if he really had a share in the garment that is less than half, however small that share might be" [S. Daiches, translation of Talmud tractate *Baba Mesia* (London: Soncino Press, 1948).]

> *Said R. Huna, "It is that he says,* 'By an oath! I possess in it a portion, and I possess in it a portion that is no more than half a share of it.'" [The claimant swears that his share is at least half (Daiches, *Baba Mesia,* 1948)].

The first issue is now resolved, and here is where the moving argument takes over. So this is our first encounter with the dialectical argument of the Talmud. It catches us unaware, by a surprising initiative.

Specifically, having asked and answered the question, we now find ourselves in an extension of the argument; the principal trait of the dialectical argument is now before us: [1], but [2] maybe the contrary is the case, so [3] what about—that is, the setting aside of a proposition in favor of its opposite. Here we come to the definitive trait of the dialectic argument: its insistence on challenging every proposal with the claim, "maybe it's the opposite?" This pestering question forces us back upon our sense of self-evidence; it makes us consider the contrary of each position we propose to set forth. It makes thought happen. True, the Talmud's voice's "but"—the whole of the dialectic in one word!—presents a formidable nuisance. But so does all criticism, and only the mature mind will welcome criticism. Dialectics is not for children, politicians, propagandists, or egoists. So the objection proceeds:

> *Then let him say,* "By an oath! The whole of it is mine!"

Why claim half when the alleged finder may as well demand the whole cloak?

But are we going to give him the whole of it? [Obviously not, there is another claimant, also taking an oath.]

The question contradicts the facts of the case: Two parties claim the cloak, so the outcome can never be that one will get the whole thing.

Then let him say, "By an oath! Half of it is mine!"

Then—by the same reasoning—why claim "no less than half," rather than simply half.

That would damage his own claim [which was that he owned the whole of the cloak, not only half of it].

The claimant does claim the whole cloak, so the proposed language does not serve to replicate his actual claim. That accounts for the language that is specified.

But here too is it not the fact that, in the oath that he is taking, he impairs his own claim? [After all, he here makes explicit the fact that he owns at least half of it. What happened to the other half?]

The solution merely compounds the problem.

[Not at all.] For he has said, "The whole of it is mine!" [And, he further proceeds,] "And as to your contrary view, by an oath, I do have a share in it, and that share is no less than half!"

We solve the problem by positing a different solution from the one we suggested at the outset. Why not start where we have concluded? Because if we had done so, we should have ignored a variety of intervening considerations and so should have expounded less than the entire range of possibilities. The power of the dialectical argument now is clear: It forces us to address not the problem and the solution alone, but the problem and the various ways by which a solution may be reached; then, when we do come to a final solution to the question at hand, we have reviewed all of the possibilities. We have seen how everything flows together, nothing is left unattended.

What we have here is not a set piece of two positions, with an analysis of each, such as formal dialogue exposes with such elegance; it is, rather, an analytical argument, explaining why this, not that, then why not that but rather this, and onward to the other thing and the thing beyond that—a linear argument in constant forward motion. When we speak of a moving argument, this is what we mean: what is not static and merely expository, but what is dynamic and always contentious. It is not an endless argument, an argument for the sake of arguing, or evidence that is important to the Bavli and other writings that use the dialectics as a principal mode of dynamic argument in process but not position. On the contrary, the passage is resolved with a decisive conclusion, not permitted to run on.

But the dialectical composition proceeds—continuous and coherent from point to point, even as it zigs and zags. We proceed to the second cogent proposition in the analysis of the cited Mishnah passage, which asks a fresh question: why an oath at all?

> M. B.M. 1:1–2 **IV.2.** [It is envisioned that each party is holding on to a corner of the cloak, so the question is raised:] Now, since this one is possessed of the cloak and standing right there, and that one is possessed of the cloak and is standing right there, why in the world do I require this oath?

Until now we have assumed as fact the premise of the Mishnah's rule, which is that an oath is there to be taken. But why assume so? Surely each party now has what he is going to get. So what defines the point and effect of the oath?

> Said R. Yohanan, "This oath [to which our Mishnah passage refers] happens to be an ordinance imposed only by Rabbis,
> "so that people should not go around gRabbing the cloaks of other people and saying, 'It's mine!'" [But, as a matter of fact, the oath that is imposed in our Mishnah passage is not legitimate by the law of the Torah. It is an act taken by sages to maintain the social order.]

We do not administer oaths to liars; we do not impose an oath in a case in which one of the claimants would take an oath for something he knew to be untrue, since one party really does own the cloak, the other really has grabbed it. The proposition solves the problem—but hardly is going to settle the question. On the contrary, Yohanan raises more problems than he solves. So we ask how we can agree to an oath in this case at all?

> *But why then not advance the following argument: since such a one is suspect as to fraud in a property claim, he also should be suspect as to fraud in oath taking?*

Yohanan places himself into the position of believing in respect to the oath what we will not believe in respect to the claim on the cloak, for, after all, one of the parties before us must be lying! Why sustain such a contradiction: gullible and suspicious at one and the same time?

> *In point of fact, we do not advance the argument: since such a one is suspect as to fraud in a property claim, he also should be suspect as to fraud in oath taking, for if you do not concede that fact, then how is it possible that the All-Merciful has ruled, "One who has*

conceded part of a claim against himself must take an oath as to the remainder of what is subject to claim"?

If someone claims that another party holds property belonging to him or her, and the one to whom the bailment has been handed over for safekeeping, called the bailee, concedes part of the claim, the bailee must then take an oath in respect to the rest of the claimed property, that is, the part that the bailee maintains does not belong to the claimant at all. So the law itself has sustained the same contradiction. That fine solution, of course, is going to be challenged:

> *Why not simply maintain, since such a one is suspect as to fraud in a property claim, he also should be suspect as to fraud in oath taking?*
> In that other case, [the reason for the denial of part of the claim and the admission of part is not the intent to commit fraud, but rather,] the defendant is just trying to put off the claim for a spell.

We could stop at this point without losing a single important point of interest; everything is before us. Starting at the beginning, without any loss of meaning or sense, we may well stop at the end of any given paragraph of thought. But the dialectics insists on moving forward, exploring, pursuing, insisting; and were we to remove a paragraph in the middle of a dialectical composite, then all that follows would become incomprehensible. That is a mark of the dialectical argument: sustained, continuous, and coherent—yet perpetually in control and capable of resolving matters at any single point. For those of us who consume, but do not produce, arguments of such dynamism and complexity, the task is to discern the continuity, that is to say, not to lose sight of where we stand in the whole movement.

Now, having fully exposed the topic, its problem, and its principles, we take a tangent indicated by the character of the principle before us: when a person will or will not lie or take a false oath. We have a theory on the matter; what we now do is expound the theory, with special reference to the formulation of that theory in explicit terms by a named authority:

> This concurs with the position of Rabbah. [For Rabbah has said, "On what account has the Torah imposed the requirement of an oath on one who confesses to only part of a claim against him? It is by reason of the presumption that a person will not insolently deny the truth about the whole of a loan in the very presence of the creditor and so entirely deny the debt. He will admit to part of the debt and deny part of it. Hence we invoke an oath in a case in which one does so, to coax out the truth of the matter."]
> For you may know, [in support of the foregoing], that R. Idi bar Abin said R. Hisda [said]: "He who [falsely] denies owing money on a loan nonetheless is suitable to give testimony, but he who denies that he holds a bailment for another party cannot give testimony."

The proposition is now fully exposed. A named authority is introduced, who will concur in the proposed theoretical distinction. He sets forth a new consideration, which of course the law always will welcome: The rational goal of finding the truth overrides the technicalities of the law governing the oath.

Predictably, we cannot allow matters to stand without challenge, and the challenge comes at a fundamental level, with the predictable give and take to follow:

> But what about that which R. Ammi bar Hama repeated on Tannaite authority: "[If they are to be subjected to an oath,] four sorts of bailees have to have denied part of the bailment and conceded part of the bailment, namely, the unpaid bailee, the borrower, the paid bailee, and the one who rents."
>
> *Why not simply maintain, since such a one is suspect as to fraud in a property claim, he also should be suspect as to fraud in oath taking?*
>
> In that case as well, [the reason for the denial of part of the claim and the admission of part is not the intent to commit fraud, but rather,] the defendant is just trying to put off the claim for a spell.
>
> *He reasons as follows: "I'm going to find the thief and arrest him." Or: "I'll find [the beast] in the field and return it to the owner."*

Once more, "if that is the case" provokes yet another analysis; we introduce a different reading of the basic case before us, another reason that we should not impose an oath:

> N. *If that is the case, then why should one who denies holding a bailment ever be unsuitable to give testimony? Why don't we just maintain that the defendant is just trying to put off the claim for a spell? He reasons as follows: "I'm going to look for the thing and find it."*
>
> O. *When in point of fact we do rule,* He who denies holding a bailment is unfit to give testimony, *it is in a case in which witnesses come and give testimony against him that at that very moment, the bailment is located in the bailee's domain, and he fully is informed of that fact, or, alternatively, he has the object in his possession at that very moment.*

The solution to the problem at hand also provides the starting point for yet another step in the unfolding exposition. Huna has given us a different resolution of matters. That accounts for No. 3, and No. 4 is also predictable:

M. B.M. 1:1–2

> IV.3.*But as to that which R. Huna has said* [when we have a bailee who offers to pay compensation for a lost bailment rather than swear it has been lost, since he wishes to appropriate the article by paying for it, (Daiches, *Baba Mesia*, 1948)], "They impose upon him the oath that the bailment is not in his possession at all,"
>
> *why not in that case invoke the principle, since such a one is*

> *suspect as to fraud in a property claim, he also should be suspect*
> *as to fraud in oath taking?*
>   *In that case also, he may rule in his own behalf, I'll give him*
> *the money.*
> **4.**   *Said R. Aha of Difti to Rabina, "But then the man clearly*
> *transgresses the negative commandment: 'You shall not covet.'"*
>   "You shall not covet" *is generally understood by people to*
> *pertain to something for which one is not ready to pay.*

Yet another authority's position now is invoked, and it draws us back to our starting point: the issue of why we think an oath is suitable in a case in which we ought to assume lying is going on; so we are returned to our starting point, but via a circuitous route:

M. B.M. 1:1–2 IV.5.

> **[6A]** *But as to that which R. Nahman said,* "They impose upon him [who denies the whole of a claim] an oath of inducement," *why not in that case invoke the principle, since such a one is suspect as to fraud in a property claim, he also should be suspect as to fraud in oath taking?*
>   *And furthermore, there is that which R. Hiyya taught on Tannaite authority:* "Both parties [employee, supposed to have been paid out of an account set up by the employer at a local store, and storekeeper] take an oath and collect what each claims from the employer," *why not in that case invoke the principle, since such a one is suspect as to fraud in a property claim, he also should be suspect as to fraud in oath taking?*
>   *And furthermore, there is that which R. Sheshet said,* "We impose upon an unpaid bailee [who claims that the animal has been lost] three distinct oaths: first, an oath that I have not deliberately caused the loss, that I did not put a hand on it, and that it is not in my domain at all," *why not in that case invoke the principle, since such a one is suspect as to fraud in a property claim, he also should be suspect as to fraud in oath taking?*

We now settle the matter:

> *It must follow that we do not invoke the principle at all, since such a one is*
> *suspect as to fraud in a property claim, he also should be suspect as to fraud in oath taking.*

What is interesting is why walk so far to end up where we started: Do we invoke said principle? No, we do not.

What we have accomplished on our wanderings is a survey of opinion on a theme, to be sure, but opinion that intersects at our particular problem as well. The moving argument serves to carry us hither and yon; its power is to demonstrate that all considerations are raised, all challenges met, all possibilities explored. This is not merely a set-piece argument, where we have proposition, evidence, analysis, conclusion; it is a different sort of thinking altogether, purposive and coherent, but also comprehensive and compelling for its admission of possibilities and attention to alternatives. The dialectical argument is the Talmud's medium of generalization from case to principle and extension from principle to new cases.

The Rabbinic sages invented the dialectical argument for the exposition of the law. There were other ways of presenting the same case, and we now turn to one of them—a famous example—to compare and contrast the Talmud's mode of discourse with that of Scripture, which the Mishnah and the Talmud mean to carry forward.

Scripture's Way of Saying through Narrative What the Mishnah Says through an Abstract Case

Can a writer in the Israelite world say "where there are equally valid claims, we split the object that is at issue equally between the claimants" in some other way than this rather tedious and technical way? To place the Mishnah and Talmud into their context in Scripture, we seek a case parallel to the one analyzed by the Talmud and supplied by the Mishnah. How about the following:

Then two harlots came to the king and stood before him. The one woman said, "Oh, my lord, this woman and I dwell in the same house; and I gave birth to a child while she was in the house. Then on the third day after I was delivered, this woman also gave birth, and we were alone; there was no one else with us in the house. Only we two were in the house. And this woman's son died in the night, because she lay on it. And she arose at midnight and took my son from beside me, while your maidservant slept, and laid it in my bosom. When I rose in the morning to nurse my child, behold, it was dead; but when I looked at it closely in the morning, behold, it was not the child that I had borne."

But the other woman said, "No, the living child is mine, and the dead child is yours."

The first said, "No, the dead child is yours, and the living child is mine."

Thus they spoke before the king.

Then the king said, "The one says, 'This is my son that is alive, and your son is dead,' and the other says, 'No, but your son is dead, and my son is the living one."

And the king said, "Bring me a sword."

So a sword was brought before the king. And the king said, "Divide the living child in two and give half to the one and half to the other."

Then the woman whose son was alive said to the king, because her heart yearned for her son, "Oh, my lord, give her the living child and by no means slay it."

But the other said, "It shall be neither mine nor yours; divide it."

Then the king answered and said, "Give the living child to the first woman and by no means slay it; she is its mother."

And all Israel heard of the judgment which the king had rendered, and they stood in awe of the king, because they perceived that the wisdom of God was in him, to render justice (1 Kings 3:16–28).[5]

Does this passage make the same point as our Mishnah paragraph? Indeed it does: There is strict justice; where there are equally valid claims, we split the object that is at issue equally between the claimants. Will the author of our Mishnah paragraph have found the principle expressed in this story surprising? So far as the rule of law is concerned, the answer of course is negative. But the point of the story before us and the purpose of the Mishnah paragraph at hand are quite different. Each author has chosen to make his own point, and he has done so, as a matter of fact, by finding a medium of expression that matches his purpose.

Our author wants to speak of principle and procedure: When is an oath required, when not? That is his main point. We know it, because it comes at the end; it is startling; there is no preparation for it; and it marks the climax and conclusion of the piece of writing at hand. When the same thing is said three times, and then something else is tacked on, our attention is drawn to that new matter.

When, then, we look back, and see how, in the prior writing, the oath has been introduced as integral, we realize what has happened. What will be the main point is introduced quite tangentially and repeated as a given; then we assume that given is not at issue. But at the end, we are told that what we took for granted is in fact not routine. An oath is required only if there is a conflict, but if each party concedes the other's claim, or if there are witnesses to establish the facts, then no oath is at issue at all. What was entirely tangential now turns up as the main point. The framer of the passage has made it certain we would be jarred and that our attention would be drawn to that surprising, and we now realize, critical issue.

The narrator in the story of Solomon and the two widows has chosen a medium suitable for his message. He sets the stage in the opening paragraph: The one party states her claim, the other the opposing claim. The rule of law is clear: Split the difference. The issue of procedure is of no consequence to our narrator, so he does not say that each party must prove her claim, for example, by taking an oath (or whatever procedure pertained at that point in Israel's history). The king then makes his elaborate preparation to carry out the rule of law. The woman who spoke first speaks again, then the other speaks as briefly as before. The king repeats the language of the first woman: "By no means slay it," now adding, "she is its mother." Is the point of the story the law that where there are equally valid claims, we split the object that is at issue equally between the claimants? Hardly! The point of the story is at the end: "And all Israel heard of the judgment which the king had rendered and stood in awe of the king because they perceived that the wisdom of God was in him, to render justice."

We see how cases of the same kind can be used for entirely different purposes, and when an author proposes to set forth his purpose, he chooses language and syntax and forms of communication that serve that purpose. The author of the story about Solomon wants to say Solomon had divine wisdom; the case makes that point by showing how Solomon transcended the limits of the law through not (mere) mercy but profound understanding of obvious facts of human nature. The author of our Mishnah paragraph is talking about different things to different people, and his choices show the difference. He gives us not narrative, which serves no purpose of his, but brief and artful clauses, each free floating, all of them joining together to create cases. He then finds for himself laconic and detached language, not the colorful and evocative phrases used by the other. Contrast the understatement with the overstatement, the one casual, the other rich in heightened and intense language:

> **this one says, "It's all mine!"—**
> **and that one says, "It's all mine!"—**
> "Oh, my lord, this woman and I dwell in the same house; and I gave birth to a child while she was in the house. Then on the third day after I was delivered, this woman also gave birth, and we were alone; there was no one else with us in the house. Only we two were in the house. And this woman's son died in the night, because she lay on it. And she arose at midnight and took my son from beside me, while your maidservant slept, and laid it in my bosom. When I rose in the morning to nurse my child, behold, it was dead; but when I looked at it closely in the morning, behold, it was not the child that I had borne."
> But the other woman said, "No, the living child is mine, and the dead child is yours."
> The first said, "No, the dead child is yours, and the living child is mine."

Contrast, again, the undramatic resolution with the tension and the resolution of the tension that form the centerpiece of the narrative:

> **this one takes an oath that he possesses no less a share of it than half,**
> **and that one takes an oath that he possesses no less a share of it than half,**
> **and they divide it up.**
> And the king said, "Bring me a sword."
> So a sword was brought before the king. And the king said, "Divide the living child in two and give half to the one and half to the other."
> Then the woman whose son was alive said to the king, because her heart yearned for her son, "Oh, my lord, give her the living child and by no means slay it."
> But the other said, "It shall be neither mine nor yours; divide it."
> Then the king answered and said, "Give the living child to the first woman and by no means slay it; she is its mother."

It is difficult to imagine two more different ways of saying more or less the same thing. The Mishnah's author speaks in brief clauses; he uses no adjectives; he requires mainly verbs. He has no actors, no "they did thus and so." He speaks only of actions people take in the established situation. No one says anything, as against, "the king said . . ." There is only the rule, no decision to be made for the case in particular. There is no response to the rule, no appeal to feeling. Indeed, the Mishnah's author knows nothing of emotions; Scripture's tells us "because her heart yearned." And the Mishnah's author knows nothing of the particularity of cases, while to the Scripture's narrator, that is the center of matters. The Mishnah presents rules, Scripture, exceptions; the Mishnah speaks of the social order, Scripture, special cases; the Mishnah addresses all Israel, and its principal player—the community at large—is never identified. Scripture tells us about the individual, embodied in the divinely chosen monarch, and relates the story of Israel through the details of his reign.

When we remember that the author of our Mishnah passage revered Scripture and knew full well the passage before us, we realize how independent-minded a writer he is. On the surface he does not even allude to Scripture's (famous) case; he does not find it necessary to copy its mode of presenting principles. And yet what differentiates the main point, "they divide it up" and "divide the living child in two"? (And who requires "and give half to the one and half to the other"!) Only these words make a material difference: *the living child*. Since our author knew Scripture, he had to have known precisely what he was doing: the affect, upon hearers or readers of his rule, of the utilization of the precise ruling of Solomon. All that changes is "living child" into "cloak." Everything is different, but everything also is the same: The law remains precisely what the narrator of the tale about Solomon knew, as a matter of fact, it was. Then the law is not the main point, either of Scripture's tale, or of the Mishnah's rule. The Torah—God's revelation to Israel—lives in the details, and through our two authors, both of them immortal for what they wrote and perfectly capable of speaking to minds and hearts of ages they could not have imagined, God speaks through the details.

The Importance of the Dialectical Argument in the Gemara

The contrast between Scripture and the Talmud's presentation of the conflicting claims highlights the Talmud's unique quality in the context of Israelite writing from Scripture to the Talmud: the provision of reasoned abstract analytical argument. What then is at stake in the dialectical argument? I see three complementary results. All of them, in my view, prove commensurate to the huge effort at concentration that is required to follow these protracted, sometimes tedious expositions.

First, we test every allegation by a counterproposition, so serving the cause of truth through challenge and constant checking for flaws in an argument.

Second, we survey the entire range of possibilities, which leaves no doubt about the cogency of our conclusion. And that means we move out of our original case, guided by its principle to new cases altogether.

Third, quite to the point, by the give and take of argument, we ourselves are enabled to go through the thought processes set forth in the subtle markings that yield our reconstruction of the argument. We not only review what people say, but how they think: the processes of reasoning that have yielded a given conclusion. Sages and disciples become party to the modes of thought; in the dialectical argument, they are required to replicate the thought processes themselves.

The Bavli empowers its disciples by inviting them to participate in its unfolding arguments. The main consequence for the Bavli of formation through dialectical analysis is simply stated. It is the power of that mode of the representation of thought to show not only the result, but also the workings, of the logical mind. By following dialectical arguments, we ourselves enter into those same thought processes, and our minds then are formed in the model of rigorous and sustained, systematic argument. The reason is simply stated. When we follow a proposal and its refutation, the consequence thereof, and the result of that, and on to challenge and response without limit, we ourselves become partners in the logical tensions and their resolutions; we are given an opening, a pass of admission into the discourse that lies before us. As soon as matters turn not upon tradition, to which we may or may not have access, but upon reason, specifically, challenge and response, proposal and counterproposal—"maybe matters are just the opposite?"—we find an open door before us.

For these are not matters of fact but of reasoned judgment, and the answer, "well, that's my opinion," in its "traditional form"—namely, that is what Rabbi X has said, so that must be so—finds no hearing. Moving from facts to reasoning, propositions to the process of counterargument, the challenge resting on the mind's own movement, its power of manipulating facts one way rather than some other and of identifying the governing logic of a fact—that process invites the reader's or the listener's participation. The author of a dialectical composite presents a problem with its internal tensions in logic and offers a solution to the problem and a resolution of the logical conflicts.

What is at stake in the capacity of the framer of a composite, or even the author of a composition, to move this way and that, always in a continuous path, but often in a crooked one? The dialectical argument opens the possibility of reaching out from one thing to something else, and the path's wandering is part of the reason. It is not because people have lost sight of their starting point or their goal in the end, but because they want to encompass, in the analytical argument as it gets underway, as broad and comprehensive a range of cases and rules as they can. The movement from point to point in reference to a single point that accurately describes the dialectical argument reaches a goal of abstraction. At the point at which we leave behind the specificities of not only cases but laws, sages carry the argument upward to the law that governs many cases, the premises that undergird many rules, and still higher to the principles that infuse diverse premises, then to the principles that generate other, unrelated premises, which, in turn, come to expression in other, still less-intersecting cases. The meandering course of argument comes to an end when we have shown how things cohere that we did not even imagine were contiguous at all.

The dialectical argument forms the means to an end. The distinctive character of the Bavli's particular kind of dialectical argument is dictated by the purpose for which dialectics is invoked. Specifically, the goal of all argument is to show in discrete detail the ultimate unity, harmony, proportion, and perfection of the law—not of the Mishnah as a document but of all the law of the same standing as that presented by the Mishnah. The dialectics shows how to read the laws in such a way as to discern that many things really say one thing. The variations on the theme then take the form of detailed expositions of this and that. Then our task is to move backward from result to the reasoning process that has yielded this result: through regression from stage to stage to identify within the case not only the principles of law that produce that result, but the processes of reasoning that link the principles to the case at hand.

Thus far we have met the dialectical argument in its abstract setting. But for the Rabbinic sages that argument sustained the quest for truth and ensured that all parties adhered to the most rigorous standard of thought and reason. The human dimensions of the matter are captured in a story about two long-time rivals in the battle for truth.

BAVLI BABA MESIA 84A

One day there was a dispute in the school house [on the following matter]: As to a sword, knife, dagger, spear, hand-saw, and scythe—at what point in making them do they become susceptible to become unclean? It is when the process of manufacturing them has been completed [at which point they are deemed useful and therefore susceptible]. And when is the process of manufacturing them completed?

R. Yohanan said, "When one has tempered them in the crucible."

R. Simeon b. Laqish said, "When one has furbished them in water."

[R. Yohanan] said to him, "Never con a con man" [lit.: a robber is an expert at robbery].

He said to him, "So what good did you ever do for me? When I was a robber, people called me, 'my lord' [lit.: Rabbi], and now people call me 'my lord.'"

He said to him, "I'll tell you what good I've done for you, I brought you under the wings of the Presence of God."

R. Yohanan was offended, and R. Simeon b. Laqish fell ill. His [Yohanan's] sister [Simeon b. Laqish's wife] came to him weeping, saying to him, "[Heal my husband,] do it for my children's sake!"

He said to her, "'Leave your fatherless children. I will preserve them alive' (Jer. 49:11)."

"Then do it on account of my widowhood!"

He said to her, "'and let your widows trust in me' (Jer. 49:11)."

R. Simeon b. Laqish died, and R. Yohanan was much distressed afterward. Rabbis said, "Who will go and restore his spirits? Let R. Eleazar b. Pedat go, because his traditions are well honed."

He went and took a seat before him. At every statement that R. Yohanan made, he comments, "There is a Tannaite teaching that sustains your view."

He said to him, "Are you like the son of Laqisha? When I would state something, the son of Laqisha would raise questions against my position on twenty-four grounds, and I would find twenty-four solutions, and it naturally followed that the tradition was broadened, but you say to me merely, 'There is a Tannaite teaching that sustains your view.' Don't I know that what I say is sound?"

So he went on tearing his clothes and weeping, "Where are you, the son of Laqisha, where are you, the son of Laqisha," and he cried until his mind turned from him. Rabbis asked mercy for him, and he died.

ENDNOTES

1. Robin Smith, "Logic," in Barnes, *Cambridge Companion to Aristotle,* 60.

2. And finds a limited place, also, in only two other Rabbinic documents, Sifra and the Yerushalmi.

3. For an equivalent exercise of hermeneutics of a contentious order, we look in vain among the other law codes and commentaries of antiquity, which tend to a certain blandness. For the Zoroastrian counterpart, see my *Judaism and Zoroastrianism at the Dusk of Late Antiquity. How Two Ancient Faiths Wrote Down Their Great Traditions* (Atlanta: Scholars Press for South Florida Studies in the History of Judaism, 1993).

4. In the Bavli, statements bearing the signal TNY, in its various forms, ordinarily bear the names of authorities who occur, also, in the Mishnah, or who are credited with the compilation of Mishnah sayings, for example, a Tosefta, such as Hiyya or Bar Qappara. But in the Bavli, the same convention does not prevail, and TNY sayings may routinely occur in the names of authorities who elsewhere figure only with figures much later than the time of the closure of the Mishnah. Whatever the intent of TNY in the Bavli, therefore, in the Yerushalmi the meaning of the signal cannot be the same. It is generally supposed that TNY in the Bavli means "a teaching out of Tannaite times." But indifference to chronology, indicated by name associations, in the Yerushalmi then bears a different meaning. There, it follows, TNY signals a status as to authority, not as to origin. And I suspect closer study of the Bavli, without the prevailing assumption as to the sense of TNY, will yield a comparable result.

5. Translation: Herbert G. May and Bruce M. Metzger, eds. *The Oxford Annotated Bible with the Apocrypha. Revised Standard Version* (NY: Oxford University Press, 1965), 419–420.

4

The Two Talmuds

The Talmud of the Land of Israel and the Talmud of Babylonia

Both Talmuds—the Talmud of the Land of Israel or Yerushalmi (Jerusalem) (400 CE), the Talmud of Babylonia or Bavli (600 CE)—are formed into commentaries to the Mishnah. They share fundamental principles of law and theology. Indeed, when we turn to consider the contents of the Talmuds, we shall have reason to cite both of them as equally representative of the Judaic system of "the Talmud." But they do not cover the same tractates. The Yerushalmi's Gemara treats the first four divisions of the Mishnah, Agriculture, Appointed Times, Women, and Damages, and the Bavli's, the second through the fifth, Appointed Times, Women, Damages, and Holy Things. Both take up the tractate Niddah, on menstrual uncleanness, of the sixth division.

The Yerushalmi was produced in the Land of Israel, to which the laws of Agriculture pertain, and the Bavli, speaking to a community of Judaism outside of the Holy Land, did not express an equivalent interest in the matter. That would explain the Yerushalmi's treating, and the Bavli's ignoring, that subject. Purities concerned rules principally pertinent to the Temple of Jerusalem, which lay in ruins, and that would account for both Talmuds' neglect of that topic. But why the Bavli devoted a huge division to Holy Things, pertaining to the routine offerings in the Temple now in ruins, and the Yerushalmi did not, we do not know.

The two Talmuds are identical in form. Both Talmuds are laid out in the same way, that is, as point-by-point treatments of phrases or even whole paragraphs of the Mishnah. The two Talmuds defined Mishnah commentary through their active program of supplying not merely information but guidance on its meaning. That formed a program of inquiry, a set of consequential issues, in place of mere information. That program derives its tasks from the character of the Mishnah and its authority, which accounts for the shared definition of the principal tasks of commentary.

Both wanted to prove the same things about the Mishnah. First, the two Talmuds concur that the law of the Mishnah derived from Scripture. This requires demonstration time and again. Second, they agree that the Mishnah does not repeat itself but exhibits perfection in language and form. That proposition serves as the point of Mishnah commentary in both documents. Both ask the same questions, for example, clarifying the language of the Mishnah, identifying the scriptural foundations of the Mishnah's rules. Not only that, but the two Talmuds look alike. Both take up a few sentences of the Mishnah and paraphrase and analyze the cited passage.

The two Talmuds accordingly make up a genus, Talmud, made up of two species, the Talmud of the Land of Israel—its Mishnah selections and its Gemara commentaries on those selections—and the Talmud of Babylonia—with its counterparts. Where the Talmuds differ, it is in the deepest layers of discourse, but not on the surface of the medium or in the messages they set forth. Both Talmuds' Gemaras invariably do to the Mishnah one of these four things, and each of these procedures will ordinarily be expressed in patterned language. It suffices here to classify the types of patterns:

1. text criticism on the wording of the Mishnah's law;
2. explanation of the meaning of the Mishnah passage, including explanatory remarks ("glosses") and amplifications;
3. addition of Scriptural proofs for the Mishnah's central propositions (a matter that will concern us later on); and
4. harmonization of one Mishnah passage with another such passage or with a statement of Tosefta.

Each of these types of composition follows a well-defined form, so that, if we were given only an account in abstract terms of the arrangement of subject and predicate or a simple account of the selection of citation language (e.g., "as it is said," "our Rabbis have taught,") we could readily predict the purpose of the composition or composite.

The Bavli and the Yerushalmi Compared: Mishnah Tractate Moed Qatan Chapter 1

To illustrate the work of the two Talmuds on the Mishnah, we turn to the Bavli's treatment of Mishnah tractate Moed Qatan, chapter 1, which deals with limitations on the work that may be done on the intermediate days of the festivals of Passover and Tabernacles. The reason that the Bavli represents both Talmuds is that as I just said they follow the same program of Mishnah commentary. Then, to show that that is the fact, I present an outline of the two Talmuds' treatment of the opening paragraphs of Mishnah tractate Moed Qatan chapter 1.

Before we turn to the Talmud, a word on the legal topic is in order. Those intermediate days come between the first and final days of the two week-long festivals. They are observed through limitations on the forms of labor that Israelites may carry out. Hard work cannot be done; work that does not have to be done on the festivals should not be done; work should not be postponed from secular days to holy days. We begin with the critical analysis of the wording of the Mishnah, with the demonstration that the exact words yield important principles, a typical initiative of the Talmuds.

The opening unit illustrates the Talmuds at their most illuminating. This kind of critical analysis defines the best work of clarification that either Talmud does with the Mishnah. Boldface type marks a citation from the Mishnah or the Tosefta, italics signal the use of Aramaic, and plain type, Hebrew.

BAVLI TO M. MOED QATAN 1:1–2 I.1
[They water an irrigated field on the intermediate days of a festival and in the Sabbatical Year, whether from a spring that first flows at that time, or from a spring that does not first flow at that time:] *since it is explicitly stated that they may water a field from a spring that flows for the first time, which may damage the soil by erosion [making necessary immediate repair of the damage during the intermediate days of the festival], is it necessary to specify that they may water from a spring that does not first flow at that time, which is not going to cause erosion?*

One may say that it is necessary to include both the latter and the former, for if the Tannaite framer had given the rule only covering a spring that first flows on the intermediate days of the festival, it is in that case in particular in which it is permitted to work on an irrigated field, but not for a rain-watered field, because the water is going to cause erosion, but in the case of a spring that does not first flow on the intermediate days, which is unlikely to cause erosion, I might have said that even a rain-watered field may be watered. So by specifying both cases the framer of the Mishnah paragraph informs us that there is no distinction between a spring that flows for the first time and one that does not flow for the first time. The rule is the same for both: an irrigated plot may be watered from it, but a rain-watered plot may not be watered from [either a new or an available spring].

Mishnah criticism presupposes perfection, namely, that the document says only what is necessary, but does not set forth in so many words rules that one may infer on the basis of what is made explicit. That premise is articulated when the Talmud asks,

since it is explicitly stated that they may water a field from a spring that flows for the first time, which may damage the soil by erosion [making necessary immediate repair of the damage during the intermediate days of the festival], is it necessary to specify that they may water from a spring that does not first flow at that time, which is not going to cause erosion?

In other words, why say the obvious? The solution demonstrates that without making the rule articulate, the Mishnah's formulation left room for misconstruction. Specifically, we can have concluded that a consideration present in one case but not in the other accounts for the lenient ruling accorded only that case. This is amply spelled out in the italicized, Aramaic commentary to the Mishnah that the Talmud provides.

Second, clarification commonly involves attention to the meanings of words and phrases, demonstration on the basis of Scripture of the sense of specific word choices. This point of insistence yielded certainty that the document formed a continuation of the Torah of Sinai.

Along these lines, in addition, the Bavli will frequently find a Scriptural basis for the rule of the Mishnah.

BAVLI TO M. MOED QATAN 1:1–2 I:2

And on what basis is it inferred that the meaning of the words **"irrigated field"** *is, a thirsty field [which has to be irrigated]?*

It is in line with that which is written: "When you were faint and weary" (Dt. 25:18), *and the Hebrew word for weary is represented in Aramaic by the word that means "exhausted."*

And how do we know that the words translated rain-watered field refer to a well-fucked field?

"For as a man has sexual relations with a maiden, so shall your sons be as husbands unto you" (Is. 62:5), *and the word in Aramaic [the lingua franca of the ancient Near East] is rendered, "Behold, as a boy fucks a girl, so your sons shall get laid in your midst."*

What is clarified here is the scriptural source for the language of the Mishnah. The Mishnah is shown to form a continuation of Scripture and to be based upon its language and its law.

Third, once the meanings of words and phrases are establish, the discussion comes to the explanation of the law. This is done phrase by phrase and brings us to the heart of the matter: the substance of the rules.

BAVLI TO MISHNAH TRACTATE MOED QATAN 1:6

They do not hew out a tomb niche or tombs on the intermediate days of a festival.

But they refashion tomb niches on the intermediate days of a festival.

They dig a grave on the intermediate days of a festival,

and make a coffin,

while the corpse is in the same courtyard.

R. Judah prohibits, unless there were boards [already sawn and made ready in advance].

Predictably, each passage of the Mishnah is given a clarification, as required; I see no amplification of any theoretical considerations or ambitious secondary developments.

BAVLI TO MISHNAH TRACTATE MOED QATAN 1:6 I.1

What are **tomb niches** *and what are* **tombs***?*

Said R. Judah, "Tomb niches are formed by digging, and tombs are formed by building."

So too it has been taught on Tannaite authority:
What are tomb niches and what are tombs? Tomb niches are formed by digging, and tombs are formed by building.

The language of the Mishnah is clarified, and parallels adduced in evidence from traditions of the same period as the Mishnah but not located in the Mishnah, which are called, we recall, Tannaite, after the word *Tanna*, repeat; thus, Tannaite = traditions that are repeated by great authorities.

MISHNAH TRACTATE MOED QATAN 1:6 II.1
But they refashion tomb niches on the intermediate days of a festival:
How do they refashion them?
Said R. Judah, "If it was too long, they may shorten it."
In a Tannaite formulation it is set forth: **One makes it broader or longer [T. Moed 1:8A–B].**

The rule is clarified; once the Mishnah says something is to be done, the natural next question is, how is it to be done?

What propositions emerge? The language of the Mishnah and of its law or Halakhah conforms to a few simple rules and is subject to definition by reference to Scripture in part, to common usage in part. The law derives from Scripture. The law of the Mishnah is expressed with exquisite care, so that redundancy is ruled out, and each detail responds to rigorous criticism. Tannaite complements to the law of the Mishnah and the Tosefta amplify and enrich the heritage of the law and cohere. There is no source of the law that calls into question the integrity of the law as spelled out in the Mishnah, and all sources of the law conform to the same rules of reason throughout. All of this represents the outcome of the analysis of the form of the law.

Let us now examine the Yerushalmi's treatment of the same Mishnah paragraphs as these are compared with the Bavli's presentation. The Yerushalmi is at the left, the Bavli at the right.

THE TALMUD OF THE LAND OF ISRAEL	THE TALMUD OF BABYLONIA
I. Yerushalmi Moed Qatan 1:1	I. Mishnah tractate Moed Qatan 1:1–2
[A] **They water an irrigated field on the intermediate days of a festival and in the Seventh Year**	A. **They water an irrigated field on the intermediate days of a festival and in the Sabbatical Year [when many forms of agricultural labor are forbidden], whether from a spring that first flows at**

1. I:1: There is no difficulty understanding why one may utilize a spring that does not first flow at that time. But in the case of a spring that first flows at that time, is this not a considerable amount of work [for the intermediate days of the festival]? The law accords with the view of R. Meir. For R. Meir has said, "From a spring that first flows on the intermediate days of a festival they irrigate [even] a field that depends upon the rain [and does not need this water]" [T. Moed 1:1 A].

[B] **whether from a spring that first flows at that time, or from a spring that does not first flow at that time.**

1. II:1: It is not difficult to understand why they may not water the irrigated field with water from a swape well [since it is laborious to get it]. But why not use collected rain water [M. 1:1C]? Said R. Yohanan, "They issued a decree concerning rain water because it is in the category of water of a swape well."

2. II:2: R. Jeremiah asked, "As to water of rain drippings which has not **that time, or from a spring that does not first flow at that time.**

1. I.1–2. Explanation of the formulation of the Mishnah's language.

2. I.3 Who is the Tannaite authority who takes this position?

B. The Sabbatical Year—how does it compare in restrictions concerning labor to the intermediate days of the festival?

1. I.4 On what count is one who on the Sabbath admonished for weeding a field or watering seedlings? Ploughing vs. sewing

2. 1:5 is it permitted to stir the soil under an olive tree in the Sabbatical Year?

3. 1:6 Flogging for plowing in the Sabbatical Year?

ceased to flow from the
hills, into what category
does it fall?"

[C] **But they do not water [an
irrigated field] with collected
rain water, or water from a
swape well.**

  1. III:1: Eleazar b. R. Yosé
asked, "As to cascades of
water, how do you treat
them? Are they in the status
of swape-well water or not?
[No answer is given.] As to
a pool that was filled with
spring water, the flow of
which then ceased, what is
the law as to watering a field
from [such a pool]?" Let us
derive the answer from the
following: But they do not
water [an irrigated field]
with collected rainwater or
water from a swape well
[M. 1:1 C]. Now how shall
we interpret that rule? If we
deal with a time in which the
rain is falling, then [why
should there be such a
prohibition]? Is it not like
irrigating the Great Sea?
But we must interpret the
passage to speak of the time
in which the rain has ceased.
If, then, it is a time that the
rain has ceased, then is it not
tantamount to a pool that
has been filled by a spring,
which has stopped flowing?
And you rule that they do
not irrigate a field from such
water. That then indicates
that in the case of a pool that

C. **But they do not water [an
irrigated field] with (1)
collected rainwater, or (2)
water from a swape well.**

  1. II.1 Explanation of the
rule of the Mishnah

  2. II.2, 3 Bodies of water that
draw from a constant source
and do not involve physical
labor in collecting the water
for irrigation; extension of
the rule of the Mishnah to
other cases.

  3. II.4, 5, 6 Tannaite
complements to the
Mishnah rule [Tosefta, then
other]

    i. II.7 Complement to
foregoing

had been filled from a
spring, which had ceased to
flow, they likewise do not
water a field from such a
pool.

**[D] And they do not dig channels
around vines.**

1. IV:1: And they dig
channels around trees [M.
1:1 D]. What are the
channels dug around a tree?
These are the ditches dug
around the roots of trees [T.
Moed 1:2B–C].

II. Yerushalmi Moed Qatan 1:2

**[A] R. Eleazar b. Azariah says,
"They do not make a new
water channel on the
intermediate days of a
festival or in the Seventh
Year." And sages say, "They
make a new water channel in
the Seventh Year, and they
repair damaged ones on the
intermediate days of a
festival."**

1. I:1: There we have
learned: [One may pile up
all his dung together. R.
Meir forbids, unless it is
heaped in a special place,
three handbreadths above or
below ground level. If he
had only a little, he may go
ahead and pile it on the
field.] R. Eleazar b. Azariah
forbids, unless it is heaped
in a special place three
handbreadths above or
below ground level [so that
it not appear to be manuring
the field], or it is laid on

**D. And they do not dig channels
around vines.**

1. III.1Explanation of the
language of the Mishnah

**E. R. Eleazar b. Azariah says,
"They do not make a new
water channel on the
intermediate days of a
festival or in the Sabbatical
Year."**

1. IV.1 Explanation of
the Mishnah's rule that
concerns the Sabbatical
Year: why is the Sabbatical
Year treated as comparable
to the intermediate days of
the festival?

2. IV.2 Explanation of
the Mishnah's rule: does the
authority before us
contradict himself?

**F. And sages say, "They make
a new water channel in the
Sabbatical Year, and they
repair damaged ones on the
intermediate days of a
festival."**

1. V.1 What is the meaning
of the language of the
Mishnah?

rocky ground [M. Sheb. 3:3]. One may interpret this matter in two ways: In one, it is a case in which the farmer had a small amount of manure stored at home on the eve of the Seventh Year. He wants to take it out into his field in the Seventh Year. Lo, he may continue adding to this manure once those who carry on ordinary labor have ceased [so that he cannot be thought to be cultivating his field during the Seventh Year]. R. Eleazar b. Azariah declares it forbidden. What is the reason for the view of R. Eleazar b. Azariah? Perhaps he will not find sufficient manure [to make piles of appropriate size, which indicates that the manure is stored, not used for fertilizing the field], and he will turn out to be merely manuring that spot [on which he is storing the manure]. [Accordingly, Eleazar requires the manure to be stored in such a way that it cannot possibly fertilize the spot on which it is located.]

[B] They repair damaged waterways in the public domain:[B] They repair damaged waterways in the public domain:

1. II:1: That is the case for one that is necessary for the festival. But in the case of

2. V.2 Speculative question on the meaning of the Mishnah's rule

   i. V.3 Illustrative case

one that is not necessary for use on the festival, it is prohibited to do so. That is the case in the instance of a channel belonging to an individual. But in the case of a channel available for public use, even in the instance of one that is not for use on the festival, it is permitted.

[C] **and dig them out. They repair roads, streets, and water pools.**

1. III:1: They dig them out [M. 1:2D]. They dig them out, in line with that which we have learned there: He who cleans out a spout removing pebbles that have collected therein.

[D] **And they do all public needs:**

1. IV:1: What are public needs? They judge capital cases, property cases, and cases involving fines [cf. M. M.Q. 3:3]. And they burn a red cow (cf. Num. chap. 19). And they break the neck of a heifer [in the case of a derelict corpse]. And they pierce the ear of a Hebrew slave [who wishes to remain with his master]. And they effect redemption for pledges of personal valuation, for things declared *herem*, for things declared consecrated, and for second tithe [through coins to be taken up to Jerusalem]. And they untie

G. **They repair damaged waterways in the public domain and dig them out. They repair roads, streets, and water pools. And they (1) do all public needs.**

1. VI.1   Close reading of the language of the Mishnah to yield a distinction that produces a clarification of the law

a shoe from the last, so long
as one does not put it back
[T. Moed 2:11 /I–O].

[E] mark off graves:

1. V:1: Interpret the passage
[to speak] of a case in which
there were heavy rains,
which washed away the
marking.

**[F] and go forth [to give
warning] against Diverse
Kinds.**

1. VI:1: And was this not
done in Adar? Interpret the
law [to speak] of a case in
which it was such a year in
which even the sprouts [in
Adar] were not discerned.

2. VI:2: And how do we
know that graves must be
marked off? R. Berekhiah,
R. Jacob, son of the
daughter of Jacob, in the
name of R. Honiah of Beth
Hauran, R. Yosé said in the
name of R. Jacob bar Aha
in the name of R. Honiah of
Beth Hauran, R. Hezekiah,
R. Uzziel son of R. Honiah
of Beth Hauran: "The leper
. . . shall cry, 'Unclean,
unclean' (Lev. 13:45). That
is so uncleanness [80 c] will
cry out with its own mouth
and say, 'Keep away.'" R.
La in the name of R. Samuel
bar Nahman: "'And when
these pass through the land
and any one sees a man's
bone, then he shall set up a
sign by it' (Ez. 39:15). It is
on the strength of that verse

H. (2) mark off graves,

1. VII.1 Indication in
Scripture that graves are to
be marked off: Ez. 44:9

i. VII.2, 3 Source of
the rule that is taken for
granted by Ez. 44:9.

ii. VII.4, 5 Further
exposition of a verse
cited in the foregoing, Ps.
50:23.

2. VII.6 Tannaite rule on
marking of graves

3. VII.7 Tannaite rule on
marking of graves

i. VII.8–13
Amplification of
foregoing

**I. and go forth [to give
warning] against what is
planted with] Diverse Kinds
[or species of crops].**

1. VIII.1 Mishnah
clarification: is this done
on the intermediate days
of the festival or prior to
the festival (of Passover)?

2. VIII.2 Mishnah
clarification: why do this
during the intermediate
days of the festival?

i. VIII.3 What defines the
mixture of seeds?

that people mark off places in which bones of a human being are found. ['A man's bone']—on this basis we prove that they mark off a place in which the backbone or skull is found. 'And he shall set' —on this basis we learn that they mark off such a place on bedrock. If you say that it is located on a rock, which is turned over, then it may wash away and impart uncleanness to some other place. 'By it'—in a place of cleanness. [That is, the marker is not set upright at the corpse matter, but beside it.] 'A sign'—On this basis that they set up a sign."

III. Yerushalmi Moed Qatan 1:3

[A] **R. Eliezer b. Jacob says, "They lead water from one tree to another, on condition that one not water the entire field.**

"Seeds that have not been watered before the festival one should not water on the intermediate days of the festival."

1. I:1: Mana stated the following without specifying an authority, while R. Abin in the name of Samuel [said], "[As to M. Sheb. 2:10: 'They may water the while soil (= ground between trees) (= ground not planted with trees),' the words of R. Simeon. R. Eliezer b. Jacob prohibits,] the dispute [at M.

II. Mishnah tractate Moed Qatan 1:3

A. **R. Eliezer b. Jacob says, "They lead water from one tree to another, on condition that one not water the entire field. "Seeds which have not been watered before the festival one should not water on the intermediate days of the festival." And sages permit in this case and in that**

1. I.1 Clarification of the rule of the Mishnah: condition operative; Tannaite allegation along the same lines.

B. **I.2, 3 Tannaite rule on the Sabbatical Year, pertinent to watering the field.**

1:3A–B] pertains to an average situation [in which the trees are not planted very closely together or very far apart]. "For how [otherwise] may we interpret the dispute about leading water from one tree to another, either in the Seventh Year or in the intermediate days of the festival? If we deal with a field in which the trees are far apart, then in the view of all parties it will be prohibited. If we deal with a field in which the trees are close together, all parties will concur that it will be permitted. Accordingly, we must deal with an average situation, in which trees are planted at the rate of ten per *seah's* space of ground. R. Eliezer b. Jacob treats such a case as if the trees were far apart, and Rabbis treat such a case as if the trees were planted close together."

[B] **And sages permit in this case and in that.**

1. II:1: What is the meaning of "in this case and in that"? [Could the meaning be,] whether they were watered before the festival and whether they were not watered before the festival? [Surely not! There will be no loss if there was no watering before the festival. The seeds cannot require

water on the festival if the
process of growth has not
been initiated by a watering
prior to the festival.] But
here we deal with a tree [in
which case it is permitted to
water, so as to prevent loss],
while there we deal with
seeds [in which case there
will not be much of a loss if
there is no watering, unless
the seeds have been
constantly irrigated up to
now].

Lo, what is the difference between the Talmud of the Land of Israel and
that of Babylonia? In the Land of Israel we want the rule and the reason. In Babylonia,
we apply the reason to new circumstances. In the former case our purpose is to
clarify and explain; in the latter, it is to extend knowledge. The mode of inquiry in
the former is to seek information, in the latter, to use information in quest of a
deeper understanding. We may reasonably invoke the analogy of syllogistic
reasoning: Both the sages of the Land of Israel and those of Babylonia have the
facts, A, B. But the Babylonians proceed to the question, if A, B, then what about
C?

The Program of the Two Talmuds

By making choices about what to discuss and how to conduct the discussion
the Talmuds, each in its own way but sharing the same values, systematically
dismantle the Mishnah. The Mishnah presents a diverse topical program, expounding
each subject in its own terms. The Talmuds ask the same questions of all topics,
imposing uniform conceptions on the various subjects that are set forth in the
Mishnah. The writers of the Mishnah created a coherent document, with a topical
program formed in accord with the logical order dictated by the characteristics of a
given topic, and with a set of highly distinctive formal traits as well. But these traits
of a cogent statement, a document of integrity, are obscured when the document is
taken apart into bits and pieces and reconstituted in the way in which the Talmuds
do this.

For now the Mishnah is read by the Talmuds as a composite of discrete
and essentially autonomous rules, a set of atoms, not an integrated molecule, so to
speak. Because of this, the most striking formal traits of the Mishnah are obliterated.
More important, the Mishnah as a whole and complete statement of a viewpoint no

longer exists. Some of its tractates, thirty-nine of sixty-three in the Yerushalmi, thirty-seven of the same corpus in the Bavli, are treated, but of the entire set of topics or tractates about a third in each case are ignored. The Mishnah's propositions are reduced to details.

Both authorships take an independent stance when facing the Mishnah, making choices, reaching decisions of their own. The second Talmud is not only independent of the Mishnah, but also of the first Talmud, which exercises no influence on the second. Both Talmuds' framers deal with Mishnah tractates of their own choice, and neither provides a Talmud to the entirety of the Mishnah. What the Mishnah therefore contributed to the Talmuds was not received in a spirit of humble acceptance by the sages who produced either of the two Talmuds.

Important choices were made about what to treat, hence what to ignore. Explaining statements clause by clause, in bits and pieces, did not have to obscure the main lines of the Mishnah's system. But it surely did so. The discrete reading of sentences, or, at most, paragraphs, denying all context, avoiding all larger generalizations except for those transcending the specific lines of tractates—this approach need not have involved the utter reversal of the paramount and definitive elements of the Mishnah's whole and integrated world view (its "Judaism"). But doing these things did facilitate the revision of the whole into a quite different pattern.

A second trait joins with the foregoing. The Mishnah rarely finds it necessary to quote sentences from the written Torah in support of its statements. The Talmuds, by contrast, find it appropriate whenever possible to cite Scriptural proof texts for the propositions of the Mishnah. (We shall return to this matter in the next chapter.) While the various tractates of the Mishnah relate in different ways to Scripture, the view of the framers of the Talmud on the same matter is not differentiated. So far as they are concerned, proof texts for Mishnaic rules are required. These will be supplied in substantial numbers. And that is the main point. The Mishnah now is systematically represented as not standing free and separate from Scripture, but dependent upon it. The authority of the Mishnah's laws then is reinforced.

But the autonomy of the Mishnah as a whole is severely compromised. Just as the Mishnah is represented in the Talmud as a set of rules, rather than as a philosophical essay, so it is presented, rule by rule, as a secondary and derivative development of Scripture. It would be difficult to imagine a more decisive effort to reformulate the Torah than is accomplished by this work.

When Do the Two Talmuds Speak for Themselves, Not for the Mishnah?

What makes the two Talmuds into something other than commentaries to the Mishnah? The question has now to be asked, when do the Talmuds speak for themselves, not for the Mishnah? Along these same lines we wonder what sorts of units of discourse contain such passages that bear what is "Talmudic" in the two Talmuds. These two questions produce the same answers for both Talmuds, allowing us to characterize the topical or propositional program of the two Talmuds together.

1. *Theoretical questions of law not associated with a particular passage of the Mishnah.* In the first of the two Talmuds there is some tendency, and in the second, a very marked tendency, to move beyond the legal boundaries set by the Mishnah's rules themselves. Sometimes in the Yerushalmi, and most of the time in the Bavli, more general inquiries are taken up. These of course remain within the framework of the topic of one tractate or another, although there are some larger modes of thought characteristic of more than a single tractate.

2. *Exegesis of Scripture separate from the Mishnah.* It is under this rubric that we find the most important instances in which the Talmuds present materials essentially independent of the Mishnah. A passage of Scripture that does not intersect with the Mishnah will be amplified and clarified in its own terms and framework. Such a passage may be formidable in size and introduce a legal or a theological topic and problem that the Mishnah does not address. Both Talmuds thus participate in the presentation of Scripture and not only of the Mishnah. In the Bavli this results in the collection of large-scale miscellanies, immense expositions of sustained passages of Scripture. For one example, the first chapter of Bavli tractate Megillah encompasses a systematic, extensive, verse-by-verse commentary to the Scroll of Esther. Mishnah tractate Megillah has nothing that compares.

3. *Historical statements.* The Talmuds contain a fair number of statements that something happened, or narratives about how something happened. While many of these are replete with biblical quotations, in general they do not provide a literal, closely articulated exegesis of Scripture, which serves merely as illustration or reference point. The Mishnah contains very little narrative and evinces slight interest in history. The two Talmuds contain massive historical narratives, as we have already seen.

4. *Stories about, and rules for, sages and disciples, separate from discussion of a passage of the Mishnah.* The Mishnah contains a tiny number of tales about Rabbis. These serve principally as precedents for, or illustrations of, rules. The Talmuds by contrast contain a sizable number of stories about sages and their relationships to other people. While Rabbinic writings encompass nothing we can call biographies, the two Talmuds do set forth sustained chapters that all together can have provided the wherewithal of biographies.

What about independent discourse, not connected to the Mishnah? When the two Gemaras present us with ideas or expressions of a world related to, but fundamentally separate from, that of the Mishnah, that is, when the Talmuds wish to say something other than what the Mishnah says and means, they will take up one of two modes of discourse. Either we find exegesis of biblical passages, with the value system of the Rabbis read into the Scriptural tales, or we are told stories about holy men and paradigmatic events, once again through tales told in such a way that a didactic purpose is served. It follows that the Talmuds are composites of three kinds of materials:

1. exegeses of the Mishnah and law (and other materials classified as authoritative, that is, Tannaite),
2. exegeses of Scripture, and
3. accounts of the men who provide both.

Both Talmuds then constitute elaborate reworkings of the two antecedent documents: the Mishnah, lacking much reference to Scripture, and Scripture itself. The Talmuds bring the two together into a synthesis of their compilers' own making, both in reading Scripture into Mishnah, and in reading Scripture alongside of, and separate from, Mishnah.

What the Two Talmuds Have in Common

If, therefore, we want to point to what is Talmudic in either of the two Talmuds, it is the exegesis of Scripture, on the one side, and the narration of historical or biographical tales about holy men, on the other. Since much of the biblical exegesis turns upon holy men of biblical times, we may say that the Talmuds speak for themselves alone, as distinct from addressing the problems of the Mishnah, when they tell about holy men now and then. But what is genuinely new in the Talmuds, in comparison and contrast to the Mishnah, is the inclusion of extensive discourse on the meaning attributed to Scripture.

It follows that the two Talmuds stand essentially secondary to two prior documents: Scripture on the one side, the Mishnah (encompassing for this purpose the whole corpus labeled Tannaite, whenever and wherever produced, much being later than the Mishnah and some being Babylonian), on the other side. The Mishnah is read in the Talmuds pretty much within the framework of meaning established by the Mishnah itself. Scripture is read as an account of a world remarkably like that of the Rabbis of the Talmuds. When the Rabbis speak for themselves, as distinct from the Mishnah, it is through exegesis of Scripture.

But any other mode of reading Scripture, to them, would have been unthinkable. They took for granted that they and Scripture's heroes and sages lived in a single timeless plane. A single logic, a uniform truth prevailed from remote antiquity to the time of the sages themselves. That uniform truth overcame the division between past and present. That indifference to history and considerations of anachronism when they read Scripture is expressed in the following manner:

"And the Lord spoke to Moses in the wilderness of Sinai in the first month of the second year after they had come out of the land of Egypt, saying, ['Let the people of Israel keep the Passover at its appointed time. On the fourteenth day of this month, in the evening, you shall keep it at its appointed time; according to all its statutes and all its ordinances you shall keep it.']" (Num. 9:1–14).

Scripture teaches you that considerations of temporal order do not apply to the sequence of scriptural stories.

For at the beginning of the present book Scripture states, "The Lord spoke to Moses in the wilderness of Sinai in the tent of meeting on the first day of the second month in the second year after they had come out of the land of Egypt" (Num. 1:1).

And here Scripture refers to "the first month," so serving to teach you that considerations of temporal order do not apply to the sequence of scriptural stories.

(Sifré to Numbers LXIV:I.1)

Now, as a matter of fact, Scripture portrays linear history, sustains narrative, and registers the sharp differentiation of present from past. In that context, the statement that considerations of temporal order do not apply jars. Yet it represents the Rabbinic view of matters.

Why is it, then, that Rabbinic writing in the Talmud and elsewhere, responding to Scripture, does not encompass sustained historical narratives or biographies and produces the fusion of times past, present, and future into one time? The Rabbinic sages substituted the quest for patterns that transcend time, called paradigmatic thinking, for historical thinking. Paradigmatic thinking generalizes and treats the past as undifferentiated from the present. The paradigm or pattern consists of generalizations concerning the human situation, patterns of conduct and consequence, and the paradigm governs present and past without distinction. That is why it is the opposite of historical.

This brings us back to the two Talmuds and their reading of the Mishnah. If we stand back and reflect on the Mishnah's program, we recognize how different is that of the Talmuds. The Mishnah covers a broad variety of topics. And each is treated in its own way. The Talmuds contribute few topics of their own but trawl across the entire surface of the Mishnah, saying the same thing about everything, as the example of the treatment of Mishnah tractate Moed Qatan shows. The Mishnah is organized topically. The Talmuds may be broken down into discrete compositions and neatly joined composites, none of them framed as freestanding, topical formations, all of them in one way or another depending upon the Mishnah for order and coherence. The Mishnah lays out rules and facts about a world beyond itself. The Talmuds negotiate rules and recast facts into propositions that concern the Mishnah—a different focus of discourse and perspective altogether.

I have argued that the character of the two Talmuds is dictated by that of the Mishnah, but now, clearly, we reverse course. For continuous with the Mishnah, the two Talmuds in point of fact redirected the Mishnah. This they did by destroying its integrity and picking and choosing with its topical (and propositional) program. At the same time they made a statement of their own. The Rabbis of the two Talmuds made a commentary. But they obliterated the text. They loyally explained the Mishnah. But they turned the Mishnah into something other than what it had been. They patiently hammered out chains of tradition, binding themselves to the authority of the remote and holy past. But it was, in the end, a tradition of their own design and choosing.

The Mishnah hides. The Talmuds spell out. The Mishnah hints. The Talmuds repeat ad nauseam. The Mishnah is subtle, the Talmuds are obvious; the one is restrained and tentative, the others aimed at full and exhaustive expression of what is already clear. The sages of the Mishnah rarely represent themselves as deciding cases. Only on unusual occasions do they declare the decided law, at best reticently spelling out what underlies their positions. The Rabbis of the Gemaras harp on who holds which opinion and how a case is actually decided, presenting a rich corpus of precedents. They seek to make explicit what is implicit in the law. The Mishnah is immaterial and spiritual, the Talmuds earthy and social. The Mishnah deals in the gossamer threads of philosophical principle, the Talmuds in the coarse rope that binds this one and that one into a social construction.

The Mishnah speaks of a world in stasis, an unchanging, eternal present tense where all the tensions of chaos are resolved. The Talmuds address the real Israel in the here and now of ever-changing times, the gross matter of disorder and history. Clearly, the central traits of the Mishnah, revealed in the document at its time of closure circa 200, were revised and transformed into those definitive of the Talmud at its time of closure circa 400 for the earlier Talmud, 600 for the later. We know only that when we compare the Mishnah to the Talmuds we find in each case two intertwined documents, quite different from one another both in style and in values. Yet they are so tightly joined that the Gemara in both cases appears in the main to provide mere commentary and amplification for the Mishnah. So in important, superficial traits the two Talmuds are indistinguishable.

The Two Talmuds Compared in Detail

But the Talmuds are distinguishable. When we compare their treatment of the same Mishnah paragraph, we readily identify the Yerushalmi's treatment of that paragraph as different from the Bavli's.

The final illustration derives from both Talmuds' reading of a brief passage of Mishnah tractate Makkot. The unity of purpose—Mishnah commentary—and the identity of proposition—the unity of the Torah, its perfection—should not obscure the simple fact that the two Talmuds do not intersect except at the Mishnah and at Scripture. Each Talmud bears its own message, but both ask the same questions. In the following abstract, as before, the Mishnah and Tosefta passages in both Talmuds are in boldface. Here is the Yerushalmi's treatment of the indicated Mishnah paragraph.

YERUSHALMI TO MISHNAH TRACTATE MAKKOT 1:8 = BAVLI
TO MISHNAH TRACTATE MAKKOT 1:10
He whose trial ended and who fled and was brought back before the same court—
they do not reverse the judgment concerning him [and retry him].
In any situation in which two proselytes up and say, "We testify concerning

Mr. So-and-so that his trial ended in the court of such-and-such, with Mr. So-and-so and Mr. So-and-so as the witnesses against him,"

lo, this one is put to death.

[Trial before] a Sanhedrin applies both in the Land and abroad.

A Sanhedrin which imposes the death penalty once in seven years is called murderous.

R. Eleazar b. Azariah says, "Once in seventy years."

R. Tarfon and R. Aqiba say, "If we were on a Sanhedrin, no one would ever be put to death."

Rabban Simeon b. Gamaliel says, "So they would multiply the number of murderers in Israel."

Now we turn to the Yerushalmi's reading of the passage of the Mishnah.

[Trial before a] Sanhedrin applies both in the Land and abroad [M. 1:8E],

as it is written, "And these things shall be for a statute and ordinance to you throughout your generations in all your dwellings" (Num. 35:29).

And why does Scripture say, "You shall appoint judges and officers in all your towns [which the Lord your God gives you]" (Dt. 16:18) In the towns of the Land of Israel.

The meaning is that in the towns of Israel they set up judges in every town, but abroad they do so only by districts.

It was taught: R. Dosetai b. R. Yannai says, "It is a religious requirement for each tribe to judge its own tribe, as it is said, 'You shall appoint *judges* and officers in all your towns which the Lord your God gives you, according to your tribes'" (Dt. 16:18).

[II] Rabban Simeon b. Gamaliel taught, "Those declared liable to the death penalty who fled from the Land abroad—they put them to death forthwith [upon recapture].

"If they fled from abroad to the Land, they do not put them to death forthwith, but they undertake a trial *de novo.*"

The Yerushalmi wants the scriptural proof for the Mishnah's allegation. The Mishnah has set forth a variety of rules. The framers of the Yerushalmi's composition therefore go in search of the scriptural foundations for those rules. The task then is to harmonize the implications at hand. Since the proof text, I.B, yields results contrary to the assumed implications of that at C, D must indicate otherwise. Unit II is an independent saying, generally relevant to M. 1:8E. It is a simple paraphrase and clarification.

Now we turn to the Bavli's reading of the same matter. The Bavli does the same thing but makes its own points. The comparison then is based on the shared program; the contrast, the different results.

BAVLI TO MISHNAH TRACTATE MAKKOT 1:10

He whose trial ended and who fled and was brought back before the same court—

they do not reverse the judgment concerning him [and retry him].

In any situation in which two get up and say, "We testify concerning Mr. So-and-so that his trial ended in the court of such-and-such, with Mr. So-and-so and Mr. So-and-so as the witnesses against him,"

lo, this one is put to death.

[Trial before] a Sanhedrin applies both in the Land and abroad.

A Sanhedrin which imposes the death penalty once in seven years is called murderous.

R. Eleazar b. Azariah says, "Once in seventy years."

R. Tarfon and R. Aqiba say, "If we were on a Sanhedrin, no one would ever be put to death."

Rabban Simeon b. Gamaliel says, "So they would multiply the number of murderers in Israel."

The Bavli's reading of the same passage is now set forth. Once more the Mishnah and Tosefta citations appear in boldface type. The use of Aramaic is signified by italics, of Hebrew by plain type. As is common in the Bavli, the statements of law are in Hebrew, the analytical discussion in Aramaic.

BAVLI TO MISHNAH TRACTATE MAKKOT 1:10 I.1

He whose trial ended and who fled and was brought back before the same court—they do not reverse the judgment concerning him [and retry him]:

Before that court in particular the judgment is not reversed, but it may be reversed before some other court! *But then it is taught further on:* In any situation in which two get up and say, "We testify concerning Mr. So-and-so that his trial ended in the court of such-and-such, with Mr. So-and-so and Mr. So-and-so as the witnesses against him," lo, this one is put to death!

Said Abbayye, "This is no contradiction. The one statement refers to a court in the Land of Israel, the other, to a court abroad."

For it has been taught on Tannaite authority:

R. Judah b. Dosetai says in the name of R. Simeon b. Shatah, "If one fled from the Land to abroad, they do not reverse the verdict pertaining to him. If he fled from abroad to the Land, they do reverse the verdict concerning him, because of the higher priority enjoyed by the Land of Israel" [Tosefta San. 3:11A–B].

BAVLI TO MISHNAH TRACTATE MAKKOT 1:10 II.1

[Trial before] a Sanhedrin applies both in the Land and abroad:

What is the source of this rule?

It is in line with that which our Rabbis have taught on Tannaite authority:

"And these things shall be for a statute of judgment to you throughout your generations in all your dwellings" (Num. 35:29)—

we learn from that statement that the Sanhedrin operates both in the Land and abroad.

If that is so, then why does Scripture state, "Judges and offices you shall make for yourself in all your gates that the Lord God gives you tribe by tribe" (Dt. 16:18) [meaning only in the tribal land, in the Land of Israel]?

G. "In your own gates you set up courts in every district and every town, but outside of the Land of Israel you set up courts in every district but not in every town."

BAVLI TO MISHNAH TRACTATE MAKKOT 1:10 III.1

A Sanhedrin which imposes the death penalty once in seven years is called murderous. R. Eleazar b. Azariah says, "Once in seventy years:"

The question was raised: does the statement, A Sanhedrin which imposes the death penalty once in seven years is called murderous *mean that even one death sentence was enough to mark the Sanhedrin as murderous, or is this merely a description of how things are?*

The question stands.

BAVLI TO MISHNAH TRACTATE MAKKOT 1:10 IV.1

A. R. Tarfon and R. Aqiba say, "If we were on a Sanhedrin, no one would ever be put to death." Rabban Simeon b. Gamaliel says, "So they would multiply the number of murderers in Israel:"

So what would they actually do?

R. Yohanan and R. Eleazar both say, "'Did you see whether or not the victim was already dying from something, or was he whole when he was killed?'" [Such a question would provide grounds for dismissing the charge of murder, if the witnesses could not answer properly.]

Said R. Ashi, "If they said that he was whole, then, 'Maybe the sword only cut an internal lesion?'"

And in the case of a charge of consanguineous sexual relations, what would they actually do?

Both Abbayye and Raba said, "'Did you see the probe in the kohl flask [actually engaged in sexual relations]?"

And as to Rabbis, what would suffice for conviction?

The answer accords with Samuel, for said Samuel, "In the case of a charge of adultery, if the couple appeared to be committing adultery [that would be sufficient evidence]."

We once again set the outlines of the two Gemaras side by side to see how they compare.

VIII. Yerushalmi Makkot 1:8	X. Bavli Mishnah Tractate Makkot 1:10
He whose trial ended and who fled and was brought back before the same court— they do not reverse the judgment concerning him [and retry him]. In any situation in which two get up and say, "We testify concerning Mr. So-and-so	He whose trial ended and who fled and was brought back before the same court— they do not reverse the judgment concerning him [and retry him]. In any situation in which two get up and say, "We testify concerning Mr. So-and-so

that his trial ended in the court of such-and-such, with Mr. So-and-so and Mr. So-and-so as the witnesses against him," lo, this one is put to death. [Trial before] a Sanhedrin applies both in the Land and abroad. A Sanhedrin which imposes the death penalty once in seven years is called murderous. R. Eleazar b. Azariah says, "Once in seventy years." R. Tarfon and R. Aqiba say, "If we were on a Sanhedrin, no one would ever be put to death." Rabban Simeon b. Gamaliel says, "So they would multiply the number of murderers in Israel."

1. I:1: [Trial before a] Sanhedrin applies both in the Land and abroad [M. 1:8E], as it is written, "And these things shall be for a statute and ordinance to you throughout your generations in all your dwellings" (Num. 35:29). And why does Scripture say, "You shall appoint judges and officers in all your towns [which the Lord your God gives you]" (Dt. 16:18).—In the towns of the Land of Israel. The meaning is that in the towns of Israel they set up judges in every town, but abroad they do so only by districts.

2. I:2: Rabban Simeon b. Gamaliel taught, "Those

that his trial ended in the court of such-and-such, with Mr. So-and-so and Mr. So-and-so as the witnesses against him," lo, this one is put to death.

1 Harmonization of conflicting implications of the Mishnah's statements.

[Trial before] a Sanhedrin applies both in the land and abroad.

1 Scriptural source for the Mishnah's rule.

A Sanhedrin which imposes the death penalty once in seven years is called murderous. R. Eleazar b. Azariah says, "Once in seventy years."

Clarification of the wording of the Mishnah.

R. Tarfon and R. Aqiba say, "If we were on a Sanhedrin, no one would ever be put to death." Rabban Simeon b. Gamaliel says, "So they would multiply the number of murderers in Israel."

So what would they actually do to accomplish

declared liable to the death penalty who fled from the Land abroad—they put them to death forthwith [upon recapture]. If they fled from abroad to the Land, they do not put them to death forthwith, but they undertake a trial de novo."

their goal? *R. Yohanan and R. Eleazar both say*, "'Did you see whether or not the victim was already dying from something, or was he whole when he was killed?'" [Such a question would provide grounds for dismissing the charge of murder, if the witnesses could not answer properly.] *Said R. Ashi, "If they said that he was whole, then, 'Maybe the sword only cut an internal lesion?'" And in the case of a charge of consanguineous sexual relations, what would they actually do? Both Abbayye and Raba said, "Did you see the probe in the kohl flask [the penis in the vagina, that is, actually engaged in sexual relations]?" And as to Rabbis, what would suffice for conviction? The answer accords with Samuel, for* said Samuel, "In the case of a charge of adultery, if the couple appeared to be committing adultery [that would be sufficient evidence]."

Standard Mishnah exegesis in both Talmuds is represented by this brief passage from Bavli Makkot. The counterpart Talmud presents numerous exercises that follow the same program. We start with I, a challenge to the implications of the stated rule, I.B yielding a dissonance, which is ironed out by a suitable distinction. We proceed to II, a scriptural source for the passage at hand. Item III raises a theoretical question meant to clarify the sense of the language before us. Entry IV reverts to the systematic glossing of the language and sense of the Mishnah. There is no kind of comment in this passage that the Yerushalmi does not provide as well; each of these types of inquiry is standard for both Talmuds.

Contrasting the Two Talmuds: How the Bavli Differs from the Yerushalmi

The two Talmuds routinely treat the same Mishnah but only very rarely intersect other than at a given Mishnah paragraph or Tosefta selection. Ordinarily, each Talmud pursues its own interests when reading a passage shared with the other.

In fact, no substantial, shared protocol or tradition of commentary, either in fully spelled-out statements in so many words, or in the gist of ideas, or in topical conventions, or in intellectual characteristics, governed the two Talmuds' reading of the same Mishnah paragraph. The Bavli presents an utterly autonomous statement, speaking in its own behalf and in its own way about its own interests. The shared traits are imposed and extrinsic: formal documents cited by one set of writers and by another. The differentiating characteristics are intrinsic and substantive: what is to be done with the shared formal statements taken from prior writings. The framers of the Bavli in no way found guidance in the processes by which the Yerushalmi's compositions and composites took shape, either in the dim past of the document, or, it goes without saying, in the results of those processes.

If in light of the comparisons already set forth we compare the way in which the two Talmuds read the same Mishnah, we discern consistent differences between them. The principal difference between the Talmuds is the same difference that distinguishes jurisprudence from philosophy. The Yerushalmi talks in details, the Bavli in large truths; the Yerushalmi tells us what the Mishnah says, the Bavli, what it means. The Bavli thinks more deeply about deep things, and, in the end, its authors also think about different things from those that occupy the writers of the Yerushalmi. How do the Talmuds compare?

1. The first Talmud analyzes evidence; the second investigates premises.

2. The first remains wholly within the limits of its case; the second vastly transcends the bounds of the case altogether.

3. The first wants to know the rule; the second asks about the principle and its implications for other cases.

The one Talmud provides an exegesis and amplification of the Mishnah, the other, a theoretical study of the law in all its magnificent abstraction—transforming the Mishnah into testimony to a deeper reality altogether: to the law behind the laws. The Bavli does commonly what the Yerushalmi does seldom and then rather clumsily. For the second Talmud, the deep structure of reason is the goal, and the only way to penetrate into how things are at their foundations is to investigate how conflicting positions rest on principles to be exposed and juxtaposed, balanced, and, if possible, negotiated, if necessary, left in the balance.

That is why the dialectical argument, which we met in chapter 3, is mostly an invention of the Bavli. There we find acute concern for the balancing of arguments, the careful formation of a counterpoint of reasons, the excessively fair representation of contradictory positions. (Why doesn't X take the position of Y? Why doesn't Y take the position of X?) The Yerushalmi as an end product is intellectually inferior to the Bavli.

What Marks the Bavli as Unique?

What characterizes the Bavli and not the Yerushalmi is the quest for the unity of the law. This is carried out through the inquiry into the premises of discrete rules. At the foundation of the rules is a common principle. The unity of the law further emerges in the statement of the emergent principles, and the comparison and contrast of those principles with the ones that derive from other cases and their premises—an inquiry without end into the law behind the laws. What the Yerushalmi ignores but the Bavli urgently seeks is how to draw attention to the premises of those positions, the reasoning behind them, the evidence that supports them, the argument that transforms evidence into demonstration. Attention turns to even the authority, among those who settle questions by expressing opinions, who can hold the combination of principles or premises that underpin a given position.

The Bavli is many times larger than the Yerushalmi. When we observe that one Talmud is longer than the other, or one Talmud gives a fuller account than the other, we realize that such an observation is trivial. Larger does not mean greater. The real difference between the Talmuds emerges from a different trait. It is the Bavli's completely different theory of what it wishes to investigate. And that difference derives from the reason that the framers of the Bavli's compositions and composites did the work to begin with. The outlines of the intellectual character of the work flow from the purpose of the project, not the reverse, and thence, the modes of thought, the specifics of analytical initiative—all these are secondary.

To state matters simply, the Yerushalmi presents and explains the laws, the rule for this, the rule for that—pure and simple; "law" bears its conventional meaning of jurisprudence. The Bavli presents the law, now in the philosophical sense of the abstract issues, the matters of theory, the principles at play far beneath the surface of detailed discussion, the law behind the laws. And that, we see, is not really "law" in any commonplace sense of jurisprudence; it is law in a deeply philosophical sense: the rules that govern the way things are, that define what is proportionate and orderly and properly composed.

What is interesting therefore is that, as in the discussion of Mishnah tractate Makkot cited earlier, even when the facts are the same, the issues identical, and the arguments matched, the Bavli's author manages to lay matters out in a very distinctive way. And that way yields as a sustained, somewhat intricate argument (requiring us to keep in the balance both names and positions of authorities and also the objective issues and facts) what the Yerushalmi's method of representation gives us as a rather simple sequence of arguments. The Bavli's presentation is one of thrust and parry, challenge and response, assertion and counterassertion, theoretical possibility and its exposure to practical facts ("if I had to rely . . . I might have supposed . . .").

The Yerushalmi's message is that the Mishnah yields clear and present rules; its medium is the patient exegesis of Mishnah passages, the provision and analysis of facts required in the understanding of the Mishnah. That medium conveys its message about not the Mishnah alone, but about the laws. The Bavli, for its part, conveys its message in a coherent and persistent manner through its ever-recurring medium of analysis and thought. Where we ask for authority behind an unstated rule and find out whether the same authority is consistent as to principle in other cases altogether, where we show that authorities are consistent with positions taken elsewhere—here above all we stand in the very heart of the Bavli's message.

The Bavli's rigorous analytical arguments are not unique, but they are characteristic of that Talmud and not routine in the prior one. And that explains why the Bavli, and not the Yerushalmi, formed the medium for the transmission of the Mishnah and its law to the coming centuries of Judaism.

Why the Bavli Won

When people speak of the Talmud without further qualification, they mean the Talmud of Babylonia. From the time of its closure to the present, the Bavli has served as the single most authoritative document, after Scripture, of Judaism. The Judaic systems that succeeded from then to now have referred back to the Bavli as authoritative; have formulated their statements in relationship to the Bavli, often in the guise of commentaries or secondary expositions of statements made in it; have taken over the Bavli as the backbone for the law and culture that these continuator and successor systems proposed to set forth.

So the definitive trait of the Judaism of the dual Torah, which emerged from late antiquity, in literary form is the statement given it by the Talmud of Babylonia. More than any other single characteristic, the hegemony of the Bavli over the intellect of that Judaism for the community of the believers distinguishes the true from the heretical in Judaism. To establish a truth, appeal to the highest court formed by those who have mastered the Bavli, its commentaries, codes, and accompanying response alone would serve. Not only so, but until the twenty-first century, all Judaisms classified as heretical formed their heresies in response to the Bavli's norms. Why did the Bavli succeed in the place of the Yerushalmi?

To some who explain the matter by appeal to practical considerations, the Bavli enjoyed hegemony because Jews of Babylonia, later Iraq, sat at the confluence of trade routes, so enjoyed superior means of communication; to others, the Bavli enjoyed priority by default, because of the decline of the Jewish community of the Land of Israel. These appeals to a class of causes of an other than intellectual character dismiss the intrinsic qualities of the document, treating as null the power of intellect, on the one side, and the force of persuasive ideas, on the other. Such arguments glide lightly over differences between the two Talmuds, which are reduced to the accidents of taste and judgment, for example, one custom over another. Along these lines, a writing resting on the Babylonian culture of beer, sesame, and barley was more suited to the taste of Jews than one that founded itself on the culture of wine, olive oil, and wheat characteristic of the Land of Israel. Then the contents of the writing mattered less than what people ate for supper.

The unproven premise of my explanation is that ideas do matter, intelligence counts, and intellect governs: People are persuaded by what they learn and respond to arguments and reasons. The Bavli exceeds the Yerushalmi not only in size but in wit, not only in comprehensive and thorough exposition of its ideas but in intellectual rigor and vigor. That is why my answer to the question of why the Bavli won appeals to not contingencies of history and politics but eternities of intellect. Now, in the setting of history explained by reference to trade routes or the sorting out of cultures, that of course is not a historical answer at all. But then, a moment of reflection will show that in its heart the question too is no question of history. In its every line, the Talmud addresses the issue of Israel's sanctification through the realization of the Torah's imperative: God's call from Sinai, "You shall be holy, for I the Lord your God am holy."

The Rabbinic sages responded to that eternal summons: For the here and now, here are the ways in which, in detail and in concrete deed, Israel, the community of Judaism, may attain that sanctification through living out the truths of the Torah. And their unique contribution was to insist that those truths formed one truth, so that understood at the most profound levels of abstraction, the Torah's rules of thought and life really could be stated in a few, simple, comprehensive, and utterly cogent ways: abstract truth sustaining concrete truths. The Bavli exceeded the Yerushalmi by its intellectual superiority—that alone, and that was more than enough.

And that brings us to the question of what is in the Talmud, beginning at the foundation: How is the Talmud—Mishnah and Gemara—part of the Torah?

5

How Is the Talmud Part of the Torah?

The Urgent Question of the Talmud

From the closure of the Torah literature in the time of Ezra, circa 450 BC to the time of the Mishnah, in 200 CE, nearly seven hundred years later, we do not have a single law code alleged to be holy and at the same time standing wholly out of relationship to the Holy Scriptures of ancient Israel. Then came the Mishnah. That document cites Scripture sparingly and makes no effort to situate itself within the framework of the Mosaic Torah. The urgent question of the Talmud — both Talmuds, really — was, how does the Mishnah relate to Scripture?

We have noted many times that the Talmud systematically cites verses of Scripture (verses of Exodus, Leviticus, Numbers, and Deuteronomy in particular) in support of the Mishnah's and the Tosefta's statements of law. These proof texts — invocations of statements from one document to validate those of another — form a principal preoccupation of the Talmuds and define a principal part of the Talmuds' program of Mishnah-commentary. Verses of Scripture play much more than a formal part in that program. It is time to ask why.

The reason derives from the politics of the Mishnah and the theology that infused the politics. The advent of the Mishnah precipitated a crisis. It is defined by these questions: Why should people accept the Mishnah's and the sages' authority? In the context of the Torah revealed by God to Moses at Sinai, what is the standing of this work, so different from all prior Israelite law codes and holy books? What authority was vested in those that enforced them, where relevant, in practical decisions that made a concrete difference? The question of authority for the new code demanded an answer, because the patriarch of the Land of Israel and the exilarch of Babylonia made the Mishnah (and related legal traditions) the practical law of the Jewish communities they governed. They furthermore employed the Rabbinic sages as the judges and clerks of their courts and administration. So the Mishnah required a theory of authority and origin, and in the nature of things, that theory would take the form of a theology of the Mishnah's and the laws' place within the Torah of Moses.

What choices presented themselves? When ancient Israelites wanted to gain for their writings the status of revelation, of Torah, or at least to link what they thought to what the Torah had said, they could do one of four things. They could sign the name of a holy man of old, for instance, Adam, Enoch, Ezra, the Twelve Patriarchs, the sons of Jacob who formed tribes, Simeon and Levi, Judah and Benjamin for instance. They could imitate the Hebrew style of Scripture, which would establish continuity with the Torah. They could claim that God had spoken to them. They could, at the very least, cite a verse of Scripture and impute to the cited passage their own opinion.

These four methods — pseudepigraphy (writing a book and signing someone else's name), stylistic imitation, a claim of direct revelation from God, and eisegesis (reading meaning into a text, as illustrated by the New Testament Gospel of Matthew chapter two and in sections of the Mishnah too, as we shall see) — found no favor with the Mishnah's framers. They exercised their imagination and formed their principal writing in a totally fresh way, making an extreme claim.

First, they signed no name to their book. The conventional attribution to Judah the Patriarch is not made articulate in the document itself, which cites the patriarch in the third person and does not hint that his is the commanding voice.

They ignored the Hebrew of Scripture and produced their own version of the language. The Mishnah's Hebrew was new in its syntax and grammar, completely unlike that of the Mosaic writings of the Pentateuch. The Rabbinic sages themselves acknowledged that their Hebrew — "the language of the sages" — differed from that of Scripture. One can translate more or less word for word from Mishnaic Hebrew and produce intelligible English or German or French or Swedish or Spanish or Italian or Portuguese, but that is not commonly the case with Scripture's Hebrew, for example.

The Mishnah's sages and heirs never claimed that God had anything to do with their opinions. We shall meet a story in which the Rabbinic sages dismiss God from participating in their debates!

And they rarely cited a verse of Scripture as authority. We have already noticed how different a law code the Mishnah is when compared to a counterpart in Scripture. It follows that, whatever the authors of the Mishnah said about their document, the implicit character of the book tells us that they did not claim God had dictated or even approved what they had to say. Why not? The framers simply ignored all the validating conventions of the social world in which they lived.

Given the character of the Torah of Moses, we cannot find surprising that laws issued to define what people were supposed to do could not stand by themselves; they had to receive the imprimatur of Heaven, that is, they had to be given the status of revelation. Accordingly, to make its way in Israelite life, the Mishnah as a constitution and code demanded for itself a theory of beginnings at Sinai, with Moses, from God.

The character of the Mishnah itself hardly won confidence that, on the face of it, the document formed part of revealed Scripture, or derived from Sinai. To understand how the document presented a problem to its sponsors we have to recall that in an age of written law codes, e.g., those of Scripture and of the Dead Sea library, the Mishnah took its own path. It was originally published through oral formulation and oral transmission, that is, in the medium of memorization. We know that that is so because the internal evidence of the Mishnah proves it. The Mishnah is carefully formulated in patterns to facilitate memorization. Formalization extends to the number of times a proposition is repeated. The Mishnah works in groups of threes or fives of multiples of three or five. That is, to make a point, a pattern is established through three or five repetitions. Three repetitions establish a series, and five correspond to the numbers of fingers of the hands. The internal evidence is supplemented by a narrative which stresses the mnemonic patterning of the Mishnah, which we shall see in due course.

But memorizing a holy book represented an anachronism. For it had been in the medium of writing that, in the view of all of Israel until about 200, God had been understood to reveal the divine word and will. The Torah was a written book, meticulously copied from generation to generation. People who claimed to receive further messages from God usually wrote them down. Josephus the Jewish historian of the first century speaks of "traditions of the fathers," but that is explicitly not part of the Torah of Sinai.

So the problem is clear. A book was holy because in style, in authorship, or in origin it continued Scripture, finding a place therefore (at least in the author's mind) within the canon, or because it provided an exposition on Scripture's meaning. But the Mishnah made no such claim. It entirely ignored the style of biblical Hebrew, speaking in a quite different kind of Hebrew altogether. It is silent on its authorship. It is attributed to Judah the Patriarch, but little internal evidence supports that claim. In any event, nowhere does the Mishnah contain the claim that God had inspired the authors of the document. These are not given biblical names and certainly are not alleged to have been biblical saints. Most of the book's named authorities flourished within the same century as its anonymous arrangers and redactors, not in remote antiquity.

Above all, the Mishnah contains scarcely a handful of exegeses of Scripture. These, where they occur, play a trivial and tangential role. So here is the problem of the Mishnah: different from Scripture in language and style, indifferent to the claim of authorship by a biblical hero or divine inspiration, stunningly aloof from allusion to verses of Scripture for nearly the whole of its discourse — yet authoritative for Israel.

Two solutions to the problem set forth by the character of the Mishnah presented themselves from the second century forward.

[1] THE MISHNAH IS SUBORDINATE TO THE WRITTEN PART OF THE TORAH BUT CAN BE SHOWN TO STAND ON THE WRITTEN TORAH'S AUTHORITY: By citing verses of Scripture to validate statements of the Mishnah, the Rabbinic sages demonstrated

point by point that the Mishnah recapitulates the laws and theology of Scripture. This response was to treat the Mishnah as subordinate to, and dependent upon, Scripture. Then what belonged to the Torah was what fell into the classification of the revelation of the Torah by God to Moses at Sinai. The way of providing what was needed within that theory was to link statements of the Mishnah to statements ("proof texts") of Scripture. The Tosefta, ca. 300, a compilation of citations of, and comments upon the Mishnah, together with some autonomous materials that may have reached closure in the period in which the work of redaction of the Mishnah was going on, as well as the Talmuds fairly systematically did just that.

That solution concerned the specific and concrete statements of the Mishnah and required a literary, not merely a theological, statement, one specific to passages of the Mishnah, one after the other. What was demanded by the claim that the Mishnah depended upon, but therefore enjoyed the standing of, Scripture, was a line-by-line commentary upon the Mishnah in light of Scripture. One of the few exegetical compositions contained in the Mishnah itself, showing what could have been the document's implicit explanation for itself as an amplification of Scripture, is the following:

MISHNAH-TRACTATE SOTAH 8:1

The anointed for battle, when he speaks to the people, in the Holy Language he did speak,

as it is said, "And it shall come to pass when you draw near to the battle, that the priest shall approach" (this is the priest anointed for battle) "and shall speak to the people" (in the Holy Language) "and shall say to them, Hear, O Israel, you draw near to battle this day" (Dt. 20:2-3) —

"against your enemies" (Dt. 20:3) — and not against your brothers,

not Judah against Simeon, nor Simeon against Benjamin.

For if you fall into their [Israelites'] hand, they will have mercy for you,

as it is said, "And the men which have been called by name rose up and took the captives and with the spoil clothed all that were naked among them and arrayed them and put shoes on their feet and gave them food to eat and something to drink and carried all the feeble of them upon asses and brought them to Jericho, the city of palm trees, unto their brethren. Then they returned to Samaria" (II Chron. 28:15).

"Against your enemies" do you go forth.

For if you fall into their hand, they will not have mercy upon you.

"Let not your heart be faint, fear not, nor tremble, neither be afraid" (Dt. 20:3).

"Let not your heart be faint" — on account of the neighing of the horses and the flashing of the swords.

"Fear not" — at the clashing of shields and the rushing of the tramping shoes.

"Nor tremble" — at the sound of the trumpets.

"Neither be afraid" — at the sound of the shouting.

For the Lord your God is with you" (Dt. 20:4) —

they come with the power of mortal man, but you come with the power of the Omnipresent.

The Philistines came with the power of Goliath. What was his end? In the end he fell by the sword, and they fell with him.

The Ammonites came with the power of Shobach [II Sam. 10:16]. What was his end? In the end he fell by the sword, and they fell with him.

But you are not thus: "For the Lord your God is he who goes with you to fight for you"

(— this is the camp of the ark).

The governing text is Dt. 20:2-3, and that is explained phrase by phrase. The aim of the glosses is to intensify the sense of Scripture, not to revise it in any way I can perceive. Citing proof texts of Scripture thus forms one way to link law to the interpretation of Scripture, organizing the exposition around a verse of Scripture and spelling out its meaning clause by clause.

Another way of linking law to Scripture is to string together a variety of topics — not just a single proposition — that are subjected to citations of relevant verses of Scripture and that yield rules of law. What renders the following exposition coherent is the repeated resort to the language, "since it is said. . . ."

MISHNAH-TRACTATE SOTAH 5:1-5

M. 5:1 "Just as the water puts her to the proof, so the water puts him [the lover] to the proof,

"since it is said, 'And it shall come...,' 'And it shall come...' (Num. 5:22, 5:24).

"Just as she is prohibited to the husband, so she is prohibited to the lover,

"since it is said, 'And she will be unclean...,' 'And she will be unclean...' (Num. 5:27, 29)," the words of R. Aqiba.

Said R. Joshua, "Thus did Zechariah b. Haqqassab expound [the Scripture]."

Rabbi says, "The two times at which, 'If she is made unclean..., She is made unclean...,' are stated in the pericope refer, one to the husband and one to the lover."

M. 5:2A. On that day did R. Aqiba expound as follows: "'And every earthen vessel into which any of them falls, whatsoever is in it conveys uncleanness' (Lev. 11:33). It does not say, 'It will be unclean, but will convey uncleanness' — that is, to impart uncleanness to other things.

"Thus has Scripture taught concerning a loaf of bread unclean in the second remove, that it imparts uncleanness in the third remove [to a loaf of bread with which it comes into contact]."

Said R. Joshua, "Who will remove the dirt from your eyes, Rabban Yohanan b. Zakkai, for you used to say, 'Another generation is going to come to declare clean a loaf of bread in the third remove [from the original source of uncleanness].

"For there is no Scripture in the Torah which indicates that it is unclean.

"But now has not Aqiba, your disciple, brought Scriptural proof from the Torah that it is indeed unclean,

"since it is said, 'And whatsoever is in it shall impart uncleanness' (Lev. 11:33)."

M. 5:3 . On that day did R. Aqiba expound as follows: "'And you shall measure without the city for the east side two thousand cubits...' (Num. 35:5).

And another Scripture says, 'From the wall of the city and outward a thousand cubits round about' (Num. 35:4).

"It is not possible to state that the required measure is a thousand amahs, for two thousand amahs already have been specified.

"But it is not possible to state that the required measure is two thousand amahs, for one thousand amahs already have been specified.

"So how shall we rule?

"A thousand amahs form the outskirts, while two thousand amahs form the Sabbath-limit."

R. Eliezer the son of R. Yosé the Galilean says, "A thousand amahs form the outskirts, and two thousand amahs cover the surrounding fields and vineyards.

M. 5:4 On that day did R. Aqiba expound as follows: "'Then sang Moses and the children of Israel this song unto the Lord and spoke saying,' (Ex. 15:1).

"Now Scripture hardly needs to add, 'Saying.'

"And why does Scripture state, 'Saying'?

"It thereby teaches that the Israelites responded word by word after Moses.

"as they do when they read the Hallel-psalms.

"Therefore, 'Saying,' is stated in this context."

R. Nehemiah says, "[They did so] as they do when they read the Shema', not as when they read the Hallel."

M. 5:5   On that day did R. Joshua b. Hurqanos expound as follows: "Job served the Holy One, blessed be He, only out of love,

"since it is said, 'Though he slay me, yet will I wait for him' (Job 13:15).

"But still the matter is in doubt [as to whether it means], 'I will wait for him,' or, 'I will not wait for him.'

"Scripture states, 'Until I die I will not put away mine integrity from me' (Job 27:5).

"This teaches that he did what he did out of love."

Said R. Joshua, "Who will remove the dirt from your eyes, Rabban Yohanan b. Zakkai. For you used to expound for your entire life that Job served the Omnipresent only out of awe,

"since it is said, 'The man was perfect and upright and one who feared God and avoided evil' (Job 1:8).

"And now has not Joshua, the disciple of your disciple, taught that he did what he did out of love."

This is not a topical exposition such as we expect to find in the Mishnah. Here we have a most unMishnaic confusion of law and theology, as well as of diverse subjects. What unifies the composition is the interest in the exegesis of the cited verses. Then the law and principles of theology are organized around formal patterns ("on that day . . . expound . . .") and the like. The Talmuds amplify the proofs and test them.

The Mishnah rarely formulates its propositions in an exegetical manner. Far more common is the formulation in abstract generalizations or in exemplary cases, all focused on a particular principle of law and theme, as in the following, the glorious writing which we met in chapter 2:

M. Baba Qamma 1:1

[There are] four generative causes of damages: (1) ox [Ex. 21:35-36], (2) pit [Ex. 21:33], (3) crop-destroying beast [Ex. 22:4], and (4) conflagration [Ex. 22:5]. What they have in common is that they customarily do damage and taking care of them is your responsibility. And when one [of them] has caused damage, the [owner] of that which causes the damage is liable to pay compensation for damage out of the best of his land [Ex. 22:4].

M. Baba Qamma 1:2

In the case of anything of that I am liable to take care, I am deemed to render possible whatever damage it may do. [If] I am deemed to have rendered possible part of the damage it may do, I am liable for compensation as if [I have] made possible all of the damage it may do.

There is no confusing the Mishnah's mode of discourse with that of any other Israelite code. In context it is unique. That position concerning the origin and authority of the Mishnah is fully exposed in the passages now in hand. But that position competed with another.

[2] THE MISHNAH AS AN AUTONOMOUS, FREESTANDING COMPONENT OF THE TORAH OF SINAI: This response was represented by the claim that the authorities of the Mishnah stood in a chain of tradition that extended back to Sinai; stated explicitly in the Mishnah's first public defense of itself, which is set forth in tractate Abot. It did not require proof texts drawn from Scripture to validate its propositions because the propositions themselves formed an oral tradition of Sinai. The Mishnah then recorded an oral tradition transmitted from master to disciple beginning with God to Moses. It enjoyed the same standing and authority as the written Torah itself.

The two solutions to the problem of the origins and authority of the Mishnah emerge in the Talmuds.

The first held that the laws of the Mishnah and related traditions derived from and depended upon the statements of Scripture. Proof texts of Scripture thus formed the foundation for the legal teachings of the Mishnah.

The second accounts for the Mishnah and associated law by appeal to a narrative of tradition. The Rabbinic sages received the law in a chain of tradition beginning at Sinai and reaching into the Mishnah itself: named authorities of the Mishnah formed links in the chain of tradition beginning at Sinai. Tractate Abot, the sayings of the Fathers, explicitly posits a chain of tradition comprised by sages and disciples from Moses at Sinai to the masters of the Mishnah.

Alongside and concomitantly, it was held as part of the theory of an independent tradition ultimately written down in the Mishnah, the Mishnah and related Rabbinic traditions were memorized in a chain of oral tradition, so that the laws as recited by the Rabbis derived from God's revelation to Moses at Sinai.

The Talmud's Provision of Proof Texts from Scripture for the Law of the Mishnah

The Bavli's paramount solution to the problem of the Mishnah lay in articulating the foundations in Scripture of the laws of the Mishnah. The Bavli succeeds through the disciplined process of clarification in imposing on the diverse topical exposition of the Mishnah a cogent and orderly framework. That is the upshot of saying the same thing about many things. What propositions emerge? The language of the Mishnah and of the Halakhah conforms to a few simple rules and is subject to definition by reference to Scripture. How this is carried out in the Bavli emerges in a simple precis of the Bavli to Mishnah-tractate Makkot ("flogging") chapters 1 and 2. The key is the recurrent formula, "How [on the basis of Scripture] do we know...?"

MISHNAH-TRACTATE MAKKOT 1:9

[6B] [If] two saw the incident from one window, and two saw it from another window,

Bavli to M. Makkot 1:9 I.1 Said R. Zutra b. Tobiah said Rab, "How on the basis of Scripture do we know that disjoined testimony is invalid? As it is said, 'At the mouth of one witness he shall not be put to death' (Dt. 17:6). *What is the meaning of the word* 'one'? *Should we say it actually means one, literally? But that fact we derive from the opening part of the clause:* 'at the mouth of two witnesses or three witnesses shall he that is worthy of death be put to death.' *So what is* 'one witness'? *It means,* 'one and the same testimony.'"

MISHNAH-TRACTATE MAKKOT 2:1A-L

These are the ones who go into exile:

Mishnah-tractate Makkot 2:1A-L I.1 [This is the governing principle: Whatever happens en route downward — the person goes into exile:] *What is the scriptural basis for these distinctions?*

Mishnah-tractate Makkot 2:1A-L 2. *Our Rabbis have taught on Tannaite authority:*

"That kills any person by error . . . unaware" (Dt. 19:4) —

Mishnah-tractate Makkot 2:1A-L 3. *Our Rabbis have taught on Tannaite authority:*

"But if he thrust him suddenly, without enmity, or have cast upon him any thing without lying in wait for him" (Num. 35:22):

Mishnah-tractate Makkot 2:1A-L 4. "and as a man goes into the wood with his neighbor" (Dt. 19:5):

just as the forest is public domain for the entry of the party who was injured and the one who did the injury, so any domain that is equally open to the entry of the injured party and the one who did the injury.

MISHNAH-TRACTATE MAKKOT 2:1M-R

[If] the iron flew from the heft and killed someone,

It has been taught on Tannaite authority:

Said Rabbi to sages, "But is it stated, 'and the iron slips from its wood' (Dt. 19:5)? What it says is, 'from the tree.' And 'tree' appears twice, just as in the first instance, the reference is to the tree that is being cut down, so in the second case, it is to the tree that is being cut down."

2. Said R. Hiyya bar Ashi said Rab, "And both parties interpret the same verse of Scripture, namely, 'and the iron slips from the tree' (Dt. 19:5).

"*Rabbi maintains that* the unvocalized letters of the text are determinative, *so we may read the word as* 'and was hurled away,' *and Rabbis hold that* the vocalization of the letters of the text is determinative, *so we can only read* 'and slipped.'"

The powerful polemic is contained in the premise of the question, "How on the basis of Scripture do we know?" The question is addressed to citations of the Mishnah, and we take for granted that the law of the Mishnah does indeed rest on Scripture, not on oral tradition alone or mainly. This other approach to the problem of showing how the Torah encompasses the Talmud proves far less dramatic than the formulation of matters in terms of an oral tradition. But it predominates in the Talmud and tends to obscure the claim of a free-standing oral Torah handed on from Sinai. The two distinct theories of the Mishnah competed for centuries, with the one illustrated here ultimately paramount. But the still more daring position, as set forth in tractate Abot and its list of Rabbinic authorities, would make its mark as well in the theology of the Mishnah as the record of the oral tradition of Sinai.

Tractate Abot and the Origins of the Law of the Mishnah in a Chain of Tradition

Here the Mishnah is represented as a free-standing, independent tradition revealed by God to Moses in addition to the written Torah. In mythic narrative that theory speaks of a memorized Torah that completes and correlates with the written one. That theory is expressed most systematically in tractate Abot. Always published along with the Mishnah but autonomous of that document in all differentiating formal attributes, the tractate Abot, the Fathers, provides the alternative account of the origin and standing of the Mishnah. How it does so requires close attention to its formal qualities.

Tractate Abot is made up of a list of sages and the wise sayings they contributed. The tractate cites authorities of the generation generally assumed to have flourished after the closure of the Mishnah and hence may be situated at ca. 250 CE — a mere guess. Tractate Abot bears no formal, or substantive, relationship to the Mishnah, its rhetorical patterns or its substantive topical program. But the tractate serves as the Mishnah's first and most important documentary defense, because it presents sayings of sages extending from Sinai to figures named in the Mishnah itself. Through these names of masters and disciples, tractate Abot therefore links the Mishnah to Sinai. It follows that, because of the authorities cited in its pages, the Mishnah constitutes part of the Torah of Sinai, for by the evidence of the chain of tradition, the Mishnah too forms a statement of revelation, that is, "Torah revealed to Moses at Sinai." This is expressed in the opening sentence:

TRACTATE ABOT 1:1

Moses received the Torah at Sinai and handed it on to Joshua, Joshua to elders, and elders to prophets. And prophets handed it on to the men of the great assembly. They said three things: Be prudent in judgment. Raise up many disciples. Make a fence for the Torah.

The verbs, receive . . . hand on . . . , in Hebrew yield the words *qabbalah*, tradition, and *masoret,* also tradition.

The theological proposition that validates the Mishnah is that the Torah is a matter of tradition. The tradition goes from master to disciple, Moses to Joshua and on through the ages to the names of Mishnah's main authorities, part of the chain begun by God with Moses at Sinai. That fact forms an implicit claim that [1] part of the Torah was, and is, orally formulated and orally transmitted, and [2] the Mishnah's authorities stand in the tradition of Sinai, so that [3] the Mishnah too forms part of the Torah of Sinai. And what is noteworthy: what the sages say does not intersect with verses of Scripture, does not cite any as proof, does not recapitulate any as a paraphrase. The sages of the Mishnah do not need to cite Scriptural proofs for their propositions. They possess an oral tradition, not in Scripture at all, from Sinai. Here is the independence of the Mishnah, which is based on oral tradition of Sinai, fully exposed.

Comparison with earlier Israelite solutions to the problem of authority affords perspective. This position is different from that taken by pseudepigraphic writers, who imitate the style of Scripture, or who claim to speak within that same gift of revelation as Moses. It is one thing to say one's holy book is Scripture because it is like Scripture, or to claim that the author of the holy book has a revelation independent of that of Moses. These two positions concede to the Torah of Moses priority over their own holy books. The Mishnah's first apologists make no such concession, when they allege that the Mishnah is part of the Torah of Moses. They appeal to the highest possible authority in the Israelite framework, claiming the most one can claim in behalf of the book which, in fact, bears the names of men who lived fifty years before the apologists themselves. The sages' apologia for the Mishnah, therefore, rests upon the persons of the sages themselves: incarnations of the Torah of Sinai in the here-and-now.

Unlike Mishnah-tractates, tractate Abot deals with no single topic, and, it follows, the document also contains no proposition that is argued in detail. But the first two chapters do set forth a proposition, which is to be discerned not from what is said but from the chain of names that is set out in those chapters. Specifically, the list of names and the way in which they are arranged contains the claim that the two great pillars of the Mishnah — the patriarch of the Jewish community in the Land of Israel, that is, Judah the Patriarch, sponsor of the document and recognized by the Roman government as ruler of the Jewish ethnic group in the country, and the sages, who studied and where relevant applied the laws of the Mishnah, stand equally in the chain of tradition backward to Sinai. This union of the patriarch and the sages forms the document's proposition concerning the sponsorship of the Mishnah and the divine authority that is accorded to its sages.

In the list of names in chapter 1, there is a clear logic of fixed association in play. The names of the listed sages form a coherent pattern. What is attributed to the sages exhibits a certain topical coherence but in substance is random and episodic. Major authorities of the Mishnah stand in a chain of tradition to Sinai; hence, the Mishnah contains the Torah of Sinai. The order of the names is therefore deliberate and unites what is attributed, though the sentences themselves bear slight connections among themselves. We encountered the opening sentence above and now turn to the remainder of chapter 1, to pay close attention to the unfolding list of names of masters/disciples from Moses through the first century CE authorities who figure in the Mishnah itself, Shammai and Hillel for example, whose disciples, the House of Shammai and the House of Hillel, very commonly participate in the exposition of the law in the Mishnah. The paragraphs are numbered for ready reference.

1:2. Simeon the Righteous was one of the last survivors of the great assembly. He would say, "On three things does the world stand: On the Torah, and on the Temple service, and on deeds of loving-kindness."

1:3. Antigonus of Sokho received [the Torah] from Simeon the Righteous. He would say, "Do not be like servants who serve the master on condition of receiving a reward, but [be] like servants who serve the master not on condition of receiving a reward. And let the fear of Heaven be upon you."

1:4. Yosé ben Yoezer of Seredah and Yosé ben Yohanan of Jerusalem received [the Torah] from them. Yosé ben Yoezer says, "Let your house be a gathering place for sages. And wallow in the dust of their feet, and drink in their words with gusto."

1:5. Yosé ben Yohanan of Jerusalem says, "Let your house be open wide. And seat the poor at your table ["make the poor members of your household"]. And don't talk too much with women. (He referred to a man's wife, all the more so is the rule to be applied to the wife of one's fellow. In this regard did sages say, So long as a man talks too much with a woman, he brings trouble on himself, wastes time better spent on studying the Torah, and ends up an heir of Gehenna.)"

1:6. Joshua ben Perahiah and Nittai the Arbelite received [the Torah] from them. Joshua ben Perahiah says, "Set up a master for yourself. And get yourself a companion-disciple. And give everybody the benefit of the doubt."

1:7. Nittai the Arbelite says, "Keep away from a bad neighbor. And don't get involved with a bad person. And don't give up hope of retribution."

1:8A. Judah ben Tabbai and Simeon ben Shetah received [the Torah] from them.

1:8B Judah ben Tabbai says, "Don't make yourself like one of those who advocate before judges [while you yourself are judging a case]. And when the litigants stand before you, regard them as guilty. But when they leave you, regard them as acquitted (when they have accepted your judgment)."

1:9. Simeon ben Shetah says, "Examine the witnesses with great care. And watch what you say, lest they learn from what you say how to lie."

1:10. Shemaiah and Abtalyon received [the Torah] from them. Shemaiah says, "Love work. Hate authority. Don't get friendly with the government."

1:11. Abtalyon says, "Sages, watch what you say, lest you become liable to the punishment of exile, and go into exile to a place of bad water, and disciples who follow you drink bad water and die, and the name of Heaven be thereby profaned."

1:12. Hillel and Shammai received [the Torah] from them. Hillel says, "Be disciples of Aaron, loving peace and pursuing grace, loving people and drawing them near to the Torah."

1:13A. He would say [in Aramaic]: "A name made great is a name destroyed, and one who does not add, subtracts.

1:13B "And who does not learn is liable to death. And the one who uses the crown, passes away."

1:14. He would say, "If I am not for myself, who is for me? And when I am for myself, what am I? And if not now, when?"

1:15. Shammai says, "Make your learning of the Torah a fixed obligation. Say little and do much. Greet everybody cheerfully."

1:16. Rabban Gamaliel says, "Set up a master for yourself. Avoid doubt. Don't tithe by too much guesswork."

1:17. Simeon his son says, "All my life I grew up among the sages, and I found nothing better for a person [the body] than silence. And the learning is not the thing, but the doing. And whoever talks too much causes sin."

1:18. Rabban Simeon ben Gamaliel says, "On three things does the world stand: on justice, on truth, and on peace. As it is said, 'Execute the judgment of truth and peace in your gates.' (Zech 8:16)"

The intent of the list is not only to establish the link to Sinai; a second polemic, which emerges in the pairs of names and how they are arranged:

Moses
Joshua
Elders
Prophets
Men of the Great Assembly
Simeon the Righteous
Antigonus of Sokho

1.	Yosé ben Yoezer	Yosé b. Yohanan
2.	Joshua b. Perahiah	Nittai the Arbelite
3.	Judah b. Tabbai	Simeon b. Shetah
4.	Shemaiah	Abtalyon
5.	Hillel	Shammai

Gamaliel
Simeon his son [that is, Simeon b. Gamaliel]
Rabban Simeon b. Gamaliel

Once the pairs end, we find Gamaliel [I], who is (later on) represented as the son of Hillel, and then Simeon, his son, Hillel's grandson.

The cogency of the list emerges when we realize that the names Gamaliel, then Simeon, are typical of the patriarchate and are continued through this same family, of primary authorities, through Gamaliel II, ruler of the Jewish community after the destruction of the second Temple in 70 CE and into the second century, then his son, Simeon b. Gamaliel, ruler of the Jewish community after the defeat of Bar Kokhba in 135 CE— and also, as it happens, the father of Judah the Patriarch, this same Judah the Patriarch who sponsored the Mishnah. Judah the Patriarch stands in the chain of tradition to Sinai. So not only the teachings of the sages of the Mishnah, but also the political sponsor of the document, who also was numbered among the sages, formed part of this same tradition. The list itself bears the message that both the patriarch and sages employed by him carry forward the tradition of Sinai.

This same point of equivalence emerges in chapter 2, which is in two parts. We consider only part of the chapter that attributes sayings to principal authorities in the chain of tradition established in chapter 1. The important point is that the list of chapter 1 continues at tractate Abot 2:1-4ff. with the Patriarch's continuators, Rabbi, then Gamaliel son of Judah the Patriarch, and then a Hillel, presumably another son of the Patriarch. This is followed by a resumption of the list involving Shammai and Hillel, now at tractate Abot 2:8 with Yohanan ben Zakkai, founder of the sages' academy after 70 C.E. . So the list goes in two continuations, the patriarchal sages and the Rabbinical ones:

TRACTATE ABOT CHAPTER 2

2:1. Rabbi says, "What is the straight path which a person should choose for himself? Whatever is an ornament to the one who follows it, and an ornament in the view of others. Be meticulous in a small religious duty as in a large one, for you do not know what sort of reward is coming for any of the various religious duties. And reckon with the loss [required] in carrying out a religious duty against the reward for doing it; and the reward for committing a transgression against the loss for doing it. And keep your eye on three things, so you will not come into the clutches of transgression. Know what is above you. An eye which sees, and an ear which hears, and all your actions are written down in a book."

2:2. Rabban Gamaliel, a son of Rabbi Judah the Patriarch says, "Fitting is learning in the Torah along with a craft, for the labor put into the two of them makes one forget sin. And all learning of the Torah which is not joined with labor is destined to be null and causes sin. And all who work with the community—let them work with them [the community] for the sake of Heaven. For the merit of the fathers strengthens them, and the righteousness which they do stands forever. And, as for you, I credit you with a great reward, as if you had done [all the work required by the community]."

2:4. Hillel [another son of the patriarch] says, "Do not walk out on the community. And do not have confidence in yourself until the day you die. And do not judge your companion until you are in his place. And do not say anything which cannot be heard, for in the end it will be heard. And do not say, 'When I have time, I shall study,' for you may never have time."

Now the sages' list resumes with another connection to Hillel and Shammai: Yohanan and his disciples:

2:8A. Rabban Yohanan ben Zakkai received [the Torah] from Hillel and Shammai. He would say, "If you have learned much Torah, do not puff yourself up on that account, for it was for that purpose that you were created." He had five disciples, and these are they: Rabbi Eliezer ben Hyrcanus, Rabbi Joshua ben Hananiah, Rabbi Yosé the Priest, Rabbi Simeon ben Nethanel, and Rabbi Eleazar ben Arakh.

2:8B. He would list their good qualities: Rabbi Eliezer ben Hyrcanus—a plastered well, which does not lose a drop of water. Rabbi Joshua—happy is the one who gave birth to him. Rabbi Yosé—a pious man. Rabbi Simeon ben Nethanel—a man who fears sin, and Rabbi Eleazar ben Arakh—a surging spring.

2:8C. He would say, "If all the sages of Israel were on one side of the scale, and Rabbi Eliezer ben Hyrcanus were on the other, he would outweigh all of them."

Gamaliel and Simeon represent the patriarchate, Yohanan ben Zakkai the Rabbinic sages. Thus the tradition of Sinai is carried forward by the patriarch and the Rabbis. There are two sectors of that tradition, [1] first, Shammai, then Hillel-Gamaliel-Simeon-Judah the Patriarch-Gamaliel-Hillel; [2] second, the continuity from Hillel, through Yohanan ben Zakkai and his disciples, so there is a separate list: Shammai, then Hillel-Yohanan ben Zakkai-Joshua-Eliezer and the others. The politics of the second century reconstruction of Israelite government in the Land of Israel comes to expression in the two chains of Torah tradition and, incidentally, validates the Mishnah by placing its own sages' authorities into position on that chain of tradition.

The Claim of the Mishnah's Deriving from Oral Tradition

The claim of a free-standing oral tradition from Sinai implicit in tractate Abot is made explicit in a narrative. It is translated into a story pertaining to the Mishnah in particular. The code is represented as a text to be memorized through repetition of the teachings of the master. God dictated the tradition to Moses, who taught it to Aaron, and on through the ages:

BAVLI ERUBIN 5:1 54A I.43

Our Rabbis have taught on Tannaite authority:
What is the order of Mishnah teaching? Moses learned it from the mouth of the All-Powerful. Aaron came in, and Moses repeated his chapter to him and Aaron went forth and sat at the left hand of Moses. His sons came in and Moses repeated their chapter to them, and his sons went forth. Eleazar sat at the right of Moses, and Itamar at the left of Aaron.

R. Judah says, "At all times Aaron was at the right hand of Moses."

Then the elders entered, and Moses repeated for them their Mishnah chapter. The elders went out. Then the whole people came in, and Moses repeated for them their Mishnah chapter. So it came about that Aaron repeated the lesson four times, his sons three times, the elders two times, and all the people once.

Then Moses went out, and Aaron repeated his chapter for them. Aaron went out. His sons repeated their chapter. His sons went out. The elders repeated their chapter. So it turned out that everybody repeated the same chapter four times.

The Rabbinic sages conducted their own classes in the manner of God's teaching to Moses. The ritual of memorization acted out the narrative of God's instruction to Moses:

BAVLI ERUBIN 5:1 54A I.46

R. Peredah had a disciple, whom he taught his lesson four hundred times before the disciple could learn it. One day he was needed for a religious duty; he repeated the lesson to him but he didn't learn it. [Peredah] said to him, "So what makes this day different from all others?"

He said to him, "From the moment that they said to the master that there is a religious duty to be carried out, I was preoccupied, and every moment I thought to myself, now the master is going to get up, or now the master is going to get up."

He said to him, "So pay attention, and I'll repeat it for you." He went and repeated it for him four hundred times more. An echo came forth and said to him, "Do you want four hundred years added to your life, or that you and your generation will have a share in the world to come?"

He said, "That I and my generation have the merit of entering the world to come."

Said to them the Holy One, blessed be He, "Give him this and that."

Once more the importance of memorization registers. When the Rabbis' disciples sat and memorized the laws of the Mishnah and associated traditions, they acted out the rite of studying the Torah that Moses our Rabbi learned from God at Sinai:

BAVLI ERUBIN 5:1 54A I.47

Said R. Hisda, "The Torah is acquired only through mnemonics, as it is said, 'Put it in their mouths' (Dt. 31:19). Don't read the word with vowels that yield 'put it,' but rather, 'its mnemonic sign.'"

R. Tahalipa of the West heard this. He went and said it before R. Abbahu. He said, "You repeat that rule on the basis of that verse, but we deduce it from this verse: 'Set up way-markers, make you' (Jer. 31:31) — derive mnemonic signs for the Torah."

And how do we know that "way-markers" *refers to mnemonics?*

Since it is written, "And any sees a man's bone, then shall he set up a sign by it" (Ezek. 39:15).

R. Eliezer said, "It is from the following: 'Say to wisdom, you are my sister, and call understanding your kinswoman' (Prov. 7:4) —devise mnemonics for the Torah."

Raba said, "Make appointed times for the Torah."

[55A] *That is in line with what Abdimi bar Hama bar Dosa said, "What is the meaning of the verse of Scripture,* 'It is not in heaven that you should say, who shall go up for us to heaven and bring it to us, nor is it beyond the sea, that you should say, who shall go over the sea for us and bring it to us' (Dt. 30:12)?

"'It is not in heaven': For if it were in heaven, you'd have had to go up after it; "'nor is it beyond the sea': And if it were, you'd have had to go over the sea after it."

Raba said, "'It is not in heaven': It won't be found in him who forms a high opinion of himself to the highest heaven; 'nor is it beyond the sea,' nor will you find it in him who is as expansive about his knowledge of it as the sea."

R. Yohanan said, "'It is not in heaven': among the arrogant; 'nor is it beyond the sea,' you won't find it among merchants or businessmen."

Accordingly, the Rabbinic sages received and handed on the Torah that is orally formulated and orally transmitted. Now recorded in the Mishnah, Tosefta, Yerushalmi, Bavli, and the various Midrash compilations of late antiquity. When tractate Abot 1:1 begins with the declaration, "Moses received Torah at Sinai and handed it on to Joshua...," the document boldly expresses the claim that Judaism is comprised by the Torah revealed at Sinai both in writing and the other in memory, that is, in oral tradition. The crisis of the Mishnah came to resolution in the story and the rites that acted out that story. But the claim in behalf of the oral part of the dual Torah would encompass a still more radical position.

The Mishnah as Part of the Torah: An Explicit Claim

The Mishnah is held in the Talmud of the Land of Israel to be equivalent to Scripture (Yerushalmi Horayot 3:5). But here the Mishnah is not called or classified as part of the Torah.

YERUSHALMI HORAYOT 3:5 I:4

It was taught in Tannaitic tradition: The arranger [of the Mishnah traditions] takes precedence over the one capable of analyzing them.

R. Samuel brother of R. Berekiah asked, "Even such as R. Ammi?"

He said to him, "How can you ask about R. Ammi? He has a first-class analytical mind."

This is what has been said: The Mishnah takes precedence over Scripture.

And the following supports this position:

For R. Simeon b. Yohai taught, "He who takes up studies in Scripture — it is a good quality that is no good quality."

Rabbis treat Scripture as equivalent to the Mishnah.

R. Samuel bar Nahman said, "The Mishnah takes precedence over the Talmud."

What is the Scriptural basis for that opinion?

Get wisdom [Mishnah], get insight [Talmud]" (Prov. 4:5).

R. Yohanan said, "The Talmud takes precedence over the Mishnah."

What is the scriptural basis for this opinion?

"To get wisdom is better than gold, to get understanding is to be chosen rather than silver" (Prov. 16:16).

How does R. Yohanan interpret the scriptural basis for the position of R. Samuel bar Nahman? Water [silver/Talmud] is cheap, wine [gold/Mishnah] is costly. Still, it is possible for the world to live without wine, but it is not possible for the world to live without water.

And how does R. Samuel bar Nahman interpret the scriptural basis of R. Yohanan's position?

Salt is cheap, and pepper is dear. It is possible for the world to live without pepper, but it is not possible for the world to live without salt.

[Q] One should always pursue the Mishnah more than the Talmud.

That is to say, "What you say (that the study of the Mishnah is preferable] refers to the time before Rabbi had embodied and abridged most of the Mishnah-traditions in his edition, but since then, run at all times after the Talmud."

Once the Mishnah entered the status of Scripture, it would take but a short step to a theory of the Mishnah as part of the revelation at Sinai — hence, oral Torah. In the first Talmud we find the first glimmerings of an effort to theorize in general, not merely in detail, about how specific teachings of Mishnah relate to specific teachings of Scripture. The citing of scriptural proof texts for Mishnah propositions, after all, would not have caused much surprise to the framers of the Mishnah; they themselves included such passages, though not often. But what conception of the Torah underlies such initiatives, and how to Yerushalmi sages propose to explain the phenomenon of the Mishnah as a whole? The following passage gives us one statement. It refers to the assertion at M. Hag. 1:8D that the laws on cultic cleanness presented in the Mishnah rest on deep and solid foundations in the Scripture.

YERUSHALMI HAGIGAH 1:7

The laws of the Sabbath [M. 1:8B]: R. Jonah said R. Hama bar Uqba raised the question [in reference to M. Hag. 1:8D's view that there are many verses of Scripture on cleanness], "And lo, it is written only, 'Nevertheless a spring or a cistern holding water shall be clean; but whatever touches their carcass shall be unclean (Lev. 11:36). And from this verse you derive many laws. [So how can M. 8:8D say what it does about many verses for laws of cultic cleanness?]"

R. Zeira in the name of R. Yohanan: "If a law comes to hand and you do not know its nature, do not discard it for another one, for lo, many laws were stated to Moses at Sinai, and all of them have been embedded in the Mishnah."

The Mishnah now is claimed to contain statements made by God to Moses. Just how these statements found their way into the Mishnah, and which passages of the Mishnah contain them, we do not know. That is hardly important, given the fundamental assertion at hand. The passage proceeds to a further, and far more consequential, proposition. It asserts that part of the Torah was written down, and part was preserved in memory and transmitted orally. In context, moreover, that distinction must encompass the Mishnah, thus explaining its origin as part of the Torah. Here is a clear and unmistakable expression of the distinction between two forms in which a single Torah was revealed and handed on at Mount Sinai, part in writing, part orally.

While the passage below does not make use of the language, Torah-in-writing and Torah-by-memory, it does refer to "the written" and "the oral." I believe myself fully justified in supplying the word Torah in square brackets. The reader will note, however, that the word Torah likewise does not occur at K, L. Only when the passage reaches its climax, at M, does it break down into a number of categories — Scripture, Mishnah, Talmud, laws, lore. It there makes the additional point that everything comes from Moses at Sinai. So the fully articulated theory of two Torahs (not merely one Torah in two forms) does not reach final expression in this passage. But short of explicit allusion to Torah-in-writing and Torah-by-memory, which (so far as I am able to discern) we find mainly in the Talmud of Babylonia, the ultimate theory of Torah of formative Judaism is at hand in what follows in the Yerushalmi's amplification of the passage just now cited.

Yerushalmi Hagigah 1:7 V

R. Zeirah in the name of R. Eleazar: "'Were I to write for him my laws by ten thousands, they would be regarded as a strange thing' (Hos. 8:12). Now is the greater part of the Torah written down? [Surely not. The oral part is much greater.] But more abundant are the matters which are derived by exegesis from the written [Torah] than those derived by exegesis from the oral [Torah]."

And is that so?

But more cherished are those matters which rest upon the written [Torah] than those which rest upon the oral [Torah].

R. Haggai in the name of R. Samuel bar Nahman, "Some teachings were handed on orally, and some things were handed on in writing, and we do not know which of them is the more precious. But on the basis of that which is written, "And the Lord said to Moses, Write these words; in accordance with these words I have made a covenant with you and with Israel' (Ex. 34:27), [we conclude] that the ones which are handed on orally are the more precious."

R. Yohanan and R. Yudan b. R. Simeon — One said, "If you have kept what is preserved orally and also kept what is in writing, I shall make a covenant with you, and if not, I shall not make a covenant with you."

The other said, "If you have kept what is preserved orally and you have kept what is preserved in writing, you shall receive a reward, and if not, you shall not receive a reward."

Here we have absolutely explicit evidence that people believed part of the Torah had been preserved not in writing but orally. Linking that part to the Mishnah remains a matter of implication. But it surely comes fairly close to the surface, when we are told that the Mishnah contains Torah traditions revealed at Sinai. From that view it requires only a small step to the allegation that the Mishnah is part of the Torah, the oral part.

Abot had held that the Mishnah contained things sages in the tradition of Moses had said. What sages said formed a chain of tradition extending back to Sinai. Hence it was equivalent to the Torah. The upshot is that words of sages enjoyed the status of the Torah. The small step beyond, I think, was to claim that what sages said *was* Torah, as much as what Scripture said was Torah. And, a further small step moved matters to the position that there were two forms in which the Torah reached Israel: one Torah in writing, the other Torah handed on orally, that is, in memory.

The final step, fully revealed in the Talmud at hand, brought the conception of Torah to its logical conclusion: what the sage said was in the status of the Torah, was Torah, because the sage was Torah incarnate. So the abstract symbol now became concrete and material once more. We recognize the many, diverse ways in which the Talmud stated that conviction. Every passage in which knowledge of the Torah yields power over this world and the next, capacity to coerce to the sage's will the natural and supernatural worlds alike, rests upon the same viewpoint. The matter is made explicit in the following famous passage:

BAVLI SHABBAT 31A/I.11 = [THE FATHERS ACCORDING TO RABBI NATHAN XV:V.1].
Our Rabbis have taught on Tannaite authority:
There was the incident of a certain gentile who came before Shammai. He said to him, "How many Torahs do you have?"
He said to him, "Two, one in writing, one memorized."
He said to him, "As to the one in writing, I believe you. As to the memorized one, I do not believe you. Convert me on condition that you will teach me only the Torah that is in writing."
He rebuked him and threw him out.
He came before Hillel. He said to him, "Convert me."
"My lord, how many Torahs were given?"
He said to him, "Two, one in writing, one memorized."
He said to him, "As to the one in writing, I believe you. As to the memorized one, I do not believe you."]
On the first day he said to him, "Alef, bet, gimel, dalet." The next day he reversed the order on him.
He said to him, "Well, yesterday, didn't you say it differently?"
He said to him, "Didn't you depend on me then? Then depend on me when it comes to the fact of the memorized Torah too."
He said to him, "My son, sit."
He wrote for him, Alef, bet. He said to him, "What is this?"
He said to him, "An alef." He said to him, "This is not an alef but a bet." He said to him, "What is this?"
He said to him, "Bet." He said to him, "This is not a bet but a gimel."
He said to him, "How do you know that this is an alef and this a bet and this a gimel? But that is what our ancestors have handed over to us — the tradition that this is an alef, this a bet, this a gimel. Just as you have accepted this teaching in good faith, so accept the other in good faith"

BAVLI SHABBAT 31A/I.12
There was another case of a gentile who came before Shammai. He said to him, "Convert me on the stipulation that you teach me the entire Torah while I am standing on one foot." He drove him off with the building cubit that he had in his hand.
He came before Hillel: "Convert me."
He said to him, "*'What is hateful to you, to your fellow don't do.'* That's the entirety of the Torah; *everything else is elaboration. So go, study.*"

The Talmud, accordingly, takes its place as a component of that Torah: part of God's revelation to Israel. But it is only one of the three parts that comprise the Torah. In the Judaism of the dual Torah, the Torah is set forth and preserved in three media, [1] a book, the Hebrew Scriptures or written Torah, [2] a memorized oral tradition, first written down in the Mishnah, ca. AD 200, and other ancient documents, and [3] the model of a sage who embodies in the here and now the paradigm of Moses, called a Rabbi.

6

How Is the Sage
Part of the Torah?

"The Torah Is not in Heaven"

If the Talmud is part of the Torah, then what does that say about the Rabbinic sage, the voice of the Talmud. He is the link to Sinai in the tradition of the master-disciple chain that produced the Mishnah and the Gemara. But how is he—his person, his convictions—part of the Torah?[1] That question is answered in a story to be examined in a moment, a story that carries to a climax the conception of the dual Torah written and oral that explains the standing and authority of the Talmud. The story maintains that the same Torah and the same logic that govern the sages govern God who revealed the Torah with its logic. The sages embody and in word and deed teach the Torah.

All depends upon the sage himself, and, it is now maintained, the sage appealing to logic and tradition can defy even God's intervention in the on-going discourse of the sages. The story concerns the two principal disciples of Yohanan ben Zakkai, those who carried him out of the besieged city, whom we met in chapter 1. They debate the status as to uncleanness of a certain kind of clay oven. The issue is not set forth in detail in the narrative, which centers on the relationship of miracles and Torah learning. In the course of the debate one party invokes Heaven's intervention, and Heaven obliges with a miracle. In the end, after several such exchanges, the sage declares Heaven outside the frame of argument: the Torah is not in heaven but is the possession of the sages. In a word, the sage possesses the Torah through his capacity to reason, and logic compels even Heaven — that is, God — to adopt the sages' position. The Mishnah is cited in bold face type, the rest of the story in plain type.

BAVLI BABA MESIA 59A-B/4:10 I.15

There we have learned: **If one cut [a clay oven] into parts and put sand between the parts,**

R. Eliezer declares [the oven broken-down and therefore useless and] insusceptible to uncleanness.

And sages declare it [useful in its new form and therefore] susceptible.

And this is what is meant by the oven of Akhenai [Mishnah-tractate Kelim 5:10].

A Tannaite statement:

On that day R. Eliezer produced all of the arguments in the world [for his position on the moot point], but they did not accept them from him. So he said to them, "If the law accords with my position, this carob tree will prove it."

The carob was uprooted from its place by a hundred cubits — and some say, four hundred cubits.

They said to him, "There is no proof from a carob tree."

So he went and said to them, "If the law accords with my position, let the stream of water prove it."

The stream of water reversed flow.

They said to him, "There is no proof from a stream of water."

So he went and said to them, "If the law accords with my position, let the walls of the school house prove it."

The walls of the school house tilted toward falling.

R. Joshua rebuked them, saying to them, "If disciples of sages are contending with one another in matters of law, what business do you have?"

They did not fall on account of the honor owing to R. Joshua, but they also did not straighten up on account of the honor owing to R. Eliezer, and to this day they are still tilted.

So he went and said to them, "If the law accords with my position, let the Heaven prove it!"

An echo came forth, saying, "What business have you with R. Eliezer, for the law accords with his position under all circumstances!"

R. Joshua stood up on his feet and said, "'It is not in heaven' (Dt. 30:12)."

What is the sense of, "'It is not in heaven' (Dt. 30:12)"?

Said R. Jeremiah, "[The sense of Joshua's statement is this:] For the Torah has already been given from Mount Sinai, so we do not pay attention to echoes, since you have already written in the Torah at Mount Sinai, 'After the majority you are to incline' (Ex. 23:2)."

R. Nathan came upon Elijah and said to him, "What did the Holy One, blessed be he, do at that moment?"

He said to him, "He laughed and said, 'My children have overcome me, my children have overcome me!'"

The story at its climax places the reason and argument of the sages above the supernatural intervention of Heaven. God himself is bound by the reason and logic of the Talmud and its Rabbinic sages. The Torah is no longer in heaven, it is now the possession of the sages. And the key to the Torah lies in the sages' arguments and contentions. The little story added on at the end portray God as confirming the courageous gesture of Joshua, Eliezer's rival.

The Sage as the Living Torah

The autonomous standing of the sage captured in this wonderful story underscores that God did not resort solely to a book to convey and preserve the divine message. It was through teachings, which could be transmitted in more than a single form: in persons as much as in books, in the living memory of disciples as much as in Scripture. Here we find in narrative form that same conception of the sage as part of a chain of tradition going back to God and Moses at Sinai that we met in chapter 5. Consequently the sage could be received as a Torah and treated as such.

An important and simple statement of that fact will prove the point. A sage himself was equivalent to a scroll of the Torah — a material, legal comparison, not merely a symbolic metaphor.

YERUSHALMI MOED QATAN 3:7.X.

He who sees a disciple of a sage who has died is as if he sees a scroll of the Torah that has been burned.

YERUSHALMI MOED QATAN 3:1.XI.

R. Jacob bar Abbayye in the name of R. Aha: "An elder who forgot his learning because of some accident that happened to him — they treat him with the sanctity owed to an ark [of the Torah]."

The sage therefore is represented as equivalent to the scroll of the Torah, and, turning the statement around, the scroll of the Torah is realized in the person of the sage. The conception is not merely figurative or metaphorical, for, in both instances, actual behavior was affected. Still more to the point, what the sage *did* had the status of law; the sage was the model of the law, thus once again enjoyed the standing of the human embodiment of the Torah. Since the sage exercised supernatural power as a kind of living Torah, his very deeds served to reveal law, as much as his word expressed revelation. That is a formidable component of the argument that the sage embodied the Torah, another way of saying that the Torah was incarnated in the person of the sage.

The capacity of the sage himself to participate in the process of revelation is illustrated in two types of materials. First of all, tales told about Rabbis' behavior on specific occasions immediately are translated into rules for the entire community to keep. Accordingly, the sage was a source not merely of good examples but of prescriptive law. Here is a simple example among thousands of candidates of how the sage's conduct formed a revelation of law:

YERUSHALMI ABODAH ZARAH 5:4 II.

R. Aha went to Emmaus, and he ate dumpling [prepared by Samaritans].
R. Jeremiah ate leavened bread prepared by them.
R. Hezekiah ate their locusts prepared by them.
R. Abbahu prohibited Israelite use of wine prepared by them.

There is no difference between the precedent of Rabbinic conduct and the public ruling issued by the sage. Along with hundreds of parallels in the Rabbinic literature these reports of what Rabbis said and did enjoyed the same authority as did citations in legal form of traditions in the names of the great authorities of old or of the day. What someone did served as a norm, if the person was a sage of sufficient standing. The precedent entered the Torah, and what a sage said became part of the oral component of the one whole Torah that God gave to Moses at Sinai. The Torah does not take form solely through sacred texts. It appeals to truth that is preserved in diverse media, books, words preserved not in books but in memorized formulas, and, finally, the lives, gestures, and deeds of holy persons.

What about women? While women rarely are represented as masters of the Torah and sages, they are portrayed as models of virtue and piety. The proper attitude in prayer is exemplified by Hannah's prayer (1 Sam. 1:10), which resulted in the birth of Samuel the prophet:

BAVLI BERAKHOT 5:1 I.16/31A-B

Said R. Hamnuna, "How many important laws concerning prayer are there to be derived from the verses of Scripture stated in connection with Hannah.

"'Now Hannah spoke from her heart' (1 Sam. 1:10). On the basis of this verse [we learn] that one who recites the Prayer has to direct his heart [to Heaven].

"'Only her lips moved.' On the basis of this verse [we learn] that one who recites the Prayer must mouth the words.

"'But her voice could not be heard.' On the basis of this verse [we learn] that it is forbidden to raise one's voice when he recites the Prayer.

"'Therefore Eli thought she was drunk.' On the basis of this verse [we learn] that one who is drunk may not recite the Prayer."

"And Eli said to her, How long will you be drunk" (1 Sam. 1:14):

Said R. Eleazar, "On the basis of this verse [we learn] that one who observes something improper in his fellow [31B] has the obligation to reprove him."

Hannah's prayer shows how people should pray. The deed of the virtuous woman provides the authoritative example for the community of the Torah.

Not only so, but the highest form of virtue is illustrated by stories of women ready to sell themselves to save their husbands. In the context of Rabbinic Judaism, with its emphasis on the priority of learning in the Torah as a means of acquiring merit, the two players — the unlettered man, the woman in each story that follows — represent outsiders. The system's norms — mastery of the Torah, consistent conformity to the law — are not met. Neither is represented as a master of Torah learning. And the self-sacrificing male in the story is an ignoramus. Neither figure in the narratives represents an embodiment of virtue either. In the setting of Rabbinic Judaism, with its stress on the long-term disciplines of the law, leading to a life of piety lived out in consistent daily discipline, the stories' make a further point. A single action accomplishes what an entire life of piety and Torah learning accomplishes.

YERUSHALMI TAANIT 1:4.I.

A certain ass driver appeared before the Rabbis the context requires: in a dream and prayed, and rain came. The Rabbis sent and brought him and said to him, "What is your trade?"

He said to them, "I am an ass driver."

They said to him, "And how do you conduct your business?"

He said to them, "One time I rented my ass to a certain woman, and she was weeping on the way, and I said to her, 'What's with you?' and she said to me, 'The husband of that woman me is in prison for debt, and I wanted to see what I can do to free him.' So I sold my ass and I gave her the proceeds, and I said to her, 'Here is your money, free your husband, but do not sin by becoming a prostitute to raise the necessary funds.'"

They said to him, "You are worthy of praying and having your prayers answered."

The ass driver clearly has a powerful lien on Heaven, so that his prayers are answered, even while those of others are not. What he did to get that entitlement? He did what no law could demand: impoverished himself to save the woman from a "fate worse than death." He had no expectation of reward. He did not ask the Rabbinic sages about his power to pray for rain, they asked him. His act of altruism was to give up his means of making a living.

YERUSHALMI TAANIT 1:4.I.

In a dream of R. Abbahu, Mr. Pentakaka ["Five sins" known to Abbahu] appeared, who prayed that rain would come, and it rained. R. Abbahu sent and summoned him. He said to him, "What is your trade?"

He said to him, "Five sins does that man [I] do every day, for I am a pimp: hiring whores, cleaning up the theater, bringing home their garments for washing, dancing, and performing before them."

He said to him, "And what sort of decent thing have you ever done?"

He said to him, "One day I was cleaning the theater, and a woman came and stood behind a pillar and cried. I said to her, 'What's with you?' And she said to me, 'That woman's my husband is in prison, and I wanted to see what I can do to free him,' so I sold my bed and cover, and I gave the proceeds to her. I said to her, 'Here is your money, free your husband, but do not sin.'"

He said to him, "You are worthy of praying and having your prayers answered."

The man has done everything sinful that one can do, and, more to the point, he has done and does wicked deeds every day. So we are shown the singularity of the act of altruism, which suffices if done only one time to outweigh a life of sin.

Here too the man sold the necessities of life to spare the woman a life of sin. In both cases — the unlettered man, the woman excluded by definition, and also the single action outweighing a life of sin — we therefore deal with outsiders who do not keep the law but are capable of acting beyond the outer requirements of the law.

Here we have located the very heart of the system: provision for the spontaneous act beyond the requirements of the law in the midst of the routine and everyday. And that singular act, which outweighs all else, embodies what God cannot command but what man can freely give: uncompensated self-sacrifice. This is beyond altruism.

How the Talmud Represents Holy Men

The Talmuds contain a huge corpus of stories about Rabbinic sages, their rulings on law, their readings of Scripture, their traits of virtue. These are episodic and do not combine to portray fully presented individuals. That fact makes all the more curious the failure of the Talmuds to encompass sustained, continuous biographies of particular, named sages. For the entire cadre of sages we do not have a single biography devoted to an individual, or even the raw materials for a sustained and systematic "life." Brief chapters and episodes in abundance, but there is nothing connected and complete. There is a further noteworthy fact. Among the documents of the formative age of Rabbinic Judaism we do not possess a single document produced by a clearly identifiable individual author, a single coherent composite of any consequence at all that concerns itself with a named figure.

The Talmud, like every document in Rabbinic literature, emerged anonymously, under public sponsorship and authorship, stripped of all marks of individual, therefore idiosyncratic, origin. Personality and individuality stood for schism, and Rabbinic literature in its very definition and character aims at the opposite, forming as it does the functional counterpart to the creeds and decisions of church councils. Framed in mythic terms, the literature aimed to make this theological statement: sages stood in a chain of tradition from Sinai, and the price of inclusion was the acceptance of the discipline of tradition — anonymity, reasoned argument to attain for a private view the status of a public judgment, a consensus statement.

The very definition of tradition that comes to expression in the character of the Talmud and the other books of the Rabbinic literature of the formative age. The sages claimed that the Rabbinic writings form components of God's revelation to Moses at Sinai received and handed on unimpaired and intact in a reliable process of instruction by masters to disciples. That claim accounts for the public, anonymous character of Rabbinic writing.

But was there no tradition of dispute? Chapter 3 stressed the role of dispute, debate, and dialectical argument in the processes of thought of Rabbinic Judaism. But people disagreed within a permitted agendum, and the protocol of disagreement always began with the premise of concurrence on all that counted. That was, as we saw, the very goal of Rabbinic dialectics: the balanced opinions, the rationality of dispute, the cogency of theology and of law as a whole. As every named saying we have examined has already shown us, dissenting views too found their properly labeled position in the Talmud, preserved in the name of the private person who registered dissent in accord with the rules governing the iron consensus of the whole.

Composites Focused upon Individual Sages

Biographical stories and sayings in the Talmuds take shape either as strings of stories about great sages of the past or as collections of sayings and comments drawn together solely because the same name stands behind all the collected sayings. These can easily have been composed into biographies. Hence the question raised here: why no gospels or biographies of the holy men, the saints in Judaism? The question is an appropriate one, because, as I shall show, there could have been. The final step — assembling available stories into a coherent narrative, with a beginning, middle, and end, for example — was not taken.

In the writing that focuses upon the sage, e.g., a paragraph of thought, a story, things that a given authority said are strung together or tales about a given authority are told at some length. In the circles responsible for making up and writing down completed units of discourse, three distinct categories of interest defined the task: (1) exegesis of the Mishnah, which we met in chapter 2, (2) exegesis of Scripture, which we met in chapter 5, and (3) preservation and exegesis, in exactly the same reverential spirit, of the words and deeds of sages. Not only so, but the kind of analysis to which Mishnah and Scripture exegesis were subjected also applied to the exegesis of sage stories.

That fact may be shown in three ways. First, just as Scripture supplied proof texts, so deeds or statements of sages provided proof texts. Second, just as a verse of Scripture or an explicit statement of the Mishnah resolved a disputed point, so what a sage said or did might be introduced into discourse as ample proof for settling a dispute. And third, it follows that just as Scripture or the Mishnah laid down Torah, so what a sage did or said laid down Torah. In the dimensions of the applied and practical reason by which the law unfolded, the sage found a comfortable place in precisely the categories defined, to begin with, by both the Mishnah and Scripture. Let us examine a few substantial examples of the sorts of sustained discourse in biographical materials turned out by circles of sages. What we shall see is an important fact. Just as these circles composed units of discourse about the meaning of a Mishnah passage, a larger theoretical problem of law, the sense of scriptural verse, and the sayings and doings of scriptural heroes seen as sages, so they did the same for living sages themselves.

In the simplest example we see that two discrete sayings of a sage are joined together. The principle of conglomeration, therefore, is solely the name of the sage at hand. One saying has to do with overcoming the impulse to do evil, and the other has to do with the classifications of sages' program of learning. What the two subjects have in common is slight. But to the framer of the passage, that fact meant nothing. For he thought that compositions joined by the same authority — the Rabbis, Levi and Simeon — should be made up.

B. BERAKHOT 1:1 III.7/5

Said R. Levi bar Hama said R. Simeon b. Laqish, "A person should always provoke his impulse to do good against his impulse to do evil,

"as it is said, 'Provoke and do not sin' (Ps. 4:5).

"If [the good impulse] wins, well and good. If not, let him take up Torah-study,

"as it is said, 'Commune with your own heart' (Ps. 4:5).

"If [the good impulse] wins, well and good. If not, let him recite the Shema,

"as it is said, '... upon your bed' (Ps. 4:5).

"If [the good impulse] wins, well and good. If not, let him remember the day of death,

"as it is said, 'And keep silent. Sela' (Ps. 4:5)."

And R. Levi bar Hama said R. Simeon b. Laqish said, "What is the meaning of the verse of Scripture, 'And I will give you the tables of stone, the law and the commandment, which I have written, that you may teach them' (Ex. 24:12).

"'The tables' refers to the Ten Commandments.

"'Torah' refers to Scripture.

"'Commandment' refers to Mishnah.

"'Which I have written' refers to the Prophets and the Writings.

"'That you may teach them' refers to the Gemara.

"'This teaches that all of them were given to Moses from Sinai.'"

The frame of the story at hand links the parts in a way unfamiliar to those accustomed to the principles of conglomeration in legal and biblical-exegetical compositions. In the former, a given problem or principle of law will tell us why one item is joined to some other. In the latter, a single verse of Scripture will account for the joining of two or more otherwise discrete units of thought. Here one passage takes up Ps. 4:5; the other Ex. 24:12. The point of the one statement hardly goes over the ground of the other. So the *sole* principle by which one item has joined the other is biographical: a record of what a sage said about topics that are, at best, contiguous, if related at all.

A second way of stringing together materials illustrative of the lives and teachings of sages is to join incidents involving a given authority or (as in the following case) two authorities believed to have stood in close relationship with one another, disciple and master, for instance. Often these stories go over the same ground in the same way. In the following, the two farewell stories make essentially the same point but in quite different language. What joins the stories is not only the shared theme but the fact that Eliezer is supposed to have studied with Yohanan b. Zakkai.

BAVLI BERAKHOT 4:2 I.2/28B.

Our Rabbis have taught on Tannaite authority:

When R. Eliezer fell ill, his disciples came in to pay a call on him. They said to him, "Our master, teach us the ways of life, so that through them we may merit the world to come."

He said to them, "Be attentive to the honor owing to your fellows, keep your children from excessive reflection, and set them among the knees of disciples of sages, and when you pray, know before whom you stand, and on that account you will merit the life of the world to come."

And when [Eliezer's master] R. Yohanan b. Zakkai fell ill, his disciples came in to pay a call on him. When he saw them, he began to cry. His disciples said to him, "Light of Israel! Pillar at the right hand! Mighty hammer! On what account are you crying?"

He said to them, "If I were going to be brought before a mortal king, who is here today and tomorrow gone to the grave, who, should he be angry with me, will not be angry forever, and, if he should imprison me, will not imprison me forever, and if he should put me to death, whose sentence of death is not for eternity, and whom I can appease with the right words or bribe with money, even so, I should weep.

"But now that I am being brought before the King of kings, the Holy One, blessed be he, who endures forever and ever, who, should he be angry with me, will be angry forever, and if he should imprison me, will imprison me forever, and if he should put me to death, whose sentence of death is for eternity, and whom I cannot appease with the right words or bribe with money,

"and not only so, but before me are two paths, one to the Garden of Eden and the other to Gehenna, and I do not know by which path I shall be brought,

"and should I not weep?"

They said to him, "Our master, bless us."

He said to them, "May it be God's will that the fear of Heaven be upon you as much as the fear of mortal man."

His disciples said, "Just so much?"

He said to them, "Would that it were that much. You should know that, when a person commits a transgression, he says, 'I hope no man sees me.'"

When he was dying, he said to them, "Clear out utensils from the house, because of the uncleanness [of the corpse, which I am about to impart when I die], and prepare a throne for Hezekiah king of Judah, who is coming."

First, we have stories about sages' farewells. Second, people took for granted, because of the lists of M. Abot 2:2ff., that Eliezer was a disciple of Yohanan b. Zakkai. Otherwise, it is difficult to explain the joining of the stories, since they scarcely make the same point, go over the same matters, or even share a common literary or rhetorical form or preference. But a framer of a composition of lives of saints, who is writing a tractate on how saints die, will have found this passage a powerful one indeed.

Yet another approach to the utilization of tales about sages was to join together stories on a given theme but told about different sages. A tractate or a chapter of a tractate on a given theme, for example, suffering and its reward, can have emerged from the sort of collection that follows. The importance of the next item is that the same kinds of stories about different sages are strung together to make a single point.

BAVLI BERAKHOT 1:1 III:15-17/5B

III:15 R. Hiyya bar Abba got sick. R. Yohanan came to him. He said to him, "Are these sufferings precious to you?"

He said to him, "I don't want them, I don't want their reward."

He said to him, "Give me your hand."

He gave him his hand, and [Yohanan] raised him up [out of his sickness].

R. Yohanan got sick. R. Hanina came to him. He said to him, "Are these sufferings precious to you?"

He said to him, "I don't want them. I don't want their reward."

He said to him, "Give me your hand."

He gave him his hand and [Hanina] raised him up [out of his sickness].

Why so? R. Yohanan should have raised himself up?

They say, "A prisoner cannot get himself out of jail."

III.16   R. Eliezer got sick. R. Yohanan came to see him and found him lying in a dark room. [The dying man] uncovered his arm, and light fell [through the room]. [Yohanan] saw that R. Eliezer was weeping. He said to him, "Why are you crying? Is it because of the Torah that you did not learn sufficiently? We have learned: 'All the same are the ones who do much and do little, so long as each person will do it for the sake of heaven.'

"If it is because of insufficient income? Not everyone has the merit of seeing two tables [Torah and riches, as you have. You have been a master of Torah and also have enjoyed wealth].

"Is it because of children? Here is the bone of my tenth son [whom I buried, so it was no great loss not to have children, since you might have had to bury them]."

He said to him, "I am crying because of this beauty of mine which will be rotting in the ground."

He said to him, "For that it certainly is worth crying," and the two of them wept together.

In the course of time, he said to him, "Are these sufferings precious to you?"

He said to him, "I don't want them, I don't want their reward."

He said to him, "Give me your hand."

He gave him his hand, and [Yohanan] raised him up [out of his sickness].

III.17   Four hundred barrels of wine turned sour on R. Huna. R. Judah, brother of R. Sala the Pious, and Rabbis came to see him (and some say it was R. Ada bar Ahba and Rabbis). They said to him, "The master should take a good look at his deeds."

He said to them, "And am I suspect in your eyes?"

They said to him, "And is the Holy One, blessed be he, suspect of inflicting a penalty without justice?"

He said to them, "Has anybody heard anything bad about me? Let him say it."

They said to him, "This is what we have heard: the master does not give to his hired hand [the latter's share of] vine twigs [which are his right]."

He said to them, "Does he leave me any! He steals all of them to begin with."

They said to him, "This is in line with what people say: 'Go steal from a thief but taste theft too!' [Simon: If you steal from a thief, you also have a taste of it.]"

He said to them, "I pledge that I'll give them to him."

Some say that the vinegar turned back into wine, and some say that the price of vinegar went up so he sold it off at the price of wine.

The foregoing composite makes the same point several times: "Not them, not their reward." Sufferings are precious, but sages are prepared to forego the benefits. The formally climactic entry makes the point that, if bad things happen, the victim has deserved punishment. In joining these several stories about sages — two involving Yohanan, the third entirely separate — the compositor of the passage made his point by juxtaposing two like biographical snippets to a distinct one. Collections of stories about saints can have served quite naturally when formed into tractates on pious virtues, expressing these virtues through strong and pictorial language such as is before us.

The foregoing sources have shown two important facts. First, a principle of composition in the sages' circles was derived from interest in the teachings associated with a given sage, as well as in tales and stories told about a sage or groups of sages. The first of the passages shows us the simplest composition of sayings, the latter, an equivalent conglomeration of related stories. So biographical materials on sages, as much as Mishnah exegesis and Scripture exegesis, came forth out of circles of sages.

The Sage and the Torah

One reason for not forming biographies of saints can have been that the sage did not stand at the level of the written Torah or of the Mishnah, the written down record of the initially oral Torah. Hence forming documents around the lives of the sages, as much as around the amplification of Scripture and the Mishnah, can have made no sense. But the opposite is the fact. The sage, as we have seen, stood at that same level of authority as did the written Torah, on the one side, and the Mishnah, on the other. Logic shared with God makes the sage an appropriate contender with God in the debates over truth. That remarkable narrative with which we began makes that point.

And there is more. God reveals the Torah not only through words handed down from Sinai in the form of the Torah, written and oral, but also through the lives and deeds of saints, that is, sages. The same modes of exegetical inquiry pertaining to the Mishnah and Scripture apply without variation to statements made by Rabbis of the contemporary period themselves.

To show that this is so, we turn to the way in which the Rabbis of the Yerushalmi proposed to resolve differences of opinion. Precisely in the same way in which talmudic Rabbis settled disputes in the Mishnah and so attained a consensus about the law of the Mishnah, they handled disputes among themselves. The importance of that fact for our argument again is simple. The Rabbis, represented in the Yerushalmi (as much as in the Bavli), treated their own contemporaries exactly as they treated the then-ancient authorities of the Mishnah. In their minds the status accorded to the Mishnah, as a derivative of the Torah, applied equally to sages' teachings. In the following instance we see how the same discourse attached to (1) a Mishnah rule is assigned as well to one in (2) the Tosefta and, at the end, to differences among (3) the Yerushalmi's authorities. We begin with the Mishnah rule.

YERUSHALMI KETUBOT 5:1.VI.

R. Jacob bar Aha, R. Alexa in the name of Hezekiah: "The law accords with the view of R. Eleazar b. Azariah, who stated, If she was widowed or divorced at the stage of betrothal, the virgin collects only two hundred zuz and the widow, a maneh. If she was widowed or divorced at the stage of a consummated marriage, she collects the full amount [M. Ket. 5:1E,D]."

R. Hananiah said, "The law accords with the view of R. Eleazar b. Azariah."

Said Abbayye, "They said to R. Hananiah, 'Go and shout [outside whatever opinion you like.' But] R. Jonah, R. Zeira in the name of R. Jonathan said, 'The law accords with the view of R. Eleazar b. Azariah.' [Yet] R. Yosa bar Zeira in the name of R. Jonathan said, 'The law does not accord with the view of R. Eleazar b. Azariah.' [So we do not in fact know the decision.]"

We proceed to the Tosefta's statement on the same issue of law.

Said R. Yosé, "We had a mnemonic: Hezekiah and R. Jonathan both say one thing."

For it has been taught:
He whose son went abroad, and whom they told, "Your son has died,"
and who went and wrote over all his property to someone else as a gift,
and whom they afterward informed that his son was yet alive —
his deed of gift remains valid.
R. Simeon b. Menassia says, "His deed of gift is not valid, for if he had known that his son was alive, he would never have made such a gift" [T. Ket. 4:14E-H].

Now come the named Rabbis to take up their place in the disputed matter.

Now R. Jacob bar Aha said, "The law is in accord with the view of R. Eleazar b. Azariah, and the opinion of R. Eleazar b. Azariah is the same in essence as that of R. Simeon b. Menassia."

Now R. Yannai said to R. Hananiah, "Go and shout [outside whatever you want]. "But, said R. Yosé bar Zeira in the name of R. Jonathan, 'The law is not in accord with R. Eleazar b. Azariah.'"

But in fact the case was to be decided in accord with the view of R. Eleazar b. Azariah.

What is important here is that the Talmud makes no distinction whatever when deciding the law of disputes (1) in the Mishnah, (2) in the Tosefta, and (3) among talmudic Rabbis. The same already-formed colloquy applied at the outset to the Mishnah's dispute is then held equally applicable to the Tosefta's.

The process of thought is the main thing, without regard to the document to which the process applies. Scripture, the Mishnah, the sage — the three spoke with equal authority. True, one had to come into alignment with the other, the Mishnah with Scripture, the sage with the Mishnah. But it was not the case that one component of the Torah, of God's word to Israel, stood within the sacred circle, another beyond. Interpretation and what was interpreted, exegesis and text, belonged together. The sage constitutes the third component in the three-part canon of the Torah, because, while Scripture and the Mishnah govern what the sage knows, in the Yerushalmi as in the Bavli it is the sage who authoritatively speaks about them. What sages were willing to do to the Mishnah in the Yerushalmi and Bavli is precisely what they were prepared to do to Scripture — impose upon it their own judgment of its meaning.

The sage speaks with authority about the Mishnah and Scripture. As much as those documents of the Torah, the sage too therefore has authority deriving from revelation. He himself may participate in the process of revelation. There is no material difference. Since that is so, the sage's teaching belongs to the Torah, that is, is revealed by God. The sage is like Moses our Rabbi, who received Torah — instruction — and wrote the Torah, the Pentateuch. So while the canon of the Torah was in three parts, Scripture, Mishnah, sage — two verbal, one incarnate — the sage, in saying what the other parts meant and in embodying that meaning in his life and thought, took primacy of place. If no document organized itself around sayings and stories of sages, it was because that was superfluous. Why so? Because all documents, equally, whether Scripture, whether the Mishnah, whether the Yerushalmi and the Bavli, gave full and complete expression of deeds and deliberations of sages, beginning, after all, with Moses, our Rabbi.

A consensus of an entire community — the Torah fully exposed — reaches its full human realization in the Rabbinic sage. That consensus will not permit individual traits of rhetoric to differentiate writer from writer or writing from writing. The individual obliterates the marks of individuality in serving the holy people by writing a work that will become part of the Torah, and stories about individuals will serve, in that context, only so far as they exemplify and realize traits characteristic of all Torah sages. So the question presents itself: what defined the content of the consensus of the Talmud? The answer, the theology of the one God of justice and mercy, now comes to the fore.

ENDNOTES

[1] See most recently Beate Ego and Helmut Merkel, editors, *Religiöses Lernen in der biblischen,, frühjüdischen und frühchristlichen Überlieferung* (Tuebingen, 2005: Mohr Siebeck).

7

How Does the Talmud Present God?

The Talmuds' Theological Consensus, Expressed in Law and Lore

Theology thinks philosophically about religion. It sets forth religious ideas and facts, deriving from Scripture for example, or from nature, or from human experience, in a systematic way so that generalizations emerge. That is to say, the religious idea of God known through self-revelation in the Torah requires analysis and harmonization. Scripture says that God is one. What does that mean, and what are the implications? Theology seeks and sets forth the answers: coherent, rational and reasonable, consistent and cogent. All the characteristic, philosophical traits of the Mishnah's and the Talmuds' modes of thought shape the theological system that sustains the Talmuds, their law and lore.

The Talmuds assign to the law the task of expounding the theology of the Torah. Expressed through norms of conduct as much as norms of conviction, the theology forms a statement of the written Torah as interpreted by the oral one. That choice of law as the theological medium is hardly surprising. The Mishnah is a code of law, and the Gemara is a systematic exposition of that law. Whatever important statements of culture or religion the Talmud makes therefore will rely on action, not only attitude, to convey the message. To be sure, the exposition encompasses not only law (in Hebrew: *halakhah*, norms of conduct) but also lore (in Hebrew, *aggadah*, norms of conviction expressed in narrative). But the law takes priority. Now having situated the Talmud and the Rabbinic sage in the setting of the dual Torah, accordingly, we come to the representation of God in that same context.

Mythic Monotheism in Theory

The written and oral Torahs join to present God as one, just, and merciful. That God is one means a single will, a single rationality governs everything. That God is just means that God is bound by reason and rationality and does nothing arbitrarily: the Judge of all the earth does justice. That God is merciful means that God takes into account the special considerations that override strict justice, as we saw in the case of the contested cloak/baby. The law embodies in detail the doctrine of the justice of God and realizes it in rites. How does the Talmud express this theology of the one all-powerful, merciful, and just God at the foundations of all that is? It is not through generalizations and syllogisms, in the manner of philosophy, but through legal and narrative modes of expression. The law embodies the principles of justice initiated by God. The narratives or myths tell the stories of the one, just and merciful God and what he says and does.

At the heart of the monotheist system we find the paradox that the wicked prosper and the righteous suffer. Called "the problem of evil" that paradox paralyzes some Judaic systems — the thought of Job and Qoheleth (Ecclesiastes) for example. But Rabbinic Judaism resolves the tension between faith and fate. Both the legal and the mythic or narrative presentations of monotheism take as the critical issue of the unity of God God's justice and the problem of evil: how can a just God tolerate the manifest injustice of the world.

The problem of evil is readily articulated: how does the one just and merciful God explain all things that happen in the world, the suffering of the righteous and the prosperity of the wicked for example? That question faces monotheism in particular: reality proves that if God is all-powerful, then he cannot be just, and if God is just, then he cannot be all powerful. The problem of evil dominates discussion about God and, today, in the aftermath of the Holocaust, gains urgency. But the Rabbinic sages pursued the same issue, which formed the heart of their theological system and supplied its dynamism, its dialectics.

To grasp the sages' answer to the problem of evil in the world, we start from the way in which polytheism works to explain the destinies of humanity. Why ask the question of evil to monotheism and not to polytheism? Life is seldom fair. Rules rarely work. To explain the reason why, polytheisms adduce multiple causes of chaos, a god per anomaly. Diverse gods do various things, so, it stands to reason, ordinarily outcomes conflict. Polytheism acknowledges no problem of evil because the many gods contend. A religion of numerous gods finds many solutions to one problem, a religion of one God alone presents one solution to many problems.

Monotheism by its nature explains many things in a single way. One God rules. Life is meant to be fair, and just rules are supposed to describe what is ordinary, all in the name of that one and only God. So in monotheism a simple logic governs to limit ways of making sense of things. But that logic contains its own dialectics as I just said. If one true God has done everything, then, since he is God all-powerful and omniscient, all things are credited to, and more to the point, are blamed on, him. In that case he can be either good or bad, just or unjust — but not both.

In company with the other authoritative works of Rabbinic Judaism the Talmuds systematically reveal the justice of the one and only God of all creation. God is not only God but also good. Appealing to the facts of Scripture and its laws, the Rabbinic sages constructed a coherent theology, a cogent structure and logical system of religious ideas, to expose the justice of the one and only God. The theology of the Talmuds conveys the picture of world order based on God's justice and equity. The working system finds its dynamic in the struggle between God's plan for creation —to create a perfect world of justice — and man's will.

Let me set forth a somewhat more elaborate synopsis of the same story in these four fundamental propositions:

1. God formed creation in accord with a plan, which the Torah reveals. World order can be shown by the facts of nature and society set forth in that plan to conform to a pattern of reason based upon justice. Those who possess the Torah — Israel — know God and those who do not — the gentiles — reject him in favor of idols. What happens to each of the two sectors of humanity, respectively, responds to their relationship with God. Israel (a theological category, not to be confused with the contemporary nation-state) in the present age is subordinate to the nations, because God has designated the gentiles as the medium for penalizing Israel's rebellion, meaning through Israel's subordination and exile to provoke Israel to repent. Private life as much as the public order conforms to the principle that God rules justly in a creation of perfection and stasis.

2. The perfection of creation, realized in the rule of exact justice, is signified by the timelessness of the world of human affairs, their conformity to a few enduring paradigms that transcend change. No conception of present, past, or future marks time, but only the recapitulation of those permanent patterns in a timeless present. Perfection is further embodied in the unchanging relationships of the social commonwealth, which assure that scarce resources, once allocated, remain in stasis.

3. Israel's condition, public and personal, marks flaws in creation. The public flaw is readily discerned: though God's people, Israel is ruled by pagan nations. The personal aspect animates the entire system: individual Israelites see no match between piety and prosperity. But there is a reason for these flaws. It invokes the figures of Adam, all humanity, and Israel, that part of humanity that is distinguished through the Torah. Because man defies God, the sin that results from man's rebellion flaws creation and disrupts world order. The paradigm of the rebellion of Adam in Eden governs, the act of arrogant rebellion leading to exile from Eden thus accounting for the condition of humanity. But, as in the original transaction of alienation and consequent exile, God retains the power to encourage repentance through punishing man's arrogance. In mercy, moreover, God exercises the power to respond to repentance with forgiveness, that is, a change of attitude evoking a counterpart change. Since, commanding his own will, man also has the power to initiate the process of reconciliation with God, through repentance, an act of humility, man may restore the perfection of that order that through arrogance he has marred.

4. God ultimately will restore that perfection that was embodied in his plan for creation. In the work of restoration death that comes about by reason of rebellious sin will die, the dead will be raised and judged for their deeds in this life,

and most of them, having been justified, will go on to eternal life in the world to come. In the paradigm of man restored to Eden is realized in Israel's return to the Land of Israel. In that world or age to come, however, that sector of humanity that through the Torah knows God will encompass all of humanity. Idolators will perish, and humanity that comprises Israel at the end will know the one, true God and spend eternity in his light.

So much for the theological system. Where in the Talmuds and their law do we find it? Accordingly, the question arises: where in the Talmud's exposition of the law does the justice of the one all-powerful, just and merciful God emerge in the exposition of law by the Mishnah and the Gemara? The answer to that question manifests how the Talmud represents God as just.

How the Talmud Portrays God's Justice

Let us turn to a systematic, legal statement of the main point of the monotheist theology: when God judges and sentences, not only is the judgment fair but the penalty fits the crime with frightening precision. But so too, when God judges and awards a decision of merit, the reward proves equally exact. These two together, the match of sin and penalty, meritorious deed and reward, then are shown by the Talmud to explain the point and purpose of one detail after another, and, all together, they add up to the portrait of a world order that is fundamentally and essentially just — the starting point and foundation of all else.

The sages stress that rules govern, rationality prevails. Here is the sages' account of God's justice, which is always commensurate to deed, both for reward and punishment, so Mishnah-tractate Sotah 1:7ff. The subject is the wife accused of adultery, the law of the written Torah spelled out at Numbers 5.

And the Lord said to Moses, "Say to the people of Israel, If any man's wife go astray and act unfaithfully against him, if a man lie with her carnally and it is hidden from the eyes of her husband, and she is undetected though she has defiled herself and there is now witness against her, since she was not taken in the act, and if the spirit of jealousy comes upon him, and he is jealous of his wife who has defiled herself; or if the spirit of jealousy comes upon him and he is jealous of his wife, though she has not defiled herself, then the man shall bring his wife to the priest, and bring the offering required of her...

""And the priest shall set the woman before the Lord and unbind the hair of the woman's head and place in her hands the cereal offering of remembrance, which is the cereal offering of jealousy. And in his hand the priest shall have the water of bitterness that brings the curse. Then the priest shall make her take an oath, saying, 'If no man has lain with you, and if you have not turned aside to uncleanness, while you were under your husband's authority, be free from this water of bitterness that brings the curse. But if you have gone astray, though you are under your husband's authority, and if you have defiled yourself, and some man other than your husband has lain with you, then (let the woman take the oath of the curse and say to the woman) 'the Lord make you an execration and an oath among your people, when the Lord makes your thigh fall away and your body swell; may this water that brings the curse pass into your bowels and make your body swell and your thigh fall away.' And the woman shall say, 'Amen, Amen.'

"And when he has made her drink the water, then, if she has defiled herself and has acted unfaithfully against her husband, the water that brings the curse shall enter into her and cause bitter pain, and her body shall swell, and her thigh shall fall away, and the woman shall become an execration among her people. But if the woman has not defiled herself and is clean, then she shall be free and shall conceive children.

What we now note is sages' identification of the precision of justice, the exact match of action and reaction, each step in the sin, each step in the response, and, above all, the immediacy of God's presence in the entire transaction. They draw general conclusions from the specifics of the law that Scripture sets forth, and that is where systematic theological thinking about takes over from exegetical learning about cases. The law now refers to the rite inflicted on the accused wife as described in Numbers 5:

MISHNAH-TRACTATE SOTAH 1:7

By that same measure by which a person metes out [to others], do they mete out to her:

She primped herself for sin, the Omnipresent made her repulsive.

She exposed herself for sin, the Omnipresent exposed her.

With the thigh she began to sin, and afterward with the belly, therefore the thigh suffers the curse first, and afterward the belly.

But the rest of the body does not escape [punishment].

We begin with sages' own general observations based on the facts set forth in Scripture. The course of response of the woman accused of adultery to her drinking of the bitter water that is supposed to produce one result for the guilty, another for the innocent, is described in Scripture in this language: "If no man has lain with you . . . be free from this water of bitterness that brings the curse . . ." (Num. 5:20-22). This is amplified and expanded, extended to the entire rite, where the woman is disheveled; then the order, thigh, belly, shows the perfect precision of the penalty. What Scripture treats as a case, sages transform into a generalization, so making Scripture yield governing rules.

The same passage proceeds to further cases, which prove the same point: where the sin begins, there the punishment also commences; but also, where an act of virtue takes its point, there divine reward focuses as well. Merely listing the following names, without spelling out details, for the cognoscenti of Scripture will have made that point: Samson, Absalom, Miriam, Joseph, and Moses.

MISHNAH-TRACTATE SOTAH 1:8

Samson followed his eyes [where they led him], therefore the Philistines put out his eyes, since it is said, "And the Philistines laid hold on him and put out his eyes" (Judg. 16:21).

Absalom was proud of his hair, therefore he was hung by his hair [2 Sam. 14:25-26].

And since he had sexual relations with ten concubines of his father, therefore they thrust ten spear heads into his body, since it is said, "And ten young men that carried Jacob's armor surrounded and smote Absalom and killed him" (2 Sam. 18:15).

And since he stole three hearts — his father's, the court's, and the Israelite's — since it is said, "And Absalom stole the heart of the men of Israel" (2 Sam. 15:6) — therefore three darts were thrust into him, since it is said, "And he took three darts in his hand and thrust them through the heart of Absalom" (2 Sam. 18:14).

Justice requires not only punishment of the sinner or the guilty but reward of the righteous and the good, and so sages find ample, systematic evidence in Scripture for both sides of the equation of justice:

MISHNAH-TRACTATE SOTAH 1:9
And so is it on the good side:
Miriam waited a while for Moses, since it is said, "And his sister stood afar off" (Ex. 2:4), therefore, Israel waited on her seven days in the wilderness, since it is said, "And the people did not travel on until Miriam was brought in again" (Num. 12:15).

MISHNAH-TRACTATE SOTAH 1:10
Joseph had the merit of burying his father, and none of his brothers was greater than he, since it is said, "And Joseph went up to bury his father . . . and there went up with him both chariots and horsemen" (Gen. 50:7, 9).

We have none so great as Joseph, for only Moses took care of his [bones].

Moses had the merit of burying the bones of Joseph, and none in Israel was greater than he, since it is said, "And Moses took the bones of Joseph with him" (Ex. 13:19).

We have none so great as Moses, for only the Holy One blessed he Be took care of his [bones], since it is said, "And he buried him in the valley" (Dt. 34:6).

And not of Moses alone have they stated [this rule], but of all righteous people, since it is said, "And your righteousness shall go before you. The glory of the Lord shall gather you [in death]" (Is. 58:8).

Scripture provides the main probative evidence for the anticipation that when God judges, he will match the act of merit with an appropriate reward and the sin with an appropriate punishment. The proposition begins, however, with general observations as to how things are, and not with specific allusions to proof texts; the character of the law set forth in Scripture is reflected upon. The accumulated cases yield the generalization.

The Tosefta in its exposition of tractate Sotah contributes further cases illustrating the exact and appropriate character of both divine justice and divine reward. What is important here is what is not made explicit; it concerns a question that the Mishnah does not raise: what about the gentiles? Does the principle of world order of justice apply to them, or are they subject to chaos? The answer given through cases here is that the same rules of justice apply to gentiles, not only Israelites such as are listed in the Mishnah's primary statement of the principle.

That point is made through the cases that are selected: Sennacherib, who besieged Jerusalem after destroying Israel comprised by the northern tribes, Nebuchadnezzar, who took and destroyed Jerusalem in the time of Jeremiah. Now the sin is the single most important one, arrogance or hubris, and the penalty is swift and appropriate, the humbling of the proud by an act of humiliation:

TOSEFTA TRACTATE SOTAH 3:18

Sennacherib took pride before the Omnipresent only through an agent, as it is said, "By your messengers you have mocked the Lord and you have said, "With my many chariots I have gone up the heights of the mountains . . . I dug wells and drank foreign waters, and I dried up with the sole of my foot all the streams of Egypt" (2 Kings 19:23-24).

So the Omnipresent, blessed be He, exacted punishment from him only through an agent, as it is said, "And that night the messenger of the Lord went forth and slew a hundred and eighty-five thousand in the camp of the Assyrians" (2 Kings 19:35).

And all of them were kings, with their crowns bound to their heads.

TOSEFTA TRACTATE SOTAH 3:19

Nebuchadnezzar said, "The denizens of this earth are not worthy for me to dwell among them. I shall make for myself a little cloud and dwell In it," as it is said, "I will ascend above the heights of the clouds, I will make myself like the Most High" (Is. 14:14).

Said to him the Omnipresent, blessed be He, "You said in your heart, 'I will ascend to heaven, above the stars of God I will set my throne on high' — I shall bring you down to the depths of the pit" (Is. 14:13, 15).

What does it say? "But you are brought down to Sheol, to the depths of the pit" (Is. 14:15).

Were you the one who said, "The denizens of this earth are not worthy for me to dwell among them"?

The king said, "Is not this great Babylon, which I have built by my mighty power as a royal residence and for the glory of my majesty? While the words were still in the king's mouth, there fell a voice from heaven, O King Nebuchadnezzar, to you it is spoken, The kingdom has departed from you, and you shall be driven from among men, and your dwelling shall be with the beasts of the field, and you shall be made to eat grass like an ox" (Dan. 4:29-32).

All this came upon King Nebuchadnezzar at the end of twelve months (Dan. 4:28-29).

As in the Mishnah, so here too, we wish to prove that justice governs not only to penalize sin but also to reward virtue. To this point we have shown the proportionate character of punishment to sin, the exact measure of justice. The first task in this other context is to establish the proportions, now of reward to punishment.

Is reward measured out with the same precision? Not at all, reward many times exceeds punishment. So if the measure of retribution is exactly proportionate to the sin, the measure of reward exceeds the contrary measure by a factor of five hundred. Later on we shall see explicit argument that justice without mercy is incomplete; to have justice, mercy is the required complement. Here we address another aspect of the same matter, that if the measure of punishment precisely matches the measure of sin, when it comes to reward for merit or virtue, matters are not that way:

TOSEFTA TRACTATE SOTAH 4:1

I know only with regard to the measure of retribution that by that same measure by which a man metes out, they mete out to him [M . Sot. 1:7A]. How do I know that the same is so with the measure of goodness [M. Sot. 1:9A]?

Thus do you say:'

The measure of goodness is five hundred times greater than the measure of retribution.

With regard to the measure of retribution it is written, "Visiting the sin of the fathers on the sons and on the grandsons to the third and fourth generation" (Ex. 20:5).

And with regard to the measure of goodness it is written, "And doing mercy for thousands' (Ex. 20:6).

You must therefore conclude that the measure of goodness is five hundred times greater than the measure of retribution.

Having made that point, we revert to the specifics of cases involving mortals, not God, and here, we wish to show the simple point that reward and punishment meet in the precision of justice.

Before proceeding to the Tosefta's extension of matters in a quite unanticipated direction, let us turn to further amplifications of the basic point concerning the exact character of the punishment for a given sin. The fact is, not only does the sinner lose what he or she wanted, but the sinner also is denied what formerly he or she had possessed, a still more mordant and exact penalty indeed. At T. Sotah 4:16, the statement of the Mishnah, "Just as she is prohibited to her husband, so she is prohibited to her lover" [M. Sot. 5:1], is transformed into a generalization, which is spelled out, and then demonstrated by a list lacking all articulation; the items on the list serve to make the point. The illustrative case — the snake and Eve — is given at T. 4:17-18, the list, at T. 4:19.

TOSEFTA SOTAH 4:16

Just as she is prohibited to her husband, so she is prohibited to her lover:

You turn out to rule in the case of an accused wife who set her eyes on someone who was not available to her:

What she wanted is not given to her, and what she had in hand is taken away from her.

TOSEFTA SOTAH 4:17

And so you find in the case of the snake of olden times, who was smarter than all the cattle and wild beasts of the field, as it is said, 'Now the serpent was smarter than any other wild creature that the Lord Cod had made'" (Gen. 3:1).

He wanted to slay Adam and to marry Eve.

The Omnipresent said to him, "I said that you should be king over all beasts and wild animals. Now that you did not want things that way, 'You are more cursed than all the beasts and wild animals of the field' (Gen. 3:14).

"I said that you should walk straight-up like man. Now that you did not want things that way, 'Upon your belly you shall go' (Gen. 3:14).

"I said that you should eat human food and drink human drink. Now: 'And dust you shall eat all the days of your life' (Gen. 3:14).

Tosefta Sotah 4:18

"You wanted to kill Adam and marry Eve? 'And I will put enmity between you and the woman' (Gen. 3:15)."

You turn out to rule, What he wanted was not given to him, and what he had in hand was taken away from him.

Here is a fine example of how a pattern signals its own details, and how knowing the native categories allows us to elaborate the pattern with little further data: What he wanted was not given to him, and what he had in hand was taken away from him. So from retributive justice and the gentiles, the subject shifts to distributive reward, shared by Abraham, the founder, and his heirs later on. Reward also is governed by exact justice, the precision of the deed matched by the precision of the response:

Tosefta tractate Sotah 4:1

And so you find in the case of Abraham that by that same measure by which a man metes out, they mete out to him.

He ran before the ministering angels three times, as it is said, "When he saw them, he ran to meet them" (Gen. 18:2), "And Abraham hastened to the tent" (Gen. 18:6), "And Abraham ran to the herd" (Gen. 18:7).

1. So did the Omnipresent, blessed be He, run before his children three times, as it is said, 'The Lord came from Sinai, and dawned from Seir upon us; he shone forth from Mount Paran" (Dt. 33:2).

Justice extends beyond the limits of a single life, when the life is Abraham's. Now justice requires that Abraham's heirs participate in the heritage of virtue that he has bequeathed. Point by point, God remembers Abraham's generous actions in favor of Abraham's children into the long future, an intimation of a doctrine involving a heritage of grace that will play a considerable role in the theological system, as we shall see in due course. Here, point by point, what Abraham does brings benefit to his heirs:

Tosefta tractate Sotah 4:2

Of Abraham it is said, "He bowed himself to the earth" (Gen. 18:2).

So will the Omnipresent, blessed be He, respond graciously to his children in time to come, "Kings will be your foster-fathers, and their queens your nursing mothers.

With their faces to the ground they shall bow down to you and lick the dust of your feet" (Is. 49:23).

Of Abraham it is said, "Let a little water be brought" (Gen. 18:4).

So did the Omnipresent, blessed be He, respond graciously and give to his children a well in the wilderness, which gushed through the whole camp of Israel, as it is said, "The well which the princes dug, which the nobles of the people delved (Num. 21:18) teaching that it went over the whole south and watered the entire desert, which looks down upon the desert" (Num. 2 1 :20).

Of Abraham it is said, 'And rest yourselves under the tree" (Gen. 18:4).

So the Omnipresent gave his children seven glorious clouds in the wilderness, one on their right, one on their left, one before them, one behind them, one above their heads, and one as the Presence among them.

The evidence is of the same character as that adduced in the Mishnah: cases of Scripture. But the power of the Tosefta's treatment of Abraham must be felt: finding an exact counterpart in Israel's later history to each gesture of the progenitor, Abraham, shows the match between the deeds of the patriarchs and the destiny of their family later on. Justice now is given dimensions we should not have anticipated, involving not only the individual but the individual's family, meaning, the entire community of holy Israel. Once more, we note, a systematic effort focuses upon details. Justice is not a generalized expectation but a very particular fact, bread/manna, calf/quail, and so on. There is where sages find the kind of detailed evidence that corresponds to the sort suitable in natural history.

The focus now shifts shift from how justice applies to the actions of named individuals — Samson, Absalom, Sennacherib, and Nebuchadnezzar — to the future history of Israel, the entire sector of humanity formed by those whom God has chosen and to whom he will give eternal life. It is a jarring initiative: of what does justice consist? The kinds of instances of justice that are given until that point concern sin and punishment, or the reward of individuals for their own actions. And these cases surely conform to the context: justice as the principle that governs what happens to individuals in an orderly world.

For sages not only accept the burden of proving, against all experience, that goodness goes to the good and evil to the wicked. They have also alleged, and here propose to instantiate, that the holy people Israel itself, its history, its destiny, conform to the principle of justice. And if claim that justice governs in the lives and actions of private persons conflicts with experience, the condition of Israel, conquered and scattered, surely calls into question any allegation that Israel's story embodies that same orderly and reasonable principle. Before us sages take one step forward in their consideration of that very difficult question, how to explain the prosperity of the idolators, the gentiles, and the humiliation of those who serve the one true God, Israel. That step consists only in matching what Abraham does with what happens to his family later on.

Measure for Measure

The rules of commensurability and proportion in judgment produce the possibility of predicting as well as explaining what will happen to sinners. Therefore to know the future and prepare for it we may appeal to the principle of measure for measure.

If we know how someone has sinned, we also know not only that but exactly how he will be penalized. And the same goes for rewards either in this world, as in the case at hand, or in the world to come. Not only individuals, but classes of sinners and of sins, will be penalized in a manner appropriate to the character of the sin. That accounts for the certainty that justice always prevails and that the one who is punished bears full responsibility for his fate. All the more urgent, then, is the concept of judgment, resurrection and life after death, and the world to come, which in its way addresses the necessary corollary of the perfection of divine justice: the manifest injustice of the workaday fate of perfectly righteous people.

When it comes to Israel, the principle of justice — commensurate response to each action — extends, also, to God's response to Israel's atonement. Israel is punished for its sin. But when Israel repents and God forgives Israel and restores the holy people's fortunes, then that same principle that all things match takes over. Hence we should not find surprising the logical extension, to the character of God's forgiveness and comfort of Israel, of the principle of measure for measure. When, specifically, Israel sins, it is punished through that with which it sins. But the sages offer the comfort that the medium of punishment will serve as the means of restoration and renewal.

Now that we have established the bases in Scripture for sages' certainty that the creation is governed by a moral order resting on the principle of justice, we have to ask, what was at stake in that conviction? Specifically we wonder what made urgent the proposition that a rational order, resting on exact justice, governed the world. At stake was making sense of the condition of the world and of Israel now and gaining access to what was going to come about. It was urgent for sages both to explain the present and also to foresee the future. On what basis? In a monotheist world, one created in accordance with rules of a reasonable character, rules upon which both God and man concur, whatever happens should lend itself to reasonable explanation by appeal to those accessible rules that govern.

The Rabbinic sages insisted upon the rationality of all things, meaning, the justice of the everyday. The system sages put forth promised to explain why things were as they were. And the possibility of explanation carried with it the promise of prediction, a model for anticipating what is going to come about. It ought, then, to follow that just as a given action will precipitate, on the part of the just God, a predictable reaction, so sages should find plausible explanations for misfortune and reliable bases for foretelling the future as well. If one suffers such-and-such a penalty for doing so-and-so, then under ordinary circumstances, if one suffers so-and-so, it is because he has committed such-and-such a deed. This is made explicit in an account of why certain calamities befall:

Mishnah-tractate Abot 5:8:

There are seven forms of punishment which come upon the world for seven kinds of transgression.

(1) [If] some people give tithes and some people do not give tithes, there is a famine from drought.

So some people are hungry and some have enough.

The match—a pattern of some giving, some not—is that some suffer, some do not. Here someone ought to say, those that do not give tithes will go hungry; that is, in fact, said in other sources. Now comes the match once more: no one gives, so everyone starves. The passage refers to the dough offering, which is a bit of dough removed before baking the bread, this is given back to the priesthood, one of God's surrogates, representing part of the grain that is used.

(2) [If] everyone decided not to tithe, there is a famine of unrest and drought.
(3) [If all decided] not to remove dough offering, there is a famine of totality.

We move from famine to pestilence, accounting for epidemics in the same reasonable way:

(4) Pestilence comes to the world on account of the death penalties which are listed in the Torah but which are not in the hands of the court [to inflict];
and because of the produce of the Seventh Year [which people buy and sell].

The sword of justice, which is rational and orderly, is replaced, when justice is delayed, by the sword of war, which is chaotic:

(5) A sword comes into the world because of the delaying of justice and perversion of justice, and because of those who teach the Torah not in accord with the law.
5:9 (6) A plague of wild animals comes into the world because of vain oaths and desecration of the Divine Name.

Now we move to the level of what happens to all Israel, not only to persons or communities. We invoke what we shall see as the three absolute sins, that is, actions that are sinful in any and all circumstances, idolatry, fornication, and murder; these bring about Israel's exile:

(7) Exile comes into the world because of those who worship idols, because of fornication, and because of bloodshed,
and because of the neglect of the release of the Land [in the year of release].

We proceed to details, worked out in response to the enumeration of the years of the Seven Year cycle that governs. In specified years, a given category of tithes is required of the farmers. Then if these are not given in the years that they are required, penalties follow:

At four turnings in the years pestilence increases: in the Fourth Year, in the Seventh Year, in the year after the Seventh Year, and at the end of the Festival [of Tabernacles] every year:

(1) in the Fourth Year, because of the poor man's tithe of the Third Year [which people have neglected to hand over to the poor];

(2) in the Seventh Year, because of the poor man's tithe of the Sixth Year;

(3) in the year after the Seventh Year, because of the dealing in produce of the Seventh Year;

and (4) at the end of the Festival every year, because of the thievery of the dues [gleanings and the like] owing to the poor [not left for them in the antecedent harvest].

Here the evidence derives not from Scripture but from an alleged correspondence of condition and its consequence, so, e.g., Abot 5:8B-C, where the drought affects some, not others. If all are guilty, the famine is complete.

Again, we see the notion of the complement and match at 5:8. The sword serves justice, politics standing for the legitimate exercise of violence; or it stands for injustice that comes through war. Then if the politics of justice does not bring about justice, the sword of justice becomes the agency of the opposite. At 5:9B the standard list of mortal sins — the triplet, idolatry, fornication, and bloodshed — is invoked to match what sages deem the insufferable penalty of exile from the Holy Land — but then mistreatment of the Land itself finds its match in exile as well, measure for measure. When, at Lev. 26:34, God through Moses threatens to penalize Israel for neglecting the Sabbatical Year that is owed to the Land through a forcible Sabbatical, Scripture says no less. The insistence upon the perfect match of crime and punishment yields a collection of illustrations; the allegation then is a given, meant to be illustrated, rather than a proposition to be proved. Here then we see what it means to maintain an exact correspondence between sin and penalty, crime and punishment.

Two motifs overspread the theology of the Talmud and related writings, the destruction of Jerusalem and its Temple and the cessation of its sacrificial service to God, and the fate of the individual; public and private affairs are governed by those same principles of order flowing from justice. When it comes to the manifest punishment represented by the loss of Jerusalem and its medium for divine service, the precision noted in the cases above gives way to a generalized conviction that an entire list of sins found the single punishment. But all of these sins fall into a single category: they are public and for them the community of Israel at large bears responsibility. That accounts for the various specific sins linked to the general ruin of Jerusalem. But there is no distinguishing sages' explanation of what happens to the individual from what happens to the people or nation. A single mode of explanation serves to account for both individual and communal fate, and that brings us to the Gemara:

Bavli-tractate Shabbat 16:2 II.42/119b

Said Abbayye, "Jerusalem was ruined only because they violated the Sabbath therein: 'And they have hidden their eyes from my Sabbaths, therefore I am profaned among them' (Ezek. 22:26)."

The Sabbath is sanctified both in public and in private. But prayer is personal and that too shapes the future:

> Said R. Abbahu, "Jerusalem was ruined only because they stopped reciting the *Shema* morning and evening: 'Woe to them that rise up early in the morning, that they may follow strong drink . . . and the harp and the lute, the tabret and the pipe and wine are in their feasts, but they do not regard the works of the Lord,' 'Therefore my people have gone into captivity for lack of knowledge' (Isa. 5:11-13)."

The fate of the Torah governs the destiny of Israel. If the Torah is neglected, if children in particular are not taught, then the entire community suffers:

> Said R. Hamnuna, "Jerusalem was ruined only because they neglected the children in the schoolmaster's household: 'pour out . . . because of the children in the street' (Jer. 6:211). Why pour out? Because the children are in the streets."

Here again, personal conduct affects public life. People sinned openly and shamelessly, so Jerusalem, not only the private home or family, was penalized:

> Said Ulla, "Jerusalem was ruined only because they were not ashamed on account of one another: 'Were they ashamed when they committed abomination? No, they were not at all ashamed, therefore they shall fall' (Jer. 6:15)."

So too, when the hierarchy of virtue and the authority of learning proved null, then the community as a whole is punished; this affects the failure to accord honor to the great; the failure of people to admonish one another; and the failure to honor disciples of sages, a set of sins of a single class:

> Said R. Isaac, "Jerusalem was ruined only because they treated equally the small and the great: 'And it shall be, like people like priest' and then, 'the earth shall be utterly emptied' (Isa. 24:2-3)."
>
> Said R. Amram b. R. Simeon bar Abba said R. Simeon bar Abba said R. Hanina, "Jerusalem was ruined only because they did not correct one another: 'Her princes are become like harts that find no pasture' (Lam. 1:6) — just as the hart's head is at the side of the other's tail, so Israel of that generation hid their faces in the earth and didn't correct one another."
>
> Said R. Judah, "Jerusalem was ruined only because they humiliated disciples of sages therein: 'But they mocked the messengers of God and despised his words and scoffed at his prophets, until the wrath of the Lord arose against his people till there was no remedy' (2 Chr. 36:16)."

None of the identified sins proves private or particular to one person only, but all require individual action or inaction.

When it comes to the private person, by contrast, sages aim at a more precise match of sin to punishment. So far as is possible, they match the character of the one with the definition of the other. Shab. 2:6:

On account of three transgressions do women die in childbirth: because they are not meticulous in the laws of (1) menstrual separation, (2) in those covering the dough offering, and (3) in those covering the kindling of a lamp for the Sabbath.

The first clearly matches in a particular way, the second and the third are more general. Various specific penalties are incurred for specific sins, and these are to be specified in the Talmud of Babylonia's amplification of that same passage of the Mishnah.

Babylonian Talmud tractate Shabbat 2:6 I.12ff./32B

I.12 It has been taught on Tannaite authority:

R. Nathan says, "On account of the sin of a man's unfulfilled vows a man's wife dies: 'If you have not wherewith to pay your vows, why should he take away your bed from under you?' (Prov. 22:27)."

Rabbi says, "On account of the sin of a man's unfulfilled vows a man's children die when they are young: 'Suffer not your mouth to cause your flesh to sin, neither say before the angel that it was an error. Wherefore should God be angry at your voice and destroy the work of your hands?' (Qoh. 5:5). What is 'the work of a man's hands'? Say: It is his sons and daughters."

I.13 Our Rabbis have taught on Tannaite authority:

"On account of the sin of unfulfilled vows children die," the words of R. Eleazar b. R. Simeon.

R. Judah the Patriarch says, "It is on account of the sin of neglect of the Torah."

In the next item if one preserves a grudge, his own household will be disrupted by discord as well, so what the man has kept going will in the end affect his own home, a principle that has been enunciated in earlier passages; what one wants one does not get, but one loses what one already has:

Babylonian Talmud tractate Shabbat 2:6 I.12ff./32B

I.17 It has been taught on Tannaite authority:

R. Nehemiah says, "For the sin of nursing a grudge [causeless hate], discord grows in someone's house, his wife will miscarry, and his sons and daughters will die young."

Since the dough offering is a mark of abundance of food, failure to give that offering leads to a scarcity of food:

Babylonian Talmud tractate Shabbat 2:6 I.12ff./32B

II.1 [The dough-offering:] R. Eleazar b. R. Judah says, "For the sin of neglect of the dough-offering, no blessing comes upon what is in storage, prices are cursed, seed is sown but others eat it up: 'I also will do this to you: I will visit you with terror, even consumption and fever, that shall consume the eyes and make the soul to pine away, and you shall sow your seed in vain, for your enemies shall eat it' (Lev. 26:16). Read the word translated as terror as though it were written, dough-offering.

"But if they give it, they are blessed: 'You shall also give to the priest the first of your dough, to cause a blessing to rest on your house' (Ezek. 44:30)."

The gathered crops are liable to the separation of grain for heave offering and tithes, which represent God's share of the crop; these are given to the surrogates, the priests, Levites, or poor, and some of the tithes also are to be consumed by the farmer in Jerusalem; here too, God has a claim, and if that is not met, then rain is withheld.

Babylonian Talmud tractate Shabbat 2:6 I.12ff./32B
II.2 For the sin of neglect of heave-offering and tithes, the heavens are shut up from bringing down dew and rain; prices are high; wages low; people pursue a living but don't catch up to it: "Drought and heat consume the snow waters, so does the grave those who have sinned" (Job 24:19).

Locusts represent thieves of the farmers' crops; for robbery, locusts come up and steal the crops:

Babylonian Talmud tractate Shabbat 2:6 I.12ff./32B
II.4 For the sin of robbery, locusts come up and famine follows, and people eat the flesh of their sons and daughters: "Hear this word, you cows of Bashan, who are in the mountain of Samaria, who oppress the poor, who crush the needy" (Amos 4:1).
And it is written, "I have smitten you with blasting and mildew; the multitude of your gardens and your vineyards and your figs trees and your olive trees has the palmer-worm devoured" (Amos 4:9); and further, "That which the palmer-worm has left has the locust eaten; that which the locust has left the cankerworm has eaten; that which the cankerworm has left the caterpillar has eaten" (Joel 1:4); "And one shall snatch on the right hand and be hungry and he shall eat on the left hand and they shall not be satisfied; they shall eat every man the flesh of his own arm" (Isa. 9:19). Don't read the consonants that yield "the flesh of his own arm" in that way but as though they bore vowels to yield "the flesh of his own seed."

The failure of the political system — of the just use of the sword for acts of legitimate violence in recompense for violation of the just law — produces political crisis: war and disruption, a view we already have seen in another context:

Babylonian Talmud tractate Shabbat 2:6 I.12ff./32B
II.5 For the transgressions of the delay of judgment, perversion of judgment, spoiling judgment, and neglect of the Torah, sword and spoil increase, pestilence and famine come, people eat and are not satisfied, and they measure out the bread that they eat by weight: "And I will bring a sword upon you, that will execute the vengeance of the covenant" (Lev. 26:25). Covenant refers only to the Torah: "But for my covenant of day and night, I had not appointed the ordinances of heaven and earth" (Jer. 33:25), and "When I break your staff of bread, ten women shall bake your bread in one oven and they shall deliver your bread again by weight" (Lev. 26:26), "Because, even because they rejected my judgments" (Lev. 26:43).

Scripture itself precipitated thought along these lines, as a reading of Leviticus 26 will readily reveal. We should not find surprising that sages turned directly to that passage to expound in general terms the particular cases set forth there:

Babylonian Talmud tractate Shabbat 2:6 I.12ff./32B

II.6 For the sin of vain oaths, false oaths, profanation of the Divine Name, and desecration of the Sabbath, wild beasts multiply, domestic ones become few, the population declines, the roads become desolate: "And if by these things you will not be rebuked by me" (Lev. 26:23); Read the letters translated by "these things" as though they bore vowels to yield "by reason of oaths" [that are false]. Further, "and I will send the beast of the field among you" (Lev. 26:22). In regard to false oaths it is written, "And you shall not swear by my name falsely, so that you profane the name of God" (Lev. 19:12), and of the profanation of the Divine Name it is written, "that you do not profane my holy name" (Lev. 22:2), and the profanation of the Sabbath is set forth, "every one who profanes it shall surely be put to death" (Ex. 31:15), and the penalty for profanation derives from the penalty for a false oath. [Freedman: Just as this is punished by the sending of wild beasts, so are the others.]

If the Temple is not kept pure and holy, God's Presence will depart from there:

Babylonian Talmud tractate Shabbat 2:6 I.12ff./32B

II.7 For the sin of bloodshed the Temple was destroyed and the Presence of God left Israel: "So you shall not pollute the land in which you are, for blood pollutes the land. And you shall not defile the land which you inhabit, in the midst of which I dwell" (Num. 35:33-4). "Lo, if you do make it unclean, you won't live there, and I won't live there."

Public sins against the social order, such as incest, idolatry, and neglect of the Sabbatical Year, are penalized by exile; others, more worthy to live in the Holy Land than Israel, will take over.

Babylonian Talmud tractate Shabbat 2:6 I.12ff./32B

II.8 For the sin of incest, idolatry, and neglect of the years of release and Jubilee, exile comes into the world, they go into exile, and others come and take their place: "For all these abominations have the men of the land done" (Lev. 18:27), "and the land is defiled, therefore I visit the iniquity thereof upon it" (Lev. 18:25), "that the land vomit you not out also when you defile it" (Lev. 18:28). With regard to idolatry: "And I will cast your carcasses upon the carcasses of your idols" (Lev. 26:30), "and I will make your cities a waste and will bring your sanctuaries into desolation" (Lev. 26:31), "and you will I scatter among the nations" (Lev. 26:33). In regard to the years of release and Jubilee Years: "Then shall the land enjoy her Sabbaths, as long as it lies desolate, and you shall be in your enemies land" (Lev. 26:34), "as long as it lies desolate it shall have rest" (Lev. 26:35).

II.9 For the sin of a foul mouth, troubles multiply, evil decrees are renewed, Israel's youth die, and the fatherless and widows cry out and are not answered: "Therefore shall the Lord not rejoice over their young men, neither shall he have compassion over their fatherless and their widows; for every one is profane and an evil doer, and every mouth speaks folly. For all this his anger is not turned away, but his hand is stretched out still" (Isa. 9:16).

So too b. Shab. 5:3 XII.12/55a-b adds the more general statement of the governing rule of justice: sin brings on death, transgression, suffering.

As is the manner of the Talmud of Babylonia, the proposition is not only stated but systematically analyzed and subjected to provocative challenge. It is not the last word that the Oral Torah has to say about death, suffering, old age, and other particulars of the common life. Measure for measure accounts for the course of a human life, perfect justice prevails. And that is the point of insistence even in the implacable position taken in the following, with the pertinent factual foundations carefully delineated:

Bavli-tractate Shabbat 5:3 XII.12/55A-B

Said R. Ammi, "Death comes about only through sin, and suffering only through transgression.

"Death comes about only through sin: 'The soul that sins, it shall die; the son shall not bear the iniquity of the father, neither shall the father bear the iniquity of the son; the righteousness of the righteous shall be upon him and the wickedness of the wicked shall be upon him' (Ezek. 18:20).

"And suffering only through transgression: 'Then will I visit their transgression with the rod and their iniquity with stripes' (Ps. 89:33)."

Now comes the challenge:

[55B] An objection was raised: Said the ministering angels before the Holy One blessed be He, "Lord of the universe, how come you have imposed the penalty of death on the first Adam?"

He said to them, "I commanded him one easy commandment, but he violated it."

Surely saints die too, what is to be said of them?

They said to him, "But isn't it the fact that Moses and Aaron, who kept the entire Torah, also died?"

He said to them, "There is one fate to the righteous and to the wicked, to the good . . . " (Qoh. 9:2).

Saints sin, and that is why they too die:

[Ammi] concurs with [the view of matters expressed by] the following Tannaite authority, as has been taught on Tannaite authority:

R. Simeon b. Eleazar says, "So, too, Moses and Aaron died on account of their sin: 'Because you didn't believe in me . . . therefore you shall not bring this assembly into the land that I have given them' (Num. 20:12) — lo, if you had believed in me, your time would not yet have come to take leave of the world."

An objection was raised: Four died on account of the snake's machinations [and not on account of their own sin]: Benjamin the son of Jacob, Amram the father of Moses, Jesse the father of David, and Caleb the son of David. But all of them are known by tradition except for Jesse, the father of David, in which case Scripture makes it clear, as it is written, "And Absalom set Amasa over the host instead of Joab. Now Amasa was the son of a man whose name was Itra the Israelite, who went in to Abigail the daughter of Nahash, sister of Zeruiah Joab's mother" (2 Sam. 17:25). Now was she the daughter of Nahash? Surely she was the daughter of Jesse: "And their sisters were Zeruiah and Abigail" (1 Chr. 2:16). But she was the daughter of him who died on account of the machinations of the snake [Nahash]. Now who is the authority here? Shouldn't we say, the Tannaite authority who stands behind the story of the ministering angels?

But there were Moses and Aaron, too. So it must be R. Simeon b. Eleazar, and that proves that there can be death without sin, and suffering without transgression. Isn't that a refutation of the position of R. Ammi?

It is a solid refutation.

That penalties for not carrying out vows prove extreme, which we have already noted, is shown by appeal to the exemplary precedent set by Jacob or by Abraham. Jacob too is shown to have sinned, and that is why even he died, and died for sins as particular to the punishment as anybody else.

If sages had to state the logic that imposes order and proportion upon all relationships — the social counterpart to the laws of gravity — they would point to justice: what accords with justice is logical, and what does not is irrational. Ample evidence derives from Scripture's enormous corpus of facts to sustain in sages view that the moral order, based on justice, governs the affairs of men and nations. We have now seen that statements of that proposition, together with evidence characteristic of sages' entire system, comes to us from the Mishnah, Tosefta, and Talmud.

Let me express the matter of the priority of justice as the first principle of all things in simple but probative way: *in sages' discourse justice never requires explanation, but violations of justice always do.* When what happens does not conform to the rule but violates the expectations precipitated by the expectation of justice, then sages pay close attention and ask why. When what happens does conform, they do not have to: their unarticulated conviction of self-evidence is embodied, therefore, in the character of their discourse: not only the speech but the silence.

Justifying God

Justice therefore defines the rational, and injustice, the irrational. To sages the principal theological task is — in the exact sense of the meaning of the word — to *justify* the condition of society by reference to conduct therein, both public and personal. So why do the wicked prosper and the righteous suffer? The premise of the question, whether addressed to Israel and the gentiles, or to the righteous and the wicked, remains the same, namely, the conviction that the moral order of justice governs.

Resurrection of the Dead: The Final Solution

The Mishnah and Talmuds solve the problem of evil and validate divine justice by appeal to the resurrection of the dead at the end of days, followed by judgment and justification for nearly all Israel.

MISHNAH-TRACTATE SANHEDRIN 10:1

All Israelites have a share in the world to come,

as it is said, "your people also shall be all righteous, they shall inherit the land forever; the branch of my planting, the work of my hands, that I may be glorified" (Is. 60:21).

And these are the ones who have no portion in the world to come:

He who says, the resurrection of the dead is a teaching which does not derive from the Torah, and the Torah does not come from Heaven; and an Epicurean.

R. Aqiba says, "Also: He who reads in heretical books,

"and he who whispers over a wound and says, 'I will put none of the diseases upon you which I have put on the Egyptians, for I am the Lord who heals you' (Ex. 15:26)."

Abba Saul says, "Also: He who pronounces the divine Name as it is spelled out."

The Talmud, along with all Rabbinic sources of the formative age, maintains that God will ultimately raise the dead for judgment. This would come about at the last days, which will correspond with, and complete, the first days of creation. Humanity is divided between those who will overcome the grave, Israel with the Torah, and those who will not, the gentiles with idolatry. The righteous suffer in this world and get their just reward in the world to come, but the wicked enjoy this world and suffer in the world to come. That conviction, critical to the system as a whole, also provided a solution to the problem of the prosperity of the wicked and the misery of the righteous. By insisting that this world does not tell the whole story of a private life, sages could promise beyond the grave what the here and now denied. The simplest statement of that position is as follows:

BAVLI TRACTATE HORAYOT 3:3 I./11A

Expounded R. Nahman bar Hisda, "What is the meaning of the verse of Scripture, 'There is a vanity that occurs on the earth, for there are the righteous who receive what is appropriate to the deeds of the wicked, and there are the wicked who receive what is appropriate to the deeds of the righteous' (Qoh. 8:14).

"Happy are the righteous, for in this world they undergo what in the world to come is assigned as recompense for the deeds of the wicked, and woe is the wicked, for in this world they enjoy the fruits of what is assigned in the world to come to the deeds of the righteous."

The righteous will enjoy the world to come all the more, and the wicked will suffer in the world to come all the more; the one has saved up his reward for eternity, the other has in this transient world already spent such reward as he may ever get. But that still begs the question:

> Said Raba, "So if the righteous enjoy both worlds, would that be so bad for them?"

Raba acts in the model of Abraham facing God before Sodom! "Will not the Judge of all the earth do justice?" But he has a better solution, making still more radical claim:

> Rather, said Raba, "Happy are the righteous, for in this world they get what is set aside for the [meritorious] deeds of the wicked in this world, and woe to the wicked, for in this world they get what is assigned for the deeds of the righteous in this world."

Raba's solution takes account of the theory of atonement through suffering. The righteous atone in the here and now, that is why they suffer. Then the world to come is all the more joyful.

Sages raise the problem of evil, characteristic of monotheism alone, at the most profound levels of their discussion of the public order and of the personal situation of households and individuals as well. That question with its answer in resurrection and eternal life defines how the Talmud represents God. The Talmuds' theological system, with the twin and complementary principles of God as merciful and as just, would endure for centuries and define the norms of Judaism, its law and theology, to the present day.

Glossary

Abot. The Fathers, the Founders, a collection of wise sayings attributed to Rabbis from Moses to the third century CE.

aggadah. Narrative, lore, theology.

Bar Kokhba. Jewish general who led a rebellion against the Roman Empire in 132–135 CE, aiming at restoring the Temple of Jerusalem and its sacrificial offerings, which had been destroyed in 70 CE.

Bavli. The Talmud of Babylonia.

BCE. Before the Common Era.

Ben Kozeba. See Bar Kokhba.

CE. Common Era, as in AD.

eisegesis. Reading meaning into a text.

exegesis. Deriving meaning from a text through interpretation of the text, word by word.

Gemara. Learning, the commentary to the Mishnah that together with the Mishnah makes up the Talmud of the Land of Israel, also known as Yerushalmi, and the Talmud of Babylonia, also know as the Bavli.

Genesis Rabbah. Rabbinic commentary to the book of Genesis, circa 450 CE.

Halakhah. The normative law, rules of correct conduct and procedure.

Hillel. First-century Pharisaic master who taught "What is hateful to yourself do not do to your neighbor. That is the entire Torah. All the rest is commentary. Now go, learn."

Judah the Patriarch. Roman-sponsored governor of the ethnic community of the Jews in the Land of Israel at the end of the second century CE.

Lamentations Rabbah. Rabbinic commentary to the other book of Lamentations; contains mourning for the destroyed Temple of 586 BCE and 70 CE.

Leviticus Rabbah. Rabbinic commentary to the book of Leviticus, circa 400 CE.

Midrash. Commentary on Scripture, a search for the deeper meanings thereof.

Mishnah. Philosophical law code organized by topical expositions in sixty-two tractates or presentations of the law on a given subject.

monotheism. Belief that God is one, unique, transcendent, merciful, and just.

Moshe Rabbenu. Moses, our lord.

mythic monotheism. Monotheism expressed through narratives, for example, of the one God and the things he did to make himself known to Israel, the holy people.

Pesiqta deRab Kahana. Rabbinic commentary on passages of Scripture read in public worship on special occasions, circa 500 CE.

philosophical monotheism. Monotheism expressed through abstract generalizations.

pseudepigraphy. Writing a book and signing someone else's name.

Rabbi. My lord.

Ruth Rabbah. Rabbinic commentary to the book of Ruth.

Shammai. Pharisaic authority in the time of Hillel, early first century.

Sinai. The mountain in the wilderness where God met Moses and gave him the Torah.

Song of Songs Rabbah. Rabbinic commentary to the book of the Song of Songs, also known as the Song of Solomon.

Talmud. A combination of the Mishnah and a commentary to the Mishnah.

Torah. God's instruction, revealed in the written Torah, Genesis, Exodus, Leviticus, Numbers, and Deuteronomy, and the oral Torah ultimately recorded in the Rabbinic writings from the Mishnah through the Bavli.

Tosefta. A collection of laws that complement those in the Mishnah.

Yerushalmi. The Talmud of the Land of Israel, produced in about 400 CE.

Yohanan ben Zakkai. Rabbi who survived the destruction of Jerusalem in 70 CE and founded an academy of Torah study after 70 and saved Judaism.

Sources of the Rabbinic Texts

Translations are my own. The Mishnah, Tosefta, Yerushalmi, and Bavli are as follows:

The Mishnah. A New Translation. New Haven and London, 1987: Yale University Press. *Choice* Outstanding Academic Book List, 1989. Second printing: 1990. Paperbound edition: 1991. CD Rom edition: Logos, 1996. CD Rom/Web edition: OakTree Software, Inc. Altamonte Springs, FL.

The Tosefta in English. I. *Zeraim, Moed, and Nashim.* Peabody, 2003: Hendrickson Publications. With a new introduction.
The Tosefta in English. II. *Neziqin, Qodoshim, and Toharot.* Peabody, 2003: Hendrickson Publications.

The Talmud of the Land of Israel. An Academic Commentary to the Second, Third, and Fourth Divisions. Atlanta, 1998-1999: Scholars Press for *USF Academic Commentary Series.* Now: Lanham, MD. University Press of America.

I.	*Yerushalmi Tractate Berakhot*
II.A.	*Yerushalmi Tractate Shabbat. Chapters 1 through 10*
II.B.	*Yerushalmi Tractate Shabbat. Chapters 11 through 24. And the Structure of Yerushalmi Shabbat*
III.	*Yerushalmi Tractate Erubin*
IV.	*Yerushalmi Tractate Yoma*
V.A.	*Yerushalmi Tractate Pesahim. Chapters 1 through 6.*
V.B.	*Yerushalmi Tractate Pesahim. Chapters 7 through 10. And the Structure of Yerushalmi Pesahim*
VI.	*Yerushalmi Tractate Sukkah*
VII.	*Yerushalmi Tractate Besah*
VIII.	*Yerushalmi Tractate Taanit*
IX.	*Yerushalmi Tractate Megillah*
X.	*Yerushalmi Tractate Rosh Hashanah*
XI.	*Yerushalmi Tractate Hagigah*
XII.	*Yerushalmi Tractate Moed Qatan*
XIII.A.	*Yerushalmi Tractate Yebamot. Chapters 1 through 10*
XIII.B.	*Yerushalmi Tractate Yebamot. Chapters 11 through 17. And the Structure of Yerushalmi Yebamot*
XIV.	*Yerushalmi Tractate Ketubot*

XV.   *Yerushalmi Tractate Nedarim*
XVI.   *Yerushalmi Tractate Nazir*
XVII.   *Yerushalmi Tractate Gittin*
XVIII.   *Yerushalmi Tractate Qiddushin*
XIX.   *Yerushalmi Tractate Sotah*
XX.   *Yerushalmi Tractate Baba Qamma*
XXI.   *Yerushalmi Tractate Baba Mesia*
XXII.   *Yerushalmi Tractate Baba Batra*
XXIII.   *Yerushalmi Tractate Sanhedrin*
XXIV.   *Yerushalmi Tractate Makkot*
XXV.   *Yerushalmi Tractate Shebuot*
XXVI.   *Yerushalmi Tractate Abodah Zarah*
XXVII.   *Yerushalmi Tractate Horayot*
XXVIII. *Yerushalmi Tractate Niddah*

The Babylonian Talmud. Translation and Commentary. Peabody, 2005: Hendrickson Publishing Co. Second printing of *The Talmud of Babylonia. An Academic Commentary.* Also published as a CD.

i.   *Berakhot*
ii.   *Shabbat*
iii.   *Erubin*
iv.   *Pesahim*
v.   *Yoma-Sukkah*
vi.   *Taanit-Megillah-Moed Qatan-Hagigah*
vii.   *Besah-Rosh Hashanah*
viii.   *Yebamot*
ix.   *Ketubot*
x.   *Nedarim-Nazir*
xi.   *Sotah-Gittin*
xii.   *Qiddushin*
xiii.   *Baba Qamma*
xiv.   *Baba Mesia*
xv.   *Baba Batra*
xvi.   *Sanhedrin*
xvii.   *Makkot-Abodah Zarah-Horayot*
xviii.   *Shebuot-Zebahim*
xix.   *Menahot*
xx.   *Hullin*
xxi.   *Bekhorot-Arakhin-Temurah*
xxii.   *Keritot-Meilah-Tamid-Niddah*

Index

Aaron, 2, 5, 151
Abbahu, R.:
  communal justice, 146;
  mnemonics, 113
Abdimi bar Hama bar Dosa, 113
Abot (the Fathers):
  definition of, 155;
  R. Nathan on, 10–12
Abot tractate, 107–13;
  on labor/Torah study, 111;
  on oral tradition of Mishnah, 112–13,
    114;
  on straight path, 111
Abraham, 141–42, 151, 153
Absalom, 137–38, 142, 151
adultery, 136–37
aggadah, 133, 155
agricultural instruments, uncleanliness of,
  68
Aha, R. See Jacob bar Abbayye, R.
Alexa, R., law of disputes, 130
altruism, 12, 123–24
Ammi bar Hama, R.:
  bailment, 61;
  death, 150;
  Mishnah precedence over Talmud, 114
Amram, R., communal justice, 146
animal sacrifice, 11–13
Aqiba, R.:
  measurement of land, 104;
  problem of evil, 152;
  recognizes Bar Kokhba as Messiah, 12;
  uncleanliness, 49–50, 103
atonement:
  collective, 2, 13–14, 143;
  individual, 12, 14–15;
  replacement of medium of, 11–14;
  rites in Rabbinic Judaism, 11–12;
  sheqel offerings for, 14, 15;
  through suffering, 153
autonomy, of Israelites, 8

Babylonia, Jewish community in, 8, 9
Babylonian Talmud. See Bavli
bailment, 35, 60–62
Bar Kokhba, 8, 12–13, 38, 111, 155
battle, 102–3
Bavli:
  communal justice, 145–51;
  composition form of, 72;
  definition of, 155;
  dialectical argument in, 50–53, 54, 59,
    67–68, 95–96;
  labor and festivals, 73–84;
  on Mishnah as part of Torah, explicit
    claim, 117;
  Mishnah topical tractates in, 40;
  Mishnah divisions covered by, 71;
  on Moses as master of Torah, 5;
  offerings/tithes neglect, 147–48;
  origin/date for closure of, 8, 9, 51;
  problem of evil, 152–53;
  punishment in, 145–51;
  robbery, 148;
  on sage as embodiment of Torah, 122–
    23;
  sages/gift of prophecy, 4;
  sin/punishment for individual, 147;
  swords, legitimate use of, 148;
  TNY in, 69n4;
  unfulfilled vows, 147.
  See also Bavli, compared with
    Yerushalmi; Bavli, individual
    sages in
Bavli, compared with Yerushalmi:
  commonalities between, 87–89;

compared in detail, 89–95;
  historical statements, 86;
  labor/festivals, 72–84;
  precedence of Bavli, 96–98;
  program of two Talmuds, 84–85;
  speaking for themselves/not Mishnah,
    85–87
Bavli, individual sages in:
  classification of sage learning program,
    126;
  given theme between two sages, 127;
  given theme shared among sages, 128–
    29;
  impulse to do evil, 126;
  suffering and reward, 128–29
BCE, definition of, 155
beast:
  consecrated/unconsecrated, 38–39;
  crop-destroying, 22, 25–26, 105
Ben Koziba. *See* Bar Kokhba
Bible, 7.
  See also Scripture
Book of the Covenant, torts/damages in,
    21–22, 24, 27, 28
bread, uncleanliness and, 103

CE, definition of, 155
chain of authority, 121
chain of tradition, 1, 111
civil law, 34–35
civil penalties, 36.
  See also punishment
cleanliness. *See* uncleanliness
cloak ownership, 55–63
communal justice, 146
conflagration. *See* fire damages
Constantine, declares Christianity licit, 8
corpses, uncleanliness of, 10, 31, 37, 74,
    80, 82, 127
courts/judges, in Balvi vs. Yerushalmi,
    89–95
Covenant, 148
crop-destroying beast, 22, 25–26, 105
Cyrus the Great, 9

damages:
  by crop-destroying beast, 22, 25–26,
    105;
  by fire, 22, 26–27, 105;
  generative causes of, 21–23, 105;
  gradations of responsibility, 23;
  by pits, 23–24
Damascus Covenant, 45–46
David (king), 2, 16–17, 151
Dead Sea library, collections of law in, 19
Dead Sea Scrolls, 6, 45
dialectical argument, 50–55, 59, 67–68,
    95–96
direct revelation from God, 100
disjoined testimony, 106
dispute law, 130
distributive reward, 141–42
Division of Agriculture, 32, 36
Division of Appointed Times, 32–33, 36
Division of Damages, 34–36
Division of Holy Things, 36
Division of Purities, 36–37
Division of Women, 33–34
divorce, 33–34
dough offering, neglect of, 147–48

Ecclesiastes, 2
Eduyyot, 30, 31
eisegesis, 100, 155
Eleazar of Modiin, judgment, 12–13
Eleazer b. Azariah, R.:
  labor/festivals, 78, 79;
  law of disputes, 130
Eli, 11, 15, 122
Eliezer, R.:
  authority of sages, 120;
  destruction of Jerusalem, 10;
  farewell story, 127;
  measurement, 104;
  mnemonics, 113;
  recognizes Bar Kokhba as Messiah, 12;
  suffering and reward, 128
evil, 126, 134, 152–53
exegesis:
  definition of, 155;
  of Scripture in Mishnah, 54, 55, 101–7;

of Scripture separate from Mishnah, 86–87
exile:
of Israel, 15–16, 144, 145;
of persons, 106, 110, 135, 149
exile among nations, 15–16

farewell story, 127
fire damages, 22, 26–27, 105
First Temple, destruction of, 10
Five Books of Moses, 1
food/drink/utensils, uncleanliness and, 36–37, 103
formative Judaism, 1
fornication, 144, 145

Gemara, 7;
analogical-contrastive reasoning in, 47–50;
closure of, 19;
comparison with Damascus Covenant, 45–46;
definition of, 155;
dialetical argument of Bavli, 50–53, 54, 59;
dialetics as medium of thought/ expression in, 53–55;
difference from Scripture, 45–47, 66–69
Genesis Rabbah, 9, 155
Greenberg, Moshe, 20
grudges, 147

Haggai, R., 4;
restoring ruler who sinned to office, 2;
written/oral law, 116
Halakhah, 38–39, 106, 133, 155
half-sheqel offering, 14
Hama bar Uqba, R., cleanliness, 115
Hamnuna, R., communal justice, 146
Hananiah, R., law of disputes, 130
Hanina, R.:
communal justice, 146;
law of disputes, 130;
suffering and reward, 128
Hannah's prayer, 122
heave-offering/tithes, neglect of, 148

Hebrew language, Scripture vs. Mishnah, 100
Herod (king), 2
Hezekiah, R., 127;
law of disputes, 130
high priest, compared/contrasted with king, 40–41
Hillel, 111, 155;
number of Torahs, 117
Hillel, House of, 109;
uncleanliness, 42–43
Hisdah, R.:
bailment, 60;
mnemonics, 113
Hiyya bar Abba, R.:
oaths, 62;
suffering and reward, 128
Hiyya bar Ashi, R., interpretation, 107
honeycombs, uncleanliness and, 42–43
Hosea, 12
Huna, R.:
bailment, 61–62;
civil duties of Rabbi, 5–7;
suffering and reward, 128–29

Idi bar Abin, R., bailment, 60
idolatry, 144, 145, 149, 152
incest, 149
individual atonement, 12, 14–15
Iranian Empire, Jews in, 9
Iranian Zoroastrian rule, end of, 9
Isaac, communal justice, 146
Isaiah, 16
Islam, 7, 9
Ismael b. Elisha, R., memory of Temple, 14
Israel:
exile among nations, 15–16;
shift from political entity to voluntary community, 13–17.
See also Jerusalem

Jacob, 82, 151
Jacob bar Abbayye, R. (R. Aha):
bailment, 62;
law of disputes, 130;
redemption, 16;

sage as embodiment of Torah, 121
Jeremiah, R.:
    authority of sages, 120;
    as model of exemplary Rabbi, 10, 11,
        12
Jerusalem:
    destruction of, 10–12;
    destruction of First Temple, 10;
    destruction of Second Temple, 8, 37–38
Jerusalem Talmud. *See* Yerushalmi
Job, 2, 104
Jonah, R.:
    law of disputes, 130
    cleanliness, 115
Jonathan, R., law of disputes, 130
Joseph, 137, 138
Josephus, 101
Joshua, 14
Joshua, R.:
    atonement, 11–12;
    authority of sages, 120–21;
    cleanliness, 103;
    destruction of Jerusalem, 10;
    on Job, 104;
    recognizes Bar Kokhba as Messiah, 12
Joshua b. Hurqanos, R., on Job, 104
Judah, R.:
    communal justice, 146;
    on order of Mishnah teaching, 112;
    tomb niches, 75
Judah the Patriarch, R., 155;
    labor/learning, 111;
    punishment for ruler who sinned, 2–3;
    as sponsor of Talmud, 100, 101, 108–9;
    sponsorship of Mishnah, 30;
    unfulfilled vows, 147
Judaism of the dual Torah, 1–2
judgment, 12–13
Julian (Roman emperor), 13

king, compared/contrasted with high
        priest, 40–41

labor:
    planning for, and festivals, 72–84;
    planning for, on Sabbath, 45–46, 73,
        75–76, 78, 82;

Torah study and, 110
Lamentations Rabbah, 155
land measurement, 104
Land of Israel:
    Jewish community in, 8;
    relationship with Roman government,
        8–9.
    See also Yerushalmi
late antiquity, 1
Levi, R., redemption, 16
Levi bar Hama, R.:
    classification of sage learning program,
        126;
    impulse to do evil, 126
Leviticus, uncleanliness in, 47–48
Leviticus Rabbah, 9, 155

Maimonides, 30
Malachi (latter prophet), 4
marriage, 33–34
master-disciple chain, 119
measurement, land, 104
memorization, 5, 101, 113, 114, 115–16
menstruation, 31, 37, 71, 147
Midrash, definition of, 155
miqveh (immersion pool), 48–50
Miriam, 137, 138
Mishnah, 7;
    authority of, 99–100, 101, 108;
    autonomy of, 105–7;
    cessation of prophecy, 4;
    classification in, 40–43;
    closure of, 8, 19, 29;
    comparison/contrast, 40–43;
    comparison with Covenant Code, torts/
        damages, 21–28;
    definition of, 155;
    difference from prior Israelite models,
        19–20;
    exegeses of Scripture in, 54, 55, 101–7;
    exemplary cases in, 104–5;
    exile, 106;
    generative causes of damages, 23, 105;
    gradations of responsibility, 23–24;
    intention, 42–43;
    Jeremiah influence on, 10;
    justice, 137–38;

language of, 100, 101;
law of disputes, 130;
mnemonic pattering in, 101;
omitted divisions/topics in, 37–39;
oral formulation of, 101;
oral tradition of, 108, 112–13, 114;
as part of Torah, explicit claim of, 114–
18;
precedence over Talmud, 114;
problem of evil, 152;
production of, 7–8;
punishment, 143–45;
relation to Scripture, 99–100;
relation to written Torah, 101–5;
repetition in, 101;
sponsorship/authorship of, 29–30, 108–
9;
supplements to (*see* Tosefta);
topical arrangement of, 19, 20, 21–22;
topical cogency/comphrehensiveness
of, 28–30;
topics of, 30–31;
tractates comprising, 30;
as tradition, 108;
uncleanliness, 42–43;
uniqueness as code of law, 28–29;
wife accused of adultery, 136–37.
See also Mishnah, regulation of Israeli
social order
Mishnah, regulation of Israeli social
order, 32–37;
in Division of Agriculture, 32, 36;
in Division of Appointed Times, 32–33,
36;
in Division of Damages, 34–36;
in Division of Holy Things, 36;
in Division of Purities, 36–37;
in Division of Women, 33–34
Mishnah Torah, 30
mnemonics, 101, 130
monotheism:
definition of, 155;
mythic, 133–36, 155;
philosophical, 155;
problem of evil in, 134
Moses, 137, 138, 151;
role as master of Torah, 4–5

Moshe Rabbenu. *See* Moses
moving argument. *See* dialectical
argument
Muhammad, 9
murder/bloodshed, 144, 145
mythic monotheism, 133–36, 155

Nahman, R., oaths, 62
Nahman bar Hisda, R., problem of evil,
152–53
nasi (patriarch), 2, 8
Nathan, R.:
authority of sages, 120;
Fathers according to, 10–12;
memory of Temple, 14;
sin/punishment for individual, 147
Nebuchadnezzar, 10, 11, 139, 142
Nehemiah, R.:
grudges, 147;
measurement of land, 104
normative Judaism, 1
Noth, Martin, 20–21

oaths, 55–66, 149
offerings, neglect of, 147–48
oral Torah, 1–2.
See also Talmud

pagan worship, restoration of, 13
participatory evaluation, 38
Patton, Michael Q., 37–38
penalty, for law infringement, 35
Peredah, R., memorization, 113
persons, as unclean, 37
Pesiqta deRab Kahana, 9, 155
philosophical monotheism, 155
pit damages, 22, 105
polytheism, problem of evil in, 134
prevailing practices, 36
Priestly Creation Narrative, 31
problem of evil, 134, 152–53
profanity, 149–50
prophets, 2, 16.
See also individual prophet
Proverbs, 2
pseudepigraphy, 100, 108, 155
punishment, 2–3, 140–41, 145–51

Qoheleth, 2
Quran, 7, 9

Raba, civil duties of Rabbi, 5, 6
Rabbi:
  as civil administrator, 5–7;
  defining, 1, 156;
  relation to partiarch, 2–3.
  See also Rabbinic sages; *individual
    Rabbi*
Rabbinic dialectics, dissent and, 124–25
Rabbinic Judaism, 1
Rabbinic sages:
  account of God's justice, 136–37;
  authority of, 120;
  autonomous standing of, 119–21;
  dialetical argument, 59–63;
  as embodiment of Torah, 121–22, 123–
    24;
  gift of prophecy and, 4;
  language of, 100;
  as part of chain of authority, 121;
  as part of chain of tradition, 124;
  relationship with prophecy, 4–5;
  representation in Talmud, 124–25;
  representation in Yerushalmi, 129–31;
  sin/punishment, 146–47
Rafram bar Pappa, civil duties of Rabbi,
    5–6
real estate, 36
redemption, 16–17
religious freedom/cultural toleration, 7
resh galuta (patriarch/ruler of ethnic
    community), 9
robbery, 148
Roman law, 7
Ruth Rabbah, 156

Sabbath:
  desecration of, 149;
  planning future work on, 45–46, 73,
    75–76, 78, 82;
  redemption and, 16–17
Sabbatical year, neglect of, 149
Samson, 137–38, 142
Samuel B. Yohai, R., Mishnah precedence
    over Talmud, 114

santification, 31–34, 38–39, 98
Saul, Abba, 152
Scripture, 29;
  adultery, 137;
  collections of law in, 19;
  difference from Gemara, 45–47, 66–69;
  exegesis in Mishnah, 54, 55, 101–7;
  exegesis separate from Mishnah, 86–
    87;
  justice, 137, 138;
  as proof texts, 102–4, 125;
  torts/damages, 21–22, 24, 27, 28;
  uncleanliness, 42, 47–48;
  Wisdom tradition of, 2
Second Temple:
  destruction of, 8, 37–38;
  impact of destruction/failure to rebuild,
    9–13
Sennacherib, 139, 142
Shammai:
  definition of, 156;
  number of Torahs, 117
Shammai, House of, 109;
  uncleanliness, 42–43
sheqels, as offerings, 14
Sheshet, R., oaths, 62
Simeon, R., uncleanliness, 48
Simeon b. Eleazar, R., death, 150–51
Simeon b. Gamaliel, R., 110–11
Simeon b. Laqish, R.:
  classification of sage learning program,
    126;
  impulse to do evil, 126;
  punishment for ruler who sinned, 2
Simeon b. Menassia, R., law of disputes,
    130
Simeon b. Yohai, R.:
  exile among nations, 15–16;
  Mishnah precedence over Talmud, 114
Simeon bar Abba, R., communal justice,
    146
Simon Gamaliel, R., labor/Torah study,
    110
Sinai, definition of, 156
Smith, Robin, 51
social order:
  punishment for sins against, 149–50;

regulation of, 32–37
Solomon (king), 2, 63–65, 156
Song of Songs Rabbah, 156
State of Israel, advent of, 9
stylistic imitation, 100
suffering and reward, 128

Tahalipa, R., mnemonics, 113
Talmud:
  age/location of production, 7–9;
  canon of (*see* Mishnah; Rabbinic sages;
    Scripture);
  commentary on law code (*see* Gemara);
  comparision with Scripture mode of
    discourse, 63–66;
  constitution/bylaws of (*see* Bavli);
  definition of, 156;
  God's justice in, 136–51;
  God's plan for creation vs. man's will,
    135–36;
  Israelite context of, 2;
  law code of (*see* Mishnah);
  living child, 63–66;
  oaths, 63–66;
  provision for proof texts from
    Scripture, 106–7;
  reasoned dialogue in, 6–7;
  sponsorship of, 100, 101, 108–9, 124;
  theological consensus expressed in law/
    lore, 133.
  See also Talmud, individual sages in
Talmud, individual sages in, 124–29;
  conglomeration, 125–29;
  given theme shared among sages, 127–
    29;
  given theme shared between two sages,
    126–27;
  individual sage, 125–26;
  suffering and reward, 127–29
Talmudic Judaism, 1
Talmud of Babylonia, Bavli. *See* Bavli
Talmud of Jerusalem. *See* Yerushalmi
Tannaite authority, 61–62, 68–69, 75
Tarfon, R., uncleanliness, 48, 49
tithes, neglect of, 148
TNY, 53, 69n4
tombs, 74–75

Torah, 7;
  definition of, 156;
  orality of, 108, 115;
  sages in, 129–31;
  written/oral, 115–16
Torah of Moses, 99, 100, 108
Torah of Sinai, 74, 101, 105–9
torts and damages, 21–28
Tosefta, 54–55, 69n4, 99, 102;
  atonement sheqels, 14;
  definition of, 156;
  distributive reward, 141–42;
  justice/reward, 138–40;
  law of disputes, 130;
  preservation of memory of Temple, 14;
  punishment for sin, 140–41;
  uncleanliness, 47–50
true value, of given object, 36

Ulla, R., communal justice, 146
uncleanliness:
  agricultural instruments, 68;
  corpses, 10, 31, 37, 74, 80, 82, 127;
  food/drink/utensils, 36–37, 103;
  honeycombs, 42–43;
  in Leviticus, 47–48;
  weapons, 68;
  women, 31, 37, 71, 103, 147
unfulfilled vows, 147
usury, 36

weapons, uncleanliness of, 68;
Wisdom tradition, of Scripture, 2
women:
  adultery and, 136–37;
  death in childbirth, 147;
  uncleanliness and, 31, 37, 71, 103, 147

Yannai, R., 130
Yerushalmi, 40;
  arrogance of Bar Kokhba, 12–13;
  cleanliness, 115;
  closure/origin of, 8;
  composition form of, 72;
  definition of, 156;
  exile among nations, 15–16;
  individual redemption, 16–17;

law of disputes, 130;
Mishnah as part of Torah, 114–17;
Misnah divisions covered by, 71;
representation of sages in, 129–31;
sage as embodiment of Torah, 121–22,
   123–24;
signal TNY, 69n4;
unique qualification of Rabbi in Torah
   learning, 2–3.
See also Bavli, compared with
   Yerushalmi
Yohanan ben Zakkai, R. (Rabban), 111,
   156;
atonement, 11–12, 14;
destruction of Jerusalem, 10–12;
disciples, 112;
farewell story, 127;
laws, 115;

Mishnah precedence over Talmud, 114;
oaths, 59–60;
suffering and reward, 128;
written/oral law, 116
Yosé bar Zeira, R., law of disputes, 130
Yudan b. R. Simeon, R., written/oral law,
   116

zealots, role in destruction of Temple, 9
Zechariah, 4
Zeira, R.:
   Mishnah laws, 115;
   written/oral Torah, 116
Zoroastrian religion, 9
   Zutra b. Tobiah, R., disjoined
      testimony, 106